Llewellynn Frederick William Jewitt

The Ballads & Songs of Derbyshire

With Illustrative Notes, and Examples of the Original Music, etc.

Llewellynn Frederick William Jewitt

The Ballads & Songs of Derbyshire
With Illustrative Notes, and Examples of the Original Music, etc.

ISBN/EAN: 9783744782135

Printed in Europe, USA, Canada, Australia, Japan

Cover: Foto ©Thomas Meinert / pixelio.de

More available books at **www.hansebooks.com**

THE BALLADS & SONGS

OF

DERBYSHIRE.

WITH ILLUSTRATIVE NOTES, AND EXAMPLES OF THE ORIGINAL MUSIC, ETC.

EDITED BY

LLEWELLYNN JEWITT, F.S.A., &c., &c.

LONDON: BEMROSE AND LOTHIAN, 21, PATERNOSTER ROW.
DERBY: BEMROSE AND SONS, IRONGATE.

MDCCCLXVII.

BEMROSE AND SONS, PRINTERS, DERBY.

TO

His Grace the Duke of Devonshire, K.G.,

Lord-Lieutenant and Custos-Rotulorum

OF THE COUNTY

WHOSE BALLADS ARE HERE FOR THE FIRST TIME COLLECTED,

THIS VOLUME IS,

AS A MARK OF PERSONAL ESTEEM,

AND AS A TRIBUTE TO THE TRUE NOBILITY OF HIS CHARACTER

AND TO

HIS HIGH INTELLECTUAL ATTAINMENTS,

MOST GRATEFULLY DEDICATED BY

The Editor.

INTRODUCTION.

IT is certainly somewhat curious that, in a county so confessedly rich in ballads and in popular songs as Derbyshire is, no attempt should hitherto have been made to collect together and give to the world even a small selection of these valuable and interesting remains. Such, however, is the fact, and the ballads, the traditions, and the lyrics of the county have remained to the present day uncollected, and, it is to be feared, uncared for, by those to whom the task of collection in days gone by would have been tolerably easy. It has therefore remained for me, with my present volume, to initiate a series of works which shall embrace these and kindred subjects, and vindicate for Derbyshire its place in the literary history of the kingdom.

In my present volume I have given a selection of upwards of fifty ballads and songs, many of them extremely curious, and all highly interesting, which are purely Derbyshire, and relate entirely to that county, to events which have happened within its bounds, or to Derbyshire families. These I have collected together from every available source, and several amongst them have never before been reprinted from the old broad-sheets and garlands in which they are contained; while others, taken down from the lips of "old inhabitants," or from the original MSS., are for the first time put into type. Knowing that in ballads it is next to, if not quite, impossible to accomplish a successful chronological arrangement, and feeling that, if accomplished, such an arrangement is open to grave objections. I have purposely avoided the attempt, and have contented myself with varying, as much as possible, the contents of my volume, and with giving to each ballad an introductory notice touching on the event commemorated, on the writer of the piece, or on the source from whence the ballad has been obtained. Having done this, the necessity for a long introduction here is obviated, and it only remains for me to announce my intention of following up my present volume with another similar one, as a "Second Series" of Derbyshire Ballads and Songs, and with others on the Poets and Poetry of Derbyshire; on the Political and Criminal songs of the county; and on its Folk-Lore and Traditions, etc. It is hoped that the present volume will find sufficient favour with the public to act as an encouragement to the early issue of the succeeding volumes, which will contain a vast amount of interesting and valuable information on points about which at present but little is known.

It will be seen that in the introductory notices to the ballads in the following pages I have acknowledged my obligations to various kind friends for the assistance they have rendered. I have now only in general terms to again tender them my thanks, and, in so doing, to ask them, and all who can in any way assist me in my labours, to continue their kind help to my future volumes, and so enable me to do justice to the rich and beautiful county which it has been my life-long study to illustrate.

As a frontispiece to my present volume, I give a facsimile of an old portrait of a Derbyshire ballad-singer of the last century, "*Singing Sam of Derbyshire*," as he was called, which I copy from the curious plate etched by W. Williams in 1760, which appeared in the "Topographer" thirty years after that time. The man was a singular character—a wandering minstrel who got his living by singing ballads in the Peak villages, and accompanying himself on his rude single-stringed instrument. Doubtless "The Beggar's Ramble" and "The Beggar's Wells," and other similar rhymes, were the production of "Singing Sam" or his compeers, and recounted his own peregrinations through the country. His instrument was as quaint and curious as himself. It consisted of a straight staff nearly as tall as himself, with a single string tied fast around it at each end. This he tightened with a fully inflated cow's bladder, which assisted very materially the tone of the rude instrument. His bow was a rough stick of hazel or briar, with a single string; and with this, with the lower end of his staff resting on the ground, and the upper grasped by his right hand, which he passed up and down to tighten or slacken the string as he played, he scraped away, and produced sounds which, though not so musical as those of Paganini and *his* single string, would no doubt harmonize with Sam's rude ballad, and ruder voice. This portrait I believe has never been reproduced until now.

On the title-page I give a small vignette showing a ballad singer of an earlier date, from a sketch by Inigo Jones, made two hundred and thirty years ago, which belongs to His Grace the Duke of Devonshire. Unlike "Singing Sam of Derbyshire," who sang his ballads from memory, and probably composed many of them as he went on, so as to suit the localities and the tastes and habits of his hearers, the man here shown sings from a printed broad-sheet, of which he carries an armful with him to dispose of to such as cared to purchase them. He is literally a "running stationer," "such as use to sing ballads and cry malignant pamphlets in the streets," and indulged their hearers in town and country with "fond bookes, ballads, rhimes, and other lewd treatises in the English tongue."

In my next volume I shall give a portrait of "Hale the Piper," another Derbyshire "worthy," and shall then take occasion to speak of the origin of Hornpipes in the locality which gave him birth.

Derby, February, 1867.

Contents.

DEDICATION	vii
INTRODUCTION	ix
KING HENRY V., His Conquest of France, in Revenge for the Affront offered by the French King, in sending him (instead of a Tribute) a Ton of Tennis-balls	1
A BALLAD OF DERBYSHIRE. By Sir Aston Cokain	6
THE MOST PLEASANT SONG OF LADY BESSY, the Eldest Daughter of King Edward the Fourth, and how she married King Henry the Seventh, of the House of Lancaster	12
DEVONSHIRE'S NOBLE DUEL WITH LORD DANBY IN THE YEAR 1687	55
THE UNCONSIONABLE BATCHELORS OF DARBY: or the Young Lasses Pawn'd by their Sweet-hearts, for a large Reckning, at Nottingham Goose Fair, when poor Susan was forc'd to pay the Shot	58
THE HUMOURS OF HAYFIELD FAIR	61
ON THE STRANGE AND WONDERFUL SIGHT THAT WAS SEEN IN THE AIR ON THE 6TH OF MARCH, 1716	64
THE DRUNKEN BUTCHER OF TIDESWELL	66
A NEW BALLAD OF ROBIN HOOD: showing his Birth, Breeding, Valour, and Marriage, at Titbury Bull-running: Calculated for the Meridian of Staffordshire, but may serve for Derbyshire or Kent	73
ROBIN HOOD AND LITTLE JOHN	85

LITTLE JOHN'S END	91
THE LAY OF THE BUCKSTONE	96
SIR RICHARD WHITTINGTON'S ADVANCEMENT: Being an Historical Account of his Education, Unexpected Fortune, Charity, &c.	104
THE DERBYSHIRE MILLER	110
TIDESWELL IN AN UPROAR, OR THE PRINCE IN THE TOWN, AND THE DEVIL IN THE CHURCH	111
THE PRINCE AT TIDESWELL	114
THE DERBY RAM	115
THE BLINK-EY'D COBLER	119
A STRANGE BANQUET; or the Devil's Entertainment by Cook Laurel, at the Peak in Darby-shire: with an Account of the several Dishes served to Table	125
THE TAYLOR'S RAMBLE, OR THE BLUES' VALOUR DISPLAYED	129
SQUIRE VERNON'S FOX-CHACE	131
THE TRUSLEY HUNTING SONG	136
SQUIRE FRITH'S HUNTING SONG	142
DERBYSHIRE MEN	145
AN ELEGY UPON THE DEATH OF THE GREATEST GENTRY IN DARLEY DALE, WHO LOVED HUNTING AND HAWKING, AND SEVERAL OTHER GAMES *Leonard Wheatcroft*	146
COCKTAIL REEL	153
LINES OCCASIONED BY A YORKSHIRE PYE SENT AS A PRESENT FROM SIR WILLIAM ST. QUINTIN TO HIS GRACE THE DUKE OF DEVONSHIRE, AT BATH, ON CHRISTMAS DAY, 1762	157
THE AGRICULTURAL MEETING	160
THE COMPLAINTE OF ANTHONIE BABINGTON	164
A NEW SONG IN PRAISE OF THE DERBYSHIRE MILITIA	182
THE FLORISTS' SONG	184

CONTENTS.

The Sorrowful Lamentation, Last Dying Speech and Confession of Old Nun's Green	187
A Traveller's Dream	188
A Poem found by Mr. * * * and Dedicated to Major Trowel	190
The Quadrupeds, &c., or Four-footed Petitioners against the Sale of Nun's Green	193
Paving and Lighting	196
The Nun's Green Rangers; or the Triple Alliance, Consisting of an old Sergeant, a Tinker, and a Bear	199
A Birch Rod for the Presbyterians	201
Lost and Dead	204
Song (satirical, on the Choir of All Saints' Church, Derby)	206
Sir Francis Leke; or the Power of Love	210
The True Lover's Knot Untied: Being the right path whereby to advise princely Virgins how to behave themselves, by the example of the renowned Princess, the Lady Arabella and the second son of the Lord Seymour, late Earl of Hertford	222
An Address to "Dickie"	226
The Driving of the Deer	230
The Ashupton Garland; or a Day in the Woodlands	237
Derbyshire Hills	243
Derbyshire Dales	246
A Rhapsody on the Peak of Derbyshire	248
The Derby Hero	249
A New Song on the great Foot Race that was contested on the London Road, near Derby, betwixt Jas. Wantling, of Derby, and Shaw, the Staffordshire Hero, for 2 Hundred Guineas	252
On the Death of the late Rev. Bache Thornhill, M.A.	255
A Journey into the Peak. To Sir Aston Cokaine	257

Epistle to John Bradshaw, Esq.	259
Hugh Stenson and Molly Green	263
The Beggar's Ramble	266
,, ,,	271
Henry and Clara	274
The Gipsies Song	280
The Flax-Dresser's Wife of Spondon, and the Pound of Tea	281
The Ashborne Foot-Ball Song	284
The Parson's Torr	286
Index of Titles, First Lines, Names, &c.	294

DERBYSHIRE BALLADS.

King Henry V.,

His Conquest of France, in Revenge for the Affront offered by the French King, in sending him (instead of the Tribute) a Ton of Tennis-balls.

THIS is one of the most curious and popular of the series of Derbyshire ballads, and one which, in its early broad-sheet form, is of great rarity. The broad-sheet from which it is here reprinted, is "Printed and Sold in Aldermary Church Yard, Bow Lane, London." It is printed broad-way of the sheet, with two short columns of three verses each beneath the engraving, and one whole column of eight verses at the side. The engraving represents a fortification, with central tower, with the Union Jack flying; the sea in front, with a ship and some small boats; and two tall soldiers in midground, evidently "on guard." Versions of this ballad have been printed by Mr. Dixon, in the volume on *Ancient Poems, Ballads, and Songs of the Peasantry of England*, edited by him for the Percy Society, and in other collections. Printed copies are to be found in the Roxburghe Collection in the British Museum, and in the Halliwell Collection in the Chetham Library, Manchester. The one here given is from the original broad-sheet in my own collection.

The ballad will be at once seen to refer to the battle of Agincourt, which was a prolific source of inspiration to the ballad and song writers of the time, and of later years. Tradition bears out the noble feature of the ballad—that of no married man or widow's son being either recruited or pressed into the service of the Sovereign over this expedition. A tradition still obtains in the Peak, among the "hills that are so free," that when Henry V. was recruiting Derbyshire and the adjoining counties, he declared that he would take no married man, and that no widow's son should be of his company, for no woman's curse should go with him in his righteous expedition.

The ballad is still not unfrequently sung in snatches by the miners and other hardy sons of the Peak, the verse being usually rendered :—

> "No married man, nor no widow's son,
> Will I ever ask to go with me ;
> For I will take no widow's curse
> From the Derby hills that are so free."

It is said that on one occasion, when George III. was reviewing a brigade of Guards in Hyde Park, he was particularly struck with the fine stalwart and manly bearing of one of the regiments,[*] and calling out to the nearest man in the ranks, asked, "Well, my fine fellow, where are you from, eh?" "Derbyshire, please your Majesty," was the reply. "Eh, Derbyshire eh! From Derby hills so free," rejoined the King, showing that he must have been acquainted with the ballad we now print.

The tune to which this Ballad was sung I here give. I am not aware that it has ever before been printed. I remember hearing it frequently sung when I was a boy, and the spirit with which it was sung is still fresh in my memory. It is as follows :—

As our king lay mus-ing on his bed, He be-thought him-self up-

---

[*] It is worthy of note, that of late years the Derbyshire Volunteers have received he marked compliment of being specially noted for their manly bearing and their distinguished appearance by her present Majesty, and by the Commander-in-Chief, H R.H. the Duke of Cambridge, on each of the occasions of general review of the Volunteer force in Hyde Park.

Another traditional version of the tune to which the ballad was sung, and which, like the one just given, is common to it and to "Robin Hood and the Pedlar," which begins—

> "I'll tell you of a pedlar bold,
> A pedlar bold he chanced to be,
> On he roll'd his pack upon his back,
> As he came tripping o'er the lea."

has been kindly supplied to me by my friend Mr. William Chappell, F.S.A., the gifted author of that admirable work, "Popular Music of the Olden Time." It is as follows :—

As our king lay musing on his bed,
He bethought himself upon a time,
Of a tribute that was due from France,
Had not been paid for so long a time.
        Fal, lal, &c.

He called for his lovely page,
His lovely page then called he;
Saying, "You must go to the King of France,
To the King of France, sir, ride speedily."
        Fal, lal, &c.

O then away went this lovely page,
This lovely page then away went he;
Lo he came to the King of France,
And then he fell down on his bended knee.
        Fal, lal, &c.

"My master greets you, worthy Sir,
Ten ton of gold that is due to he,
That you will send him his tribute home,
Or in French land you soon will him see."
        Fal, lal, &c.

"Your master's young, and of tender years,
Not fit to come into my degree;

And I will send him three Tennis-Balls,
That with them he may learn to play."
   Fal, lal, &c.

O then returned this lovely page,
This lovely page then returned he,
And when he came to our gracious King,
Low he fell down on his bended knee.
   Fal, lal, &c.

"What news? What news? my trusty page,
What is the news you have brought to me?"
"I have brought such news from the King of France,
That he and you will ne'er agree.
   Fal, lal, &c.

"He says, you're young, and of tender years,
Not fit to come into his degree;
And he will send you three Tennis-Balls,
That with them you may learn to play."
   Fal, lal, &c.

"Recruit me Cheshire and Lancashire,
And Derby Hills that are so free;
No marry'd man, or widow's son,
For no widow's curse shall go with me."
   Fal, lal, &c.

They recruited Cheshire and Lancashire,
And Derby Hills that are so free;
No marry'd man, nor no widow's son,
Yet there was a jovial bold company.
   Fal, lal, &c.

O then we march'd into the French land,
With drums and trumpets so merrily ;
And then bespoke the King of France,
" Lo ! yonder comes proud King Henry."
   Fal, lal, &c.

The first shot that the Frenchmen gave,
They kill'd our Englishmen so free :
We kill'd ten thousand of the French,
And the rest of them they run away.
   Fal, lal, &c.

And then we marched to Paris gates,
With drums and trumpets so merrily,
O then bespoke the King of France,
" The Lord have mercy on my men and me !
   Fal, lal, &c.

" O I will send him his tribute home,
Ten ton of gold that is due to he,
And the finest flower that is in all France,
To the Rose of England I will give free."
   Fal, lal, &c.

A Ballad of Darbyshire.

BY SIR ASTON COKAIN.

SIR ASTON COKAIN, the most illustrious member of the famous family of Cokain, of Ashborne, was the son of Thomas Cokain, of Ashborne and of Pooley, by his wife Ann, daughter of Sir John Stanhope,[*] of Elvaston, by Derby. He was born at Elvaston, in

---

[*] Ancestor of the present Earl of Harrington, of Elvaston.

1608, was educated at Cambridge, and received the honour of knighthood in 1641. He was one of the most eminent poets of the day, and was the intimate friend of Donne, Suckling, Randolph, Drayton, Massinger, Habbington, Sandys, May, Jonson, and other wits of the age. He was cousin to Charles Cotton, to whom he addressed many of his writings. Sir Aston married Mary, daughter of Sir Gilbert Kniveton, of Mercaston, near Derby. In 1671 he, with his son, Thomas Cokain, sold his estates in the neighbourhood of Ashborne to Sir William Boothby; and he also sold his estate of Pooley. In 1683 Sir Aston Cokain died at Derby, and was buried at Polesworth. His son Thomas, who married Mary, co-heiress of Carey Sherry, was the last male heir of the family, and died without issue.

In 1658 Sir Aston Cokain published his volume, *Small Poems of Divers Sorts*, a volume of 508 pages, which is now of great rarity. Some few copies have a portrait—a laureated bust—of Cokain, with the verse—

"Come, Reader, draw thy purse, and be a guest
To our Parnassus; 'Tis the Muses feast,
The entertainment needs must be divine—
Appollo's th' Host where Cockains heads ye Sign."

This portrait is of excessive rarity. Curiously enough, the copperplate was used as the portrait of Ovid in North's translation of Plutarch's Lives, and it has also more than once been re-engraved. The volume contains also two dramatic pieces, "The Obstinate Lady, a Comedy written by Aston Cokain," which was first published in 1657, and "Trappolin suppos'd a Prince, an Italian Trage-Comedy." Cokain also wrote the "Tragedy of Ovid," and other things, and several editions of his works, under different titles, were issued.

I.

Dear *Polyhymnie*, be
Auspicious unto me,
That I may spread abroad
Our Shire's worth in an ode,
Merrily chanting.

They that our Hills do blame,
Have no cause for the same ;
Seeing the Muses lye
Upon *Parnassus* high,
    Where no joy's wanting.

2.

Upon *Olympus* Hill
Hebe Heaven's cup doth fill :
And *Iove* of *Candy* Isle
Doth the Gods reconcile,
    When they do wrangle.
In *France* at *Agincourt*
(Where we fought in such sort)
Behind an hill we did
Make our Archers lye hid,
    Foes to entangle.

3.

The long commanding *Rome*,
And old *Byzantium*,
Lisbon in *Portugal*,
Are situated all
    Upon Hills strongly :
All therefore that protest
Hilly ground's not the best,
Are of their wits bereav'd,
And all of them deceiv'd,
    And censure wrongly.

4.

The Peer of *England* known
Darby's Earldom to own,

Is honoured by the style
Of King of *Mona's* Isle
    Hereditary.
Why hath *Orantus* found
A Channel under ground
Where t'lye hid, but for shame
When it hears *Darwin's** name,
    Which Fame doth carry?

5.

Why do the Nymphs (believe)
Of *Nile*, it down Rocks drive;
Unless it be for fear
Trent's glory should go near
    To overgo them?
The *Spaw Luick* Land hath,
And *Sommerset* the *Bath*:
Buxtons (dear County) be
As famous unto thee
    As they unto them.

6.

For King *Mausolus* Tomb,
Lango's known by each Groom;
And the *Campanian* Lake
Doth very famous make
    Italies confines;
The walls of burned stone
Eternise *Babylon*:
And the large Devil's vault
Doth *Darbyshire* exalt,
    Wherein no sun shines.

---

* *Darwin*, the river Derwent.

7.
The Pike to *Tennariff*
An high repute doth give :
And the Coloss of brass,
Where under ships did pass,
    Made *Rhodes* aspire.
Tunbridge makes *Kent* renown'd
And *Epsome Surryes* Ground :
Pools-hole, and St. *Anne's* Well
Makes *Darbyshire* excell
    Many a shire.

8.
Here on an Hill's side steep
Is *Elden* hole, so deep,
That no man living knowes
How far it hollow goes :
    Worthy the knowing.
Here also is a Well
Whose Waters do excell
All waters thereabout ;
Both being in and out
    Ebbing and flowing.

9.
Here's Lead, whereof is made
Bullets for to invade
Them whose pride doth prevail
So far, as to assail
    Our Brittish borders.
Our Lead so much may do,
That it may win *Peru* ;

And (if we chance to meet
A *Spanish* silver Fleet)
    Commit great murthers.

10.

Diana's Fane to us
Extolleth *Ephesus:*
The Sand-hil, and deaf stone,
Do *Darbyshire* renown,
    Worth Admiration.
Windsor Berks doth commend,
And *Essex Audley-end:*
We of our *Chatsworth* boast,
A glory to our coast,
    And the whole Nation.

11.

Spain doth vaunt of its sack,
And *France* of Claret crack;
Of Rhenish *Germany:*
And of thy Ale speak free,
    My gallant County.
Now I have made an end,
I wish you to commend
Either the author's wit,
Or me for singing it,
    Out of your bounty.

THE MOST PLEASANT

Song of Lady Bessy,

The Eldest Daughter of King Edward the Fourth, and how she married King Henry the Seventh, of the House of Lancaster.

THIS fine old ballad concerning the Princess Elizabeth of York, wife of Henry VII. of Lancaster, relates to the Earl of Derby, the Earl of Shrewsbury, and others connected with Derbyshire. It is supposed to have been written by Humphrey Brereton. There are two versions of this curious ballad. The version here given is from a MS. copy of the time of Charles II., belonging to the late Mr. Bateman. It was edited by Mr. Halliwell for the Percy Society.

FOR Jesus sake be merry and glad,
   Be blythe of blood, of bone, and blee,
And of your words be sober and sad,
   And a little while listen to me:
I shall tell you how Lady Bessy made her moan,
   And down she kneeled upon her knee
Before the Earle of Darby her self alone,
   These were her words fair and free:—
Who was your beginner, who was your ground,
   Good father Stanley, will you tell me?
Who married you to the Margaret Richmond,
   A Dutchess of a high degree?
And your son the Lord George Strange
   By that good lady you had him by.

And Harden lands under your hands,
  And Moules dale also under your fee,
Your brother Sir William Stanley by parliament,
  The Holt Castle who gave him truely ?
Who gave him Brome-field, that I now ment ?
  Who gave him Chirk-land to his fee ?
Who made Him High Chamberlain of Cheshire ?
  Of that country farr and near
They were all wholly at his desire,
  When he did call they did appear ;
And also the Forrest of Delameer,
  To hunt therin both day and night
As often as his pleasure were,
  And to send for baron and knight ;
Who made the knight and lord of all ?
  Good father Stanley, remember thee !
It was my father, that king royall,
  He set you in that room so high.
Remember Richmond banished full bare,
  And lyeth in Brittain behind the sea,
You may recover him of his care,
  If your heart and mind to him will gree :
Let him come home and claim his right,
  And let us cry him King Henry !
And if you will maintain him with might,
  In Brittain he needeth not long to tarry.
Go away, Bessy, the Lord said then,
  I tell thee now for certainty,
That fair words make oft fooles full faine,
  When they be but found vain glory.

Oh! father Stanley, to you I call,
  For the love of God remember thee,
Since my father King Edward, that king royall,
  At Westminster on his death bed lee;
He called to him my unckle Richard,
  So he did Robert of Brackenbury,
And James Terrill he was the third;
  He sent them to Ludlow in the west countrey,
To fetch the Duke of York, and the Duke of Clarence,
  These two lords born of a high degree.
The Duke of York should have been prince,
  And king after my father free,
But a balle full game was them among,
  When they doomed these two lords to dye:
They had neither justice nor right, but had great wrong,
  Alack! it was the more pitty!
Neither were they burried in St. Maries,
  In church or churchyard or holy place:
Alas! they had dolefull destinies,
  Hard was their chance, worse was their disgrace!
Therefore, help good father Stanley, while you have space,
  For the love of God and mild Mary,
Or else in time to come you shall, alas!
  Remember the words of Lady Bessy!
Good Lady Bessy, be content,
  For tho' your words be never so sweet,
If King Richard knew, you must be shent,
  And perchance cast into prison deep;
Then had you cause to waill and weep,
  And wring your hands with heavy chear;

Therefore, good lady, I you beseek
  To move me no more in this matter.
Oh! good father Stanley, listen now and hear;
  Heare is no more but you and I:
King Edward that was my father dear.
  On whose estate God had mercy,
In Westminster as he did stand,
  On a certain day in a study,
A book of reason he had in his hand,
  And so sore his study he did apply,
That his tender tears fell on the ground,
  All men might see that stood him by:
There were both earls and lords of land,
  But none of them durst speak but I.
I came before my father the king,
  And kneeled down upon my knee;
I desired him lowly of his blessing,
  And full soon he gave it unto me:
And in his arms he could me thring,
  And set me in a window so high;
He spake to me full sore weeping,—
  These were the words he said to me:
Daughter, as thou wilt have my blessing,
  Do as I shall councell thee,
And to my words give good listening,
  For one day they may pleasure thee:
Here is a book of Reason, keep it well,
  As you will have the love of me;
Neither to any creature do it tell,
  Nor let no liveing lord it see,

Except it be the Lord Stanley,
  The which I love full heartiley:
All the matter to him show you may,
  For he and his thy help must be;
As soon as the truth to him is shown
  Unto your words he will agree;
For their shall never son of my body be gotten
  That shall be crowned after me,
But you shall be queen and wear the crown,
  So doth expresse the prophecye!
He gave me tax and toland,
  And also diamonds to my degree,
To get me a prince when it pleaseth Christ,
  The world is not as it will be:
Therefore, good father Stanley, grant my request
  For the love of God I desire thee;
All is at your commandment down in the west,
  Both knight and squire and the commentie;
You may choose then where you like best,
  I have enough both of gold and fee;
I want nothing but the strength of men,
  And good captains two or three.
Go away, Bessy, the lord said then,
  To this will I never agree,
For women oft time cannot faine,
  These words they be but vain glory!
For and I should treason begin
  Against King Richard his royalty,
In every street within London
  The Eagle's foot should be pulled down,

Derbyshire Ballads.

And as yet in his great favour I am,
    But then shoud I loose my great renowne !
I shoud be called traitor thro' the same
    Full soon in every markett towne !
That were great shame to me and my name,
    I had rather spend ten thousand pounde.
O father Stanley, to you I mak my moane,
    For the love of God remember thee ;
It is not three days past and gone,
    Since my unckle Richard sent after me
A batchelor and a bold baron,
    A Doctor of Divinitye,
And bad that I should to his chamber gone,
    His love and his leman that I should bee ;
And the queen that was his wedded feere,
    He would her poyson and putt away ;
So would he his son and his heir,
    Christ knoweth he is a proper boy !
Yet I had rather burn in a tunne
    On the Tower Hill that is so high,
Or that I would to his chamber come,
    His love and his leman will I not be !
I had rather be drawn with wild horses five,
    Through every street of that citty,
Or that good woman should lose her life,
    Good father, for the love of mee.
I am his brother's daughter dear ;
    He is my uncle, it is no nay ;
Or ever I would be his wedded feere,
    With sharp swords I will me slay ;

At his bidding if I were then,
    And follow'd also his cruel intent,
I were well worthy to suffer pain,
    And in a fire for to be brent.
Therefore, good father Stanley, some pity take
    On the Earl Richmond and me,
And the rather for my father's sake,
    Which gave thee the Ile of Man so free;
He crowned thee with a crown of lead,
    He holpe the first to that degree;
He set thee the crown upon thy head,
    And made thee the lord of that countrey;
That time you promised my father dear,
    To be to him both true and just,
And now you stand in a disweare.
    Oh! Jesu Christ, who may men trust?
O good lady, I say againe
    Your fair words shall never move my mind;
King Richard is my lord and sov'raign,
    To him I will never be unkind.
I will serve him truly till I die,
    I will him take as I him find;
For he hath given to mine and me,
    His bounteous gifts do me so bind.
Yet good father Stanley, remember thee,
    As I have said so shall it prove,
If he of his gift be soe free,
    It is for fear and not for love;
For if he may to his purpose come,
    You shall not live these years three,

For these words to me he did once move
  In Sandall Castle underneath a tree :
He said there shall no branch of the eagle fly
  Within England, neither far nor nigh ;
Nor none of the Talbots to run him by,
  Nor none of their lineage to the ninth degree ;
But he would them either hang or head,
  And that he swear full grievously.
Therefore help, gentle lord, with all speed ;
  For when you would fain it will not be.
Your brother dwellith in Holt Castle,
  A noble knight forsooth is he ;
All the Welsh-men love him well,
  He may make a great company.
Sir John Savage is your sister's son.
  He is well beloved within his shire,
A great company with him will come,
  He will be ready at your desire.
Gilbert Talbott is a captain pure,
  He will come with main and might ;
To you he will be fast and sure,
  Against my uncle king and knight.
Let us raise an host with him to fight,
  Soon to the ground we shall him ding.
For God will stand ever with the right,
  For he hath no right to be king !
Go away, Bessy, the Lord can say ;
  Of these words, Bessy, now lett be ;
I know king Richard woud not me betray,
  For all the gold in Christantye.

I am his subject, sworn to be true:
    If I should seek treason to begin,
I and all mine full sore should rue,
    For we were as like to lose as winne.
Beside that, it were a deadly sin
    To refuse my king, and him betray:
The child is yet unborne that might moan in time,
    And think upon that woefull day.
Wherefore, good lady, I do you pray,
    Keep all things close at your hart root;
So now farr past it is of the day,
    To move me more it is no boot.
Then from her head she cast her attire,
    Her colour changed as pale as lead,
Her faxe that shoan as the gold wire
    She tair it of besides her head,
And in a swoon down can she swye,
    She spake not of a certain space!
The Lord had never so great pitty
    As when he saw her in that case,
And in his arms he can her embrace;
    He was full sorry then for her sake.
The tears fell from her eyes apace,
    But at the last these words she spake,
She said, to Christ my soul I betake,
    For my body in Tem'ms drow'nd shall be!
For I know my sorrow will never slake,
    And my bones upon the sands shall lye!
The fishes shall feed upon me their fill;
    This is a dolefulle destinye!

And you may remedy this and you will,
    Therefore the bone of my death I give to thee !
And ever she wept as she were woode,
    The Earle on her had so great pitty,
That her tender heart turned his mood.
    He said, stand up now, Lady Bessye,
As you think best I will agree
    Now I see the matter you do not faine,
I have thought in this matter as much as yee :
    But it is hard to trust women,
For many a man is brought into great woe,
    Through telling to women his privity :
I trust you will not serve me so
    For all the gold in Christantie.
No, father, he is my mortall foe,
    On him fain wrooken woud I bee !
He hath put away my brethren two,
    And I know he would do so by me ;
But my trust is in the Trinity,
    Through your help we shall bale to him bring,
And such a day on him to see
    That he and his full sore shall rue !
O Lady Bessye, the Lord can say,
    Betwixt us both forecast we must
How we shall letters to Richmond convey,
    No man to write I dare well trust ;
For if he list to be unjust
    And us betray to King Richard,
Then you and I are both lost ;
    Therefore of the scribe I am afraid.

You shall not need none such to call.
    Good father Stanley, hearken to me
What my father, King Edward, that king royal,
    Did for my sister, my Lady Wells, and me:
He sent for a scrivener to lusty London,
    He was the best in that citty;
He taught us both to write and read full soon,
    If it please you, full soon you shall see:
Lauded be God, I had such speed,
    That I can write as well as he,
And also indite and full well read,
    And that (Lord) soon shall you see,
Both English and alsoe French,
    And also Spanish, if you had need.
The earle said, You are a proper wench,
    Almighty Jesus be your speed,
And give us grace to proceed out,
    That we may letters soon convey
In secrett wise and out of doubt
    To Richmond, that lyeth beyond the sea.
We must depart, lady, the earle said then;
    Wherefore keep this matter secretly.
And this same night, betwixt nine and ten,
    In your chamber I think to be.
Look that you make all things ready,
    Your maids shall not our councell hear,
For I will bring no man with me
    But Humphrey Brereton, my true esquire.
He took his leave of that lady fair,
    And to her chamber she went full tight,

And for all things she did prepare,
    Both pen and ink, and paper white.
The lord unto his study went,
    Forecasting with all his might
To bring to pass all his intent;
    He took no rest till it was night.
And when the stars shone fair and bright,
    He him disguised in strange mannere,
He went unknown of any wyght,
    No more with him but his esquire.
And when he came her chamber near,
    Full privily there can he stand,
To cause the lady to appeare
    He made a signe with his right hand;
And when the lady there him wist,
    She was as glad as she might be.
Char-coals in chimneys there were cast,
    Candles on sticks standing full high;
She opened the wickett and let him in,
    And said, welcome, lord and knight soe free!
A rich chair was set for him,
    And another for that fair lady.
They ate the spice and drank the wine,
    He had all things at his intent;
They rested them as for a time,
    And to their study then they went.
Then that lady so fair and free,
    With rudd as red as rose in May,
She kneeled down upon her knee,
    And to the lord thus can she say:

Good father Stanley, I you pray,
    Now here is no more but you and I ;
Let me know what you will say,
    For pen and paper I have ready.
He saith, commend me to my son George Strange,
    In Latham Castle there he doth lye,
When I parted with him his heart did change,
    From Latham to Manchester he road me by.
Upon Salford Bridge I turned my horse againe,
    My son George by the hand I hent ;
I held so hard forsooth certaine,
    That his formast finger out of the joint went :
I hurt him sore, he did complain,
    These words to him then I did say :
Son, on my blessing, turne home againe,
    This shall be a token another day.
Bid him come like a merchant of Farnfield,
    Of Coopland, or of Kendall, wheather that it be,
And seven with him, and no more else,
    For to bear him company.
Bid him lay away watch and ward,
    And take no heed to mynstrel's glee ;
Bid him sit at the lower end of the board,
    When he is amongst his meany,
His back to the door, his face to the wall,
    That comers and goers shall not him see ;
Bid him lodge in no common hall,
    But keep him unknowne right secretly.
Commend me to my brother Sir William so dear,
    In the Holt Castle there dwelleth hee ;

Since the last time that we together were,
  In the forest of Delameere both fair and free,
And seven harts upon one hearde,
  Were brought to the buck sett to him and me;
But a forester came to me with a whoore bearde,
  And said, good sir, awhile rest ye,
I have found you a hart in Darnall Park,
  Such a one I never saw with my eye.
I did him crave, he said I shoud him have;
  He was brought to the broad heath truely;
At him I let my grayhound then slipp,
  And followed after while I might dree.
He left me lyeing in an ould moss pit,
  A loud laughter then laughed hee;
He said, Rise up, and draw out your cousin;
  The deer is dead, come you and see.
Bid him come as a marchant of Carnarvon,
  Or else of Bew-morris whether it be;
And in his company seven Welshmen,
  And come to London and speak to me;
I have a great mind to speak with him,
  I think it long since I him see.
Commend me to Sir John Savage, that knight,
  Lady, he is my sister's sone,
Since upon a friday at night
  Before my bedside he kneeled downe:
He desired me as I was uncle dear,
  Many a time full tenderly,
That I would lowly King Richard require
  If I might get him any fee.

I came before my soveraigne Lord,
   And kneeled down upon my knee,
So soon to me he did accord,
   I thanked him full courteously,
A gatt him an hundred pounds in Kent
   To him and his heirs perpetually,
Also a manor of a duchy rent,
   Two hundred pounds he may spend thereby,
And high sheriff of Worcestershire,
   And also the park of Tewksbury.
He hath it all at his desire,
   Therewith dayley he may make merry.
Bid him come as a merchant man
   Of West Chester, that fair city,
And seven yeomen to wait him on,
   Bid him come to London and speak with me.
Commend me to good Gilbert Talbott,
   A gentle esquire forsooth is he ;
Once on a Fryday, full well I woot
   King Richard called him traitour high :
But Gilbert to his fawchon prest,
   A bold esquire forsooth is he ;
Their durst no sarjant him arreast,
   He is called so perlous of his body.
In the Tower Street I meet him then
   Going to Westminster to take sanctuarie ;
I light beside my horse I was upon,
   The purse from my belt I gave him truely ;
I bad him ride down into the North-West,
   Perchance a knight in England I might him see :

Wherefore pray him at my request
   To come to London to speak with me.
Then said the royall Lord so just,
   Now you have written, and sealed have I,
There is no messenger that we may trust,
   To bring these writeings into the West Countrey.
Because our matter it is so high,
   Least any man wou'd us descry.
Humphrey Brereton, then said Bessye,
   Hath been true to my father and me;
He shall take the writeings in hand,
   And bring them into the West Countrey:
I trust him best of all this land
   On this message to go for me.
Go to thy bed, Father, and sleep full soon,
   And I shall wake for you and me,
By tomorrow at the riseing of the sune,
   Humphrey Brereton shall be with thee.
She brings the Lord to his bed so trimly dight
   All that night where he should lye,
And Bessy waked all that night,
   There came no sleep within her eye:
In the morning when the day can spring,
   Up riseth young Bessye,
And maketh hast in her dressing;
   To Humphrey Brereton gone is she:
But when she came to Humphrey's bower bright,
   With a small voice called she,
Humphrey answered that lady bright,
   Saith, Who calleth on me so early?

I am King Edward's daughter right,
  The Countesse clear, young Bessy,
In all hast with mean and might
  Thou must come speak with the Earle of Darby.
Humphrey cast upon him a gowne,
  And a pair of slippers upon his feet;
Alas! said Humphrey, I may not ride,
  My horse is tired as you may see;
Since I came from London city,
  Neither night nor day, I tell you plain,
There came no sleep within my eye;
  On my business I thought certaine.
Lay thee down, Humphrey, he said, and sleep,
  I will give space of hours three:
A fresh horse I thee bechyte,
  Shall bring thee through the West Countrey.
Humphrey slept not hours two,
  But on his journey well thought hee;
A fresh horse was brought him tooe,
  To bring him through the West Countrey.
Then Humphrey Brereton with mickle might,
  Hard at Latham knocketh hee;
Who is it, said the porter, this time of the night,
  That so hastily calleth on mee?
The porter then in that state,
  That time of the night riseth hee,
And forthwith opened me the gate,
  And received both my horse and me.
Then said Humphrey Brereton, truely
  With the Lord Strange speak would I faine,

From his father the Earle of Darby.
   Then was I welcome that time certaine ;
A torch burned that same tide,
   And other lights that he might see ;
And brought him to the bedd side
   Where as the Lord Strange lie.
The lord mused in that tide,
   Said, Humphrey Brereton, what mak'st thou here?
How fareth my father, that noble lord,
   In all England that hath no peer?
Humphrey took him a letter in hand,
   And said, Behold, my lord, and you may see.
When the Lord Strange looked the letter upon,
   The tears trickled downe from his eye :
He said, we must come under a cloud,
   We must never trusted bee ;
We may sigh and make a great moane,
   This world is not as it will bee.
Have here, Humphrey, pounds three,
   Better rewarded may thou bee ;
Commend me to my father dear,
   His daily blessing he would give me ;
He said also in that tide,
   Tell him all thus from me ;
If I be able to go or ride,
   This appointment keep will I.
When Humphrey received the gold, I say,
   Straight to Manchester rideth hee.
The sun was light up of the day,
   He was aware of the Warden and Edward Stanley ;

The one brother said to the other,
  As they together their matins did say :
Behold, he said, my own dear brother,
  Yonder comes Humphrey Brereton, it is no nay,
My father's servant at command,
  Some hasty tydeings bringeth hee.
He took them either a letter in hand,
  And bad them behold, read and see :
They turn'd their backs shortly tho',
  And read those letters readily.
Up they leap and laughed too,
  And also they made game end glee,—
Fair fare our father, that noble lord,
  To stirr and rise now beginneth hee :
Buckingham's blood shall be wroken,
  That was beheaded in Salsbury ;
Fare fall that countesse, the king's daughter,
  That fair lady, young Bessye.
We trust in Jesus in time hereafter,
  To bring thy love over the sea.
Have here, Humphrey, of either of us shillings ten,
  Better rewarded may thou bee.
He took the gold of the two gentlemen,
  To sir John Savage then rideth hee ;
He took him then a letter in hand,
  And bad him behold, read and see :
When sir John Savage looked the letter upon,
  All blackned the knight's blee ;
Woman's wisdom is wondrous to hear, loe,
  My uncle is turned by young Bessye :

Derbyshire Ballads.

Whether it turn to waile or woe,
   At my uncle's bidding will I bee.
To Sheffield Castle at that same tide,
   In all the hast that might bee,
Humphrey took his horse and forth could ride
   To Gilbert Talbot fair and free.
He took him a letter in his hand,
   Behold, said Humphrey, read and see;
When he the letter looked upon,
   A loud laughter laughed hee,—
Fare fall that Lord in his renowne there,
   To stirr and rise beginneth hee:
Fair fall Bessie that countesse clear,
   That such councell cou'd give truely;
Commend me to my nephew nigh of blood,
   The young Earle of Shrewsbury,
Bid him neither dread for death nor good;
   In the Tower of London if he bee,
I shall make London gates to tremble and quake,
   But my nephew borrowed shall bee.
Commend me to the countess that fair make,
   King Edward's daughter, young Bessy:
Tell her I trust in Jesu that hath no pear,
   To bring her love over the sea.
Commend me to that lord to me so dear,
   That lately was made the Earle of Darby;
And every hair of my head
   For a man counted might bee,
With that lord without any dread,
   With him will I live and dye.

Have here, Humphrey, pounds three,
    Better rewarded may thou bee:
Look to London gates thou ride quickly,
    In all the hast that may bee;
Commend me to that countesse young Bessy,
    She was King Edward's daughter dear,
Such a one she is, I say truely,
    In all this land she hath no peer.
He took his leave at that time,
    Strait to London rideth he,
In all the hast that he could wind,
    His journey greatly he did apply.
But when he came to London, as I weene,
    It was but a little before the evening,
There was he warr, walking in a garden,
    Both the earle, and Richard the king.
When the earle did Humphrey see,
    When he came before the king,
He gave him a privy twink then with his eye,
    Then down falls Humphrey on his knees kneeling;
Welcome, Humphrey, says the lord,
    I have missed thee weeks three.
I have been in the west, my lord,
    There born and bred was I,
For to sport and play me certaine,
    Among my friends far and nigh.
Tell me, Humphrey, said the earle then,
    How fareth all that same countrey?
Of all the countreys I dare well say,
    They be the flower of chivalry;

For they will bycker with their bowes,
    They will fight and never fly.
Tell me, Humphrey, I thee pray,
    How fareth King Richard his commenty?
When King Richard heard him say so,
    In his heart he was right merry;
He with his cap that was so dear.
    He thanked that lord most courteously:
And said, father Stanley, thou art to me near,
    You are the chief of our poor commenty;
Half England shall be thine,
    It shall be equall between thee and me;
I am thine and thou art mine,
    So two fellows will we bee.
I swear by Mary, that mild maiden,
    I know no more such under the skye;
When I am king and wear the crown, then
    I will be chief of the poor commenty:
Task nor mize I will make none,
    In no countrey farr nor nigh;
If their goods I shoud take and pluck them downe,
    For me they woud fight full faintly:
There is no riches to me so rich,
    As is the love of our poor commenty.
When they had ended all their speeches,
    They take their leave full heartiley;
And to his bower King Richard is gone.
    The earle and Humphrey Brereton
To Bessy's bower anon were gone;
    When Bessy Humphrey did see anon,

She took him in her arms and kissed him times three.
   Welcome, she said, Humphrey Brereton ;
How hast thou spedd in the West Countrey
   I pray thee tell me quickly and anon.
Into a parlour they went from thence,
   There were no more but he and shee :
Humphrey, said Bessy, tell me e're we go hence
   Some tideings out of the West Countrey ;
If I shall send for yonder prince
   To come over the sea, for the love of me,
And if King Richard shoud him convince,
   Alas ! it were great ruthe to see,
Or murthered among the Stanley's blood to be,
   Indeed that were great pitty :
That sight on that prince I woud not see,
   For all the gold in Christantie !
Tell me, Humphrey, I thee pray,
   How hast thou spedd in the West Countrey ?
What answer of them thou had now say,
   And what reward they gave to thee.
By the third day of May it shall be seen.
   In London all that they will bee ;
Thou shalt in England be a queen,
   Or else doubtless that they will dye.
Thus they proceed forth the winter then,
   Their councell they kept close all three,
The earle he wrought by prophecy certaine,
   In London he would not abide or bee,
But in the subburbs without the city
   An ould inn chosen hath hee.

A drew an Eagle foot on the door truely,
　　That the western men might know where he did lye.
Humphrey stood on a high tower then,
　　He looked into the West Countrey;
Sir William Stanley and seven in green,
　　He was aware of the Eagle drawne;
He drew himselfe so wonderous nigh,
　　And bad his men go into the towne.
And drink the wine and make merry;
　　Into the same inn he went full prest,
Whereas the earle his brother lay.
　　Humphrey full soon into the west
Looks over a long lee;
　　He was aware of the Lord Strange and seven in green,
Come rideing into the city.
　　When he was aware of the Eagle drawn,
He drew himself so wonderously nigh,
　　He bad his men go into the towne certain,
And drink the wine and make merry:
　　And he himselfe drew then,
Where as his father in the inne lay.
　　Humphrey looked in the west, I say,
Sixteen in green then did he see;
　　He was aware of the Warden and Edward Stanley,
Come rideing both in one company.
　　When they were aware of the Eagle drawne,
The gentlemen they drew it nee:
　　And had their men go into the towne,
And drink the wine and make merry.
　　And did go themselves into the same inn full prest,

Where the earle their father lay.

Yet Humphrey beholdeth into the west,
And looketh towards the north countrey;

He was aware of Sir John Savage and Sir Gilbert Talbot,
Came rideing both in one company.

When they were aware of the Eagle drawn,
Themselves drew it full nigh,

And bad their men go into the towne,
To drink the wine and make merry.

They did go themselves into the same inn,
Where as the earle and Bessy lye.

When all the lords together were,
Amongst them all Bessy was full buissy;

With goodly words Bessy then said there,
Fair lords, what will you do for me?

Will you relieve yonder prince,
That is exiled beyond the sea?

I woad not have King Richard him to convince,
For all the gold in Christentye.

The Earle of Darby came forth then,
These words he said to young Bessye,—

Ten thousand pounds will I send,
Bessy, for the love of thee,

And twenty thousand Eagle feet,
The Queen of England for to make thee;

Then Bessy most lowly the earle did greet,
And thankt his honor most heartiley.

Sir William Stanley came forth then,
These words he said to fair Bessy:

Remember, Bessy, another time,

Who doth the most, Bessy, for thee ;
   Ten thousand coats, that shall be red certaine,
In an hours warning ready shall bee ;
   In England thou shalt be our queen,
Or doubtlesse I will dye.
   Sir John Savage came forth then,
These words he said to young Bessye,—
   A thousand marks for thy sake certaine,
Will I send thy love beyond the sea.
   Sir Gilbert Talbott came forth then,
These were the words he said to Bessy :
   Ten thousand marks for thy sake certaine,
I will send to beyond the sea.
   The Lord Strange came forth then,
These were the words he said to Bessy :
   A little money and few men,
Will bring thy love over the sea ;
   Let us keep our gold at home, said he,
For to wage our company ;
   For if we should send it over the sea,
We shoud put our gold in jeopartie.
   Edward Stanley came forth then,
These were the words he said to Bessye :
   Remember, Bessye, another time,
Who that now doth the best for thee,
   For there is no power that I have,
Nor no gold for to give thee ;
   I will be under my father's banner, if God me save,
There either to live or dye.
   Bessye came forth before the lords all,

And downe she falleth upon her knee :
  Nineteen thousand pound of gold, I shall
Send my love behind the sea,
  A love letter, and a gold ring,
From my heart root rite will I.
  Who shall be the messenger the same to bring,
Both the gold and the writeing over the sea ?
  Humphrey Brereton, said Bessy,
I know him trusty and true certaine,
  Therefore the writeing and the gold truely
By him shall be carried to Little Brittaine.
  Alas, said Humphry, I dare not take in hand.
To carry the gold over the sea ;
  These galley shipps they be so strange,
They will me night so wonderously ;
  They will me robb, they will me drowne.
They will take the gold from me.
  Hold thy peace, Humphrey, said Bessye then,
Thou shalt it carry without jepordye ;
  Thou shalt not have any caskett nor any male,
Nor budgett, nor cloak sack, shall go with thee ;
  Three mules that be stiff and strong withall,
Sore loaded with gold shall they bee,
  With saddle-side skirted I do tell thee
Wherein the gold sowe will I :
  If any man faine whose is the shipp truely
That saileth forth upon the sea,
  Say it is the Lord Lislay,
In England and France well beloved is he.
  Then came forth the Earle of Darby.

These words he said to young Bessy :
He said, Bessye, thou art to blame
 To appoint any shipp upon the sea :
I have a good shipp of my owne,
 Shall carry Humphrey with the mules three ;
An eagle shall be drawne upon the mast top,
 That the Italians may it see :
There is no freak in all France
 The eagle that dare come nee
If any one ask whose ship it is, then
 Say it is the Earles of Darby.
Humphrey took the three mules then,
 Into the west wind wou'd hee.
Without all doubt at Liverpoole
 He took shipping upon the sea :
With a swift wind and a liart,
 He so saild upon the sea,
To Beggrames Abbey in Little Brittain,
 Where as the English Prince lie ;
The Porter was a Cheshire man,
 Well he knew Humphrey when he him see ;
Humphrey knockt at the gate truely,
 Where as the porter stood it by,
And welcomed me full heartiley,
 And received then my mules three ;
I shall thee give in this breed
 To thy reward pounds three ;
I will none of thy gold, the porter said,
 Nor Humphrey none of the fee,
I will open thee the gates certaine

To receive thee and the mules three;
For a Cheshire man born am I certain,
    From the Malpas but miles three.
The porter opened the gates that time,
    And received him and the mules three.
The wine that was in the hall that time
    He gave to Humphrey Brereton truely.
Alas! said Humphrey, how shoud I doe,
    I am strayed in a strange countrey,
The Prince of England I do not know,
    Before I never did him see.
I shall thee tell, said the porter then,
    The Prince of England know shall ye,
Low where he siteth at the butts certaine,
    With other lords two or three;
He weareth a gown of velvet black
    And it is cutted above the knee.
With a long visage and pale and black
    Thereby know that prince may ye;
A wart he hath, the porter said,
    A little alsoe above the chinn,
His face is white, his wart is redd.
    No more than the head of a small pinn:
You may know the prince certaine,
    As soon as you look upon him truely.—
He received the wine of the porter, then
    With him he took the mules three.
When Humphrey came before that prince
    He falleth downe upon his knee,
He delivereth the letters which Bessy sent.

And so did he the mules three,
   A rich ring with a stone,
     Thereof the prince glad was hee:
He took the ring of Humphrey then,
   And kissed the ring times three.
Humphrey kneeled still as any stone,
   As sure as I do tell to thee;
Humphrey of the prince answer gott none,
   Therefore in heart was he heavy;
Humphrey stood up then full of skill,
   And then to the prince said he:
Why standest thou so still at thy will,
   And no answer dost give to me?
I am come from the Stanleys' blood so dear.
   King of England for to make thee,
A fairer lady then thou shalt have to thy fair,
   There is not one in all christantye;
She is a countesse, a king's daughter, Humphrey said,
   The name of her it is Bessye,
She can write, and she can read,
   Well can she work by prophecy;
I may be called a lewd messenger,
   For answer of thee I can gett none,
I may sail home with heavy cheare,
   What shall I say when I come home?
The prince he took the Lord Lee,
   And the Earle of Oxford was him nee,
The Lord Ferris wou'd not him beguile truely,
   To councell they are gone all three:
When they had their councell taken,

To Humphrey then turned he :
Answer, Humphrey, I can give none truely
   Within the space of weeks three ;
The mules into a stable were taken anon,
   The saddle skirts unopened were,
Therein he found gold great plenty
   For to wage a company.
He caused the abbot to make him chear:
   In my stead now let him be,
If I be king and wear the crown
   Well acquited Abbott shalt thou be.
Early in the morning they made them knowne,
   As soon as the light they cou'd see ;
With him he taketh his lords three,
   And straight to Paris he took his way.
An herriott of arms they made ready,
   Of men and money they cou'd him pray,
And shipps to bring him over the sea,
   The Stanleys' blood for me hath sent,
The King of England for to make me,
   And I thank them for their intent,
For if ever in England I wear the crowne,
   Well acequited the King of France shall be :
Then answered the King of France anon,
   Men nor money he getteth none of me,
Nor no shipps to bring him over the sea ;
   In England if he wear the crowne,
Then will he claim them for his own truely :
   With this answer departed the prince anon,
And so departed the same tide.

   And the English lords three
To Beggrames Abbey soon coud the ride,
   There as Humphrey Brereton then lee ;
Have Humphrey a thousand mark here,
   Better rewarded may thou be :
Commend me to Bessy that Countesse clear,
   Before her never did I see :
I trust in God she shall be my feer,
   For her I will travell over the sea ;
Commend me to my father Stanley, to me so dear,
   My owne mother married hath he,
Bring him here a love letter full right
   And another to young Bessye,
Tell her, I trust in Jesus full of might
   That my queen that she shall bee ;
Commend me to Sir William Stanley,
   That noble knight in the west countrey,
Tell him that about Michaelmas certaine
   In England I do hope to be ;
At Millford haven I will come inn
   With all the power that make may I,
The first town I will come inn
   Shall be the towne of Shrewsbury ;
Pray Sir William Stanley, that noble knight,
   That night that he will look on me :
Commend me to Sir Gilbert Talbot, that royall knight,
   He much in the north countrey,
And Sir John Savage, that man of might,
   Pray them all to look on me,
For I trust in Jesus Christ so full of might,

In England for to abide and bee.
I will none of thy gold, sir prince, said Humphrey then.
   Nor none sure will I have of thy fee,
Therefore keep thy gold thee within,
   For to wage thy company ;
If every hair were a man,
   With thee, sir prince, will I be :
Thus Humphrey Brereton his leave hath tane,
   And sailed forth upon the sea,
Straight to London he rideth then,
   There as the earle and Bessy lay ;
And bad them behold, read and see.
The earle took leave of Richard the king,
And into the west wind wou'd he ;
   He left Bessye in Leicester then
And bad her lye in pryvitye,
   For if King Richard knew thee here anon,
In a fire burned thou must be.
   Straight to Latham the earle is gone,
There as the Lord Strange then lee ;
   He sent the Lord Strange to London,
To keep King Richard company.
   Sir William Stanley made anone
Ten thousand coats readily,
   Which were as redd as any blood,
Thereon the hart's head was set full high,
   Which after were tryed both trusty and good
As any cou'd be in Christantye.
   Sir Gilbert Talbot ten thousand doggs
In one hour's warning for to be,

And Sir John Savage fifteen white hoods,
Which wou'd fight and never flee;
Edward Stanley had three hundred men,
There were no better in Christantye;
Sir Rees ap Thomas, a knight of Wales certain,
Eight thousand spears brought he.
Sir William Stanley sat in the Holt Castle,
And looked over his head so high;
Which way standeth the wind, can any tell?
I pray you, my men, look and see.
The wind it standeth south east,
So said a knight that stood him by.
This night yonder prince, truely
Into England entereth hee.
He called a gentleman that stood him nigh,
His name was Rowland of Warburton.
He bad him go to Shrewsbury that night,
And bid yonder prince come inn:
But when Rowland came to Shrewsbury,
The portculles was let downe;
They called him Henry Tydder, in scorn truely,
And said, in England he shou'd wear no crowne:
Rowland bethought him of a wyle then,
And tied a writeing to a stone,
And threw the writeing over the wall certain,
And bad the bailiffs to look it upon:
They opened the gates on every side,
And met the prince with procession:
And wou'd not in Shrewsbury there abide,
But straight he drest him to Stafford towne.

King Richard heard then of his comeing,
He called his lords of great renowne;
　The Lord Pearcy he came to the king
And upon his knees he falleth downe,
　I have thirty thousand fighting men
For to keep the crown with thee.
　The Duke of Northfolk came to the king anone,
And downe he falleth upon his knee;
　The Earle of Surrey, that was his heir,
Were both in one company;
　We have either twenty thousand men here,
For to keep the crown with thee.
　The Lord Latimer, and the Lord Lovell,
And the Earle of Kent he stood him by,
　The Lord Ross, and the Lord Scrope, I you tell,
They were all in one company;
　The Bishopp of Durham, he was not away,
Sir William Bonner he stood him by,
　The good Sir William of Harrington, as I say,
Said, he wou'd fight and never fly.
　King Richard made a messenger,
And sent him into the west countrey,
　And bid the Earle of Darby make him bowne,
And bring twenty thousand men unto me,
　Or else the Lord Strange his head I will him send,
And doubtless his son shall dye;
　For hitherto his father I took for my friend,
And now he hath deceived me.
　Another herald appeared then
To Sir William Stanley that doughty knight,

Bid him bring to me ten thousand men,
Or else to death he shall be dight.
 Then answered that doughty knight,
And spake to the herald without letting ;
 Say, upon Bosseworth Field I meen to fight,
Uppon Monday early in the morning :
 Such a breakfast I him behight,
As never did knight to any king.
 The messenger home can him gett,
To tell King Richard this tydeing.
 Fast together his hands then cou'd he ding,
And said, the Lord Strange shou'd surely dye ;
 And putt him into the Tower of London,
For at liberty he shou'd not bee.
 Lett us leave Richard and his lords full of pride,
And talk we more of the Stanleys' blood,
 That brought Richmond over the sea with wind and tyde,
From Litle Brittain into England over the flood.
 Now is Earle Richmond into Stafford come,
And Sir William Stanley to Litle Stoone ;
 The prince had rather then all the gold in Christantye,
To have Sir William Stanley to look upon ;
 A messenger was made ready anone,
That night to go to Litle Stoon ;
 Sir William Stanley he rideth to Stafford towne,
With a solemn company ready bowne.
 When the knight to Stafford was comin,
That Earle Richmond might him see,
 He took him in his arms then,
And there he kissed him times three ;

The welfare of thy body doth comfort me more
Then all the gold in Christantye.
    Then answered that royall knight there,
And to the prince these words spake he,—
    Remember, man, both night and day,
Who doth now the most for thee :
    In England thou shalt wear a crown, I say,
Or else doubtless I will dye ;
    A fairer lady then thou shalt have for thy feer,
Was there never in Christanty ;
    She is a countesse, a king's daughter,
And there to both wise and witty ;
    I must this night to Stone, my soveraigne,
For to comfort my company.
    The prince he took him by the hand,
And said, farewell, Sir William, fair and free.
    Now is word come to Sir William Stanley there,
Early in the Monday, in the morning,
    That the Earle of Darby, his brother dear,
Had given battle to Richard the king.
    That wou'd I not, said Sir William anone,
For all the gold in Christantye,
    That the battle shou'd be done ;
Straight to Lichfield cou'd he ride,
    In all the hast that might bee.
And when he came to Lichfield that tyde,
    All they cryed King Henry :
Straight to Bolesworth can they go
    In all the hast that might be,
But when he came Bolesworth Field unto,

Derbyshire Ballads.

There met a royall company ;
The Earle of Darby thither was come,
   And twenty thousand stood him by :
Sir John Savage, his sister's son,
   He was his nephew of his blood so nigh,
He had fifteen hundred fighting men,
   That wou'd fight and never flye :
Sir William Stanley, that royall knight, then
   Ten thousand red coats had he,
They wou'd bicker with their bows there,
   They wou'd fight and never flye :
The Red Rosse, and the Blew Boar.
   They were both a solemn company ;
Sir Rees ap Thomas he was thereby,
   With ten thousand spears of mighty tree :
The Earle of Richmond went to the Earle of Darby,
   And downe he falleth upon his knee,
Said, father Stanley, full of might,
   The vaward I pray you give to me,
For I am come to claime my right,
   And faine revenged wou'd I bee.
Stand up, he said, my son, quickly,
   Thou hast thy mother's blessing truely,
The vaward, son, I will give to thee,
   So that thou wilt be ordered by me :
Sir William Stanley, my brother dear,
   In the battle he shall be ;
Sir John Savage, he hath no peer,
   He shall be a wing then to thee ;
Sir Rees ap Thomas shall break the array,

For he will fight and never flee ;
I myselfe will hove on the hill, I say,
   The fair battle I will see.
King Richard he hoveth upon the mountaine :
   He was aware of the banner of the bould Stanley,
And saith, Fetch hither the Lord Strange certain,
   For he shall dye this same day ;
To the death, Lord, thee ready make,
   For I tell thee certainly
That thou shalt dye for thy uncle's sake,
   Wild William of Stanley.
If I shall dye, said the Lord Strange then,
   As God forbid it shou'd so bee,
Alas ! for my lady that is at home,
   It should be long or she see me,
But we shall meet at doomsday,
   When the great doom shall be.
He called for a gent in good fay,
   Of Lancashire, both fair and free,
The name of him it was Lathum ;
   A ring of gould he took from his finger,
And threw it to the gent then,
   And bad him bring it to Lancashire,
To his lady that was at home ;
   At her table she may sit right,
Or she see her lord it may be long.
   I have no foot to fligh nor fight,
I must be murdered with the king :
   If fortune my uncle Sir William Stanley loose the field,
As God forbid it shou'd so bee,

Pray her to take my eldest son and child,
And exile him over behind the sea ;
   He may come in another time
By feild or fleet, by tower or towne,
   Wreak so he may his father's death in fyne,
Upon Richard of England that weareth the crown.
   A knight to King Richard then did appeare,
The good Sir William of Harrington.
   Let that Lord have his life, my dear
Sir king, I pray you grant me this boone,
   We shall have upon this field anon,
The father, the son, and the uncle all three :
   Then shall you deem, lord, with your own mouth then,
What shall be the death of them all three.
   Then a block was cast upon the ground,
Thereon the lord's head was laid,
   A slave over his head can stand,
And thus that time to him thus said :
   In faith there is no other booty tho',
But need that thou must be dead.
   Harrington in hart was full woe,
When he saw that the lord must needs be dead.
   He said, our ray breaketh on ev'ry side,
We put our feyld in jepordie.
   He took up the lord that tyde,
King Richard after did him never see.
   Then they blew up their bewgles of brass,
That made many a wife to cry alas !
   And many a wive's child fatherlesse ;
They shott of guns then very fast,

Over their heads they could them throw :
Arrows flew them between,
   As thick as any hayle or snowe,
As then that time might plaine be seene ;
   Then Rees ap Thomas with the black raven,
Shortly he brake their array ;
   Then with thirty thousand fighting men
The Lord Pearcy went his way ;
   The Duke of Northefolke wou'd have fledd with a good
With twenty thousand of his company,   [will,
   They went up to a wind millne uppon a hill,
That stood soe fayre and wonderousse hye ;
   There he met Sir John Savage, a royall knight,
And with him a worthy company ;
   To the death was he then dight.
And his sonne prisoner taken was he :
   Then the Lord Alroes began for to flee,
And so did many other moe ;
   When King Richard that sight did see,
In his heart hee was never soe woe :
   I pray you, my merry men, be not away,
For upon this field will I like a man dye,
   For I had rather dye this day,
Then with the Standley prisoner to be.
   A knight to King Richard can say there,
Good Sir William of Harrington ;
   He said, sir king, it hathe no peer,
Upon this feyld to death to be done,
   For there may no man these dints abide :
Low, your horse is ready at your hand :

Sett the crown upon my head that tyde,
Give me my battle axe in my hand;
 I make a vow to myld Mary that is so bright,
I will dye the king of merry England.

Besides his head they hewed the crown down right,
That after he was not able to stand;
 They dinge him downe as they were woode,
They beat his bassnet to his heade,

Until the braynes came out with the bloode;
They never left him till he was dead.
 Then carryed they him to Leicester,
And pulled his head under his feet.

Bessye mett him with a merry cheare,
And with these words she did him greete;
 How like you the killing of my brethren dear?
Welcome, gentle uncle, home!

Great solace ytt was to see and hear,
When the battell yt was all done;
 I tell you, masters, without lett,
When the Red Rosse soe fair of hew,

And young Bessye together mett,
It was great joy I say to you.
 A bishopp then marryed with a ringe
The two bloods of great renowne.

Bessy said, now may we singe,
Wee two bloods are made all one.
 The Earle of Darby hee was there,
And Sir William Stanley, that noble knight,

Upon their heads he set the crown so fair,
That was made of gould so bright.

And there he came under a cloud,
That some time in England looked full high ;
   But then the hart he lost his head,
That after no man cou'd him see.
   But Jesus, that is both bright and shine,
And born was of mylde Mary,
   Save and keepe our noble kinge,
And also the poore commentie. Amen.

The other version of this ballad, to which I have referred, is preserved in the Harleian MSS. It differs considerably from the one here printed, as will be at once apparent from the following opening passage :—

God that is moste of myghte,
   And born was of a mayden free,
Save and kepe our comlye queene.
   And also the poore comynalitie ;
For wheras Kynge Richard, I understande.
   Had not reigned yeares three.
But the beste Duke in all this lande
   He caused to be headit at Salysburye ;
That tyme the Standleyes without dowte
   Were dred over England ferre and nee.
Next Kynge Richard that was soe stowte
   Of any lorde in England free.
There was a ladye faire on moulde,
   The name of hir was litiil Bessie ;
She was yonge, she was not oulde.
   Bot of the yeares of one and twentye ;
She colde wryte and she coulde reede,

Well she coulde wyrke by propesye;
She sojorned in the cetye of London
   That tyme with the Earle of Derbye.
Upon a tyme, as I you tell,
   There was noe moe bot the Earle and she,
She made complaynte one Richard the Kynge,
   That was hir uncle of blode soe nee.

There are many other ballads having reference to the Stanleys, Earls of Derby; but this will be sufficient as a present example.

Devonshire's Noble Duel

WITH LORD DANBY IN THE YEAR 1687.

F this curious ballad, which is also known by the name of "The Long Armed Duke," there are several versions. The one here given is printed from a broad-sheet, and is, perhaps, the most complete of any of the versions which has come under my notice. The circumstance which gave rise to the ballad has not as yet been satisfactorily explained. It has been suggested that its origin was the quarrel in which the Earl of Devonshire, Lord Delamere, and Colonel Colepepper were engaged. It is traditionally said that the arms of the "Long Armed Duke" were so long that he could garter his stockings below the knee without stooping down or being seated!

Good people give attention to a story you shall hear,
Between the King and my Lord Delamere
A quarrel arose in the Parliament House,
Concerning the Taxes to be put in force.
      With my fal de ral de ra.

I wonder, I wonder, that James our good King,
So many hard Taxes upon the poor should bring ;
So many hard Taxes, as I have heard them say
Makes many a good farmer to break and run away.

Such a rout has been in the Parliament, as I hear,
Betwixt a Dutch lord and my Lord Delamere.
He said to the King, as he sat on the throne,
" If it please you, my Liege, to grant me a boon."

" Oh, what is thy boon ? Come let me understand."
" 'Tis to give me all the poor you have in the land ;
I'll take them down to Cheshire, and there I will sow
Both hemp seed and flax seed, and hang them in a row.

It's better, my Liege, they should die a shorter death,
Than for your Majesty to starve them on earth."
With that up starts a Dutch Lord, as we hear,
And he says, " Thou proud Jack," to my Lord Delamere,

" Thou ought to be stabbed," and he turned him about,
" For affronting the King in the Parliament House."
Then up got a brave Duke, the Duke of Devonshire,
Who said, " I will fight for my Lord Delamere :—

He is under age, as I'll make it appear ;
So I'll stand in defence of my Lord Delamere."
A stage then was built, and to battle they went,
To kill or be killed it was their intent.

The very first blow, as we understand.
Devonshire's rapier went back to his hand ;
Then he muséd awhile, but not a word spoke
When against the King's armour his rapier he broke.

Oh, then he stept backward, and backward stept he,
And then stept forward my Lord Willoughby;
He gave him a rapier, and thus he did say,
"Play low, Devonshire, there's treachery, I see."

He knelt on his knee, and he gave him the wound;
With that the Dutch Lord fell dead on the ground.
The King call'd his soldiers, and thus he did say,
"Call Devonshire down, take the dead man away."

He answered, "My Liege, I've killed him like a man,
And it is my intent to see what clothing he's got on.
O treachery! O treachery! as I well may say,
It was your intent, O King, to take my life away.

He fought in *your* armour, while I fought him bare,
And thou, King, shalt win it before thou dost it wear;
I neither do curse King, Parliament, or Throne,
But I wish every honest man may enjoy his own.

The rich men do flourish with silver and gold,
While poor men are starving with hunger and cold;
And if they hold on as they have begun,
They'll make little England pay dear for a King."

Another version, which I have in MS., has, besides many minor variations, these additional verses:—

Oh the Duchess of Devonshire was standing hard by,
Upon her dear husband she cast her lovely eye;
"Oh, fie upon treachery—there's been treachery, I say,—
It was your full intent to have ta'en my Duke's life away."

Then away to the Parliament these votes all went again,
And there they acted like just and honest men.
I neither curse my King, nor kingdom, crown or throne,
But I wish every honest man to enjoy but what is his own.

One of the versions of this ballad gives the name of Lord Delaware —

" In the Parliament House a great rout has been there,
  Betwixt our good King and the Lord Delaware."

And it also gives the locality for sowing " hemp seed and flax seed " to " Lincolnshire." This same version speaks of the Duke of Devonshire as—

" Up sprung a Welch Lord, the brave Duke of Devonshire."

There can be no doubt, however, that Lord Delamere is the peer intended to be commemorated, and that Cheshire is the county to which he is made to refer, and to which indeed he belonged.

The Unconsionable Batchelors of Darby:

Or the Young Lasses Pawn'd by their Sweet-hearts, for a large Reckning, at Nottingham Goose-Fair, where poor Susan was forced to pay the Shot.

To the tune of *To thee, to thee, &c.*

THIS curious ballad I reprint from a black-letter broad-sheet in the Roxburghe Collection in the British Museum, where it is adorned with three curious wood-cuts. Nottingham Goose

Fair, it may be well to remark, is still the most popular fair in the Midland Counties, and is annually attended by many of the "Lasses of Darby," who "with young men" go "to Goose-fair for recreation," by special trains and otherwise. The distance of Nottingham from Derby by turnpike road, along which the lasses and young men of the ballad must have travelled, is fifteen miles. Goose-fair formerly lasted for twenty-one days.

> You lovers of mirth attend a while
>   a merry new Ditty here I write
> I know it will make you laugh and smile
>   for every line affords delight :
> The Lasses of Darby with young Men
>   they went to Goose-fair for recreation
> But how these Sparks did serve them then
>   is truly worth your observation :
> Truly, truly, worth your observation,
>   therefore I pray observe this Ditty
> The Maids did complain they came there in vain
>   and was not, was not that a pity.
>
> So soon as they came into the Fair
>   the Batchellers made them conjues low
> And bid them a thousand welcomes there
>   this done, to a tipling-school they go :
> How pleasant was honest Kate and Sue?
>   believing they should be richly treated,
> But Neighbours and Friends as I am true
>   no Lasses ever was so cheated :
> Cheated, cheated, very farely cheated
>   they were left alone to make their moan
> And was not, was not that a pity.

The innocent Lasses fair and gay
    concluded the Men was kind and free
Because they pass'd the time away
    a plenty of cakes and ale they see;
For sider and mead they then did call
    and whatever else the House afforded
But Susan was forc'd to pay for all
    out of the money she had hoarded
Hoarded, hoarded, money she had hoarded
    it made her sing a doleful Ditty
And so did the rest with grief opprest
    and was not, was not that a pity.

Young Katy she seemed something coy
    because she would make them eager grow,
As knowing thereby she might enjoy
    what beautiful Damsels long to know.
On compliments they did not stand
    nor did they admire their charming features
For they had another game in hand
    which was to pawn those pretty Creatures:
Creatures, creatures, loving loving creatures
    which was so charming fair and pretty
The Men sneak'd away and nothing did pay
    and was not, was not that a pity?

Though 'f out of the door they enterd first
    and left them tipling there behind
Those innocent Maids did not mistrust
    that Batchelors could be so unkind;
Quoth Susan, I know their gone to buy
    the fairings which we do require

And they will return, I know, for why
    they do our youthful charms admire,
Therefore, therefore stay a little longer
    and I will sing a pleasant Ditty
But when they found they were catch'd in the pound
    they sigh'd and weep'd the more's the pity.

Now finding the Men returned no more
    and that the good People would not trust
They presently call'd to know the score
    it chanc'd to be fifteen shillings just :
Poor Kate had but five pence in her purse
    but Sue had a crown besides a guinney ;
And since the case had happen'd thus
    poor Soul she paid it e'ry penny :
Penny, penny, e'ry, e'ry penny
    tho' with a sad and doleful Ditty
Said she for this I had not a kiss
    and was not, was not that a pity ?

        Printed for J. Bessel, in West-Smithfield.

The Humours of Hayfield Fair.

THIS ballad, copied from a broad-sheet, has been printed in Hutchinson's "Tour through the High Peak of Derbyshire," 1809. It will be seen to be a version—whether the original one or not remains to be seen—of the favourite ballad usually called "Come Lasses and Lads," of which the earliest known copy appears to have been printed in 1672, under the title of "The Rural Dance about the May-pole," and which has again been printed in "Pills to purge Melancholy," in "Tixhall poetry," and also, with the music, in Chappel's "Popular Music of the Olden Time," as well as in several other works. It ought to be stated that the ballad I here reprint—" The Humours of Hayfield Fair,"—although I speak of it as a version of the "Rural Dance about the May-pole," is, with the exception of here and there a verse, or part of a verse, totally distinct from it. It will, of course, be seen to go to the same tune. Hayfield is a village near Chapel-en-le-Frith, in the High Peak of Derbyshire,—in the midst of a district as wild in its superstitions as in its ballad poetry, and in its traditions as in its scenery. It has two fairs in the year, which were formerly much frequented by the "Lads and Lasses" of the district, whether they had "leave of their dads" or not.

 Come, lasses and lads, take leave of your dads,
  And away to the fair let's hie ;
 For every lad has gotten his lass,
  And a fiddler standing by ;
 For Jenny has gotten her Jack,
  And Nancy has gotten her Joe,
 With Dolly and Tommy, good lack,
  How they jig it to and fro !
Ritum, raddledum, raddledum ; ritum raddledum ri :
Ritum, raddledum, raddledum ; ritum raddledum ri.

 My heart 'gain ribs ga' thumps,
  When I went to th' wake or fair,
 Wi' a pair of new sol'd pumps,
  To dance when I got there :
 I'd ride grey nag I swore,
  And were mounted like a king,
 Cousin Dickey walked on a'fore,
  Driving a pig tied wi' a string.
   Ritum raddledum, &c.

Pally Sampson too was there,
   Wi' "Neighbour how do you do?"
There were all the world at the fair,
   And drunk 'till they were fou';
'Twas neither heigh! nor gee!
   For soon as I sold my cow,
The fiddler shog'd his knee,
   And I danced my pumps clean through.
      Ritum raddledum, &c.

"You're out," says Dick—"I'm not," says Nick,
   "The fiddler plays it false;"
And so says Hugh, and so says Sue,
   And so says nimble Alice:
The fiddler did agree,
   To right us in a crack,
Dance face to face, says he,
   And then dance back to back.
      Ritum raddledum, &c.

Thus after an hour they tript to a bower
   To play for ale and cakes,
And kisses too—until they were due,
   The maidens held the stakes;
The women then began
   To quarrel with the men,
And bad them *take their kisses back*,
   And gi' 'em their *own again*.
      Ritum raddledum, &c.

Thus they sat, until it were late,
   And they tir'd the fiddler quite,

Wi' singing and playing, without any paying,
  From morning until it were night:
They told the fiddler then
  They'd pay him for his play.
And each gave two-pence,
  (Speaking) (Ey, they gave him two pence a piece)
And then they hopp'd away.
    Ritum raddledum, &c.

Come Dolly, says I, now homeward hie,
  And I'll go wi' thee a mile:
She twinkled her eyes wi' a sigh
  As I handed her over the style;
Then I cuddled, and kissed her face,
  Were I much to blame?
Had you been in my place,
(Speaking) I don't mean you in the smock frock dancing a hornpipe—I mean that sly looking fellow smoking his pipe in the corner,)
  I vow you'd ha' done the same.
    Ritum raddledum, &c.

ON THE

Strange and Wonderful Sight

That was seen in the Air on the 6th of March, 1716.

THIS ballad occurs in "The Garland of Merriment: containing Three New Songs. 1st. A Game at Cards for a Kingdom, or Mar routed. 2d. A Comical Scotch Dialogue between a

Highlander and his Wife about the last Battle. 3d. A Copy of Verses on the Death of my Lord Derwentwater. 4th. On the Wonderful Sight that was seen in the Air on the 6th of March last. Nottingham: Printed by William Ayscough in Bridlesmith Gate." I am not aware that it has ever been reprinted, except by myself in "The Reliquary" for April 1866. The appearances were probably those of the Aurora borealis. On the title-page of this curious chap-book, which was printed in 1716-7, is a wood-cut of four persons playing cards at a table.

THE sixth of March, kind neighbours this is true,
A wonder in the Sky came to my View;
I pray believe it, for I tell no Lye,
There's many more did see it as well as I.

I was on a Travel, and was very late,
To speak the truth just about Day-light' gate;
My Heart did tremble being all alone,
To see such Wonders—the like was never known.

The first of all so dark it was to me,
That much ado my Way I had to see;
I turn'd me round to see some Lights appear,
And then I saw those Wonders in the air.

These Lights to me like great long spears did show,
Sharp at one end, kind neighbours this is true:
I was so troubled I could not count them o'er,
But I suppose there was above a score.

Then I saw like Blood it did appear,
And that was very throng among those spears;
I thought the Sky would have opened in my View,
I was so daunted I knew not what to do.

F

The next I saw two Clouds meet fierce together
As if they would have fought one another;
And darkened all these Spears excepting one,
They gave a Clash and quickly they were gone.

The very last Day in the same month I am told
Many People did strange Sights behold;
At *Hartington*, the truth I will not spare,
That Night they saw Great Wonders in the Air.

This *Hartington* it is in *Darbyshire*,
And credible persons living there,
They have declared what Wonders they did view
The very last night in *March* its certain true.

About Eleven a'Clock late in that Night,
A very dark Cloud which did them sore afright;
Great smoke there came, it was perfect to their view,
They cried out, O Lord, what must we do?

They saw Great Lights which did amaze them sore,
The like was never seen in any *Age* before,
They went into their Houses for to Pray,
We must Repent whilst it is call'd to Day.

The Drunken Butcher of Tideswell.

TIDESWELL is one of the largest and most important villages in the High Peak of Derbyshire, and has been more than once, as will be seen in the present volume, celebrated in song and ballad. It is situated about seven miles from Buxton, and the same from Bakewell, in a highly romantic and wildly picturesque neighbourhood. Its church is a fine building, containing many interesting monuments, among which are those to the Foljambes, Meverells, &c., and one to Bishop Pursglove. The following ballad is the production of William Bennett, the author of "The King of the Peak," "The Cavalier," etc. Of this ballad Mr. Bennett thus spoke in the "Reliquary," in which it appeared:—"The ballad (the subject of which is as well known in the Peak as that Kinder Scout is the highest hill, and Tideswell Church the most stately and beautiful church in it) will perhaps appear a little modernised to some, who have only heard the tale from the mouths of unsober topers, accustomed to use ancient provincial and obsolete words, which not only render the sense less distinguishable, but also mar the flow of the rhythm. I confess, therefore, to having taken some liberties with the grammar, the orthography, and the metre; but in all other respects I have strictly adhered to the original; and my honesty in this respect will be recognized and admitted by many persons to whom these minstrel relics are precious.

"The legend is still so strong in the Peak, that numbers of the inhabitants do not concur in the sensible interpretation put upon the *appearance* by the Butcher's wife, but pertinaciously believe that the drunken man was beset by an evil spirit, which either ran by his horse's side, or rolled on the ground before him, faster than his horse could gallop, from Peak Forest to the sacred inclosure of Tideswell churchyard, where it disappeared; and many a bold fellow, on a moonlight night, looks anxiously around as he crosses Tideswell Moor, and gives his nag an additional touch of the spur, as he hears the bell of Tideswell Church swinging midnight to the winds, and remembers the tale of the 'Drunken Butcher of Tideswell.'"

OH, list to me, ye yeomen all,
    Who live in dale or down!
My song is of a butcher tall,
    Who lived in Tiddeswall town.
In bluff King Harry's merry days,
    He slew both sheep and kine;
And drank his fill of nut brown ale,
    In lack of good red wine.

Beside the Church this Butcher lived,
  Close to its gray old walls ;
And envied not, when trade was good,
  The Baron in his halls.
No carking cares disturbed his rest,
  When off to bed he slunk ;
And oft he snored for ten good hours,
  Because he got so drunk.

One only sorrow quelled his heart,
  As well it might quell mine—
The fear of sprites and grisly ghosts,
  Which dance in the moonshine :
Or wander in the cold Churchyard,
  Among the dismal tombs ;
Where hemlock blossoms in the day,
  By night the nightshade blooms.

It chanced upon a summer's day,
  When heather-bells were blowing,
Bold Robin crossed o'er Tiddeswall Moor,
  And heard the heath-cock crowing :
Well mounted on a forest nag,
  He freely rode and fast ;
Nor drew a rein, till Sparrow Pit,*
  And Paislow Moss† were past.

---

* Sparrow Pit is a small hamlet about two miles from Chapel-en-le-Frith, situated at the "four lane ends," where the Buxton and Castleton and the Chapel-en-le-Frith and Tideswell roads intersect each other.

† Paislow Moss, about half way between Sparrow Pit and Sandy Way Head.

Then slowly down the hill he came,
    To the Chappelle en le firth,*
Where, at the Rose of Lancaster,
    He found his friend the Smith :
The Parson, and the Pardoner too,
    There took their morning draught ;
And when they spied a Brother near,
    They all came out and laughed.

" Now draw thy rein, thou jolly Butcher ;
    " How far hast thou to ride ?"
" To Waylee-Bridge,† to Simon the Tanner,
    To sell this good cow-hide."
" Thou shalt not go one foot ayont,
    'Till thou light and sup with me ;
And when thou'st emptied my measure of liquor,
    I'll have a measure wi' thee."

" Oh no, oh no, thou drouthy Smith !
    I cannot tarry to-day :
The Wife, she gave me a charge to keep ;
    And I durst not say her nay."
" What likes o' that," said the Parson then,
    " If thou'st sworn, thou'st ne'er to rue :
Thou may'st keep thy pledge, and drink thy stoup,
    As an honest man e'en may do."

" Oh no, oh no, thou jolly Parson !
    I cannot tarry, I say ;

---

* Chapel-en-le-Frith is a considerable and important market town, about six miles from Buxton.

† Whaley Bridge, near Chapel-en-le-Frith.

I was drunk last night, and if I tarry,
    I'se be drunk again to-day."
"What likes, what likes." cried the Pardoner then,
    "Why tellest thou that to me?
Thou may'st e'en get thee drunk this blessed night;
    And well shrived for both thou shalt be."

Then down got the Butcher from his horse,
    I wot full fain was he;
And he drank 'till the summer sun was set,
    In that jolly company:
He drank 'till the summer sun went down,
    And the stars began to shine;
And his greasy noddle was dazed and addle,
    With the nut brown ale and wine.

Then up arose those four mad fellows,
    And joining hand in hand,
They danced around the hostel floor,
    And sung, tho' they scarce could stand,
"We've aye been drunk on yester night,
    And drunk the night before;
And sae we're drunk again to-night,
    If we never get drunk any more."

Bold Robin the Butcher was horsed and away;
    And a drunken wight was he;
For sometimes his blood-red eyes saw double;
    And then he could scantly see.
The forest trees seemed to featly dance,
    As he rode so swift along;
And the forest trees, to his wildered sense,
    Resang the jovial song.

Derbyshire Ballads.

Then up he sped over Paislow Moss,
    And down by the Chamber Knowle : *
And there he was scared into mortal fear
    By the hooting of a barn owl :
And on he rode, by the Forest Wall,
    Where the deer browsed silently ;
And up the Slack, 'till, on Tiddeswall Moor,
    His horse stood fair and free.

Just then the moon, from behind the rack,
    Burst out into open view ;
And on the sward and purple heath
    Broad light and shadow threw ;
And there the Butcher, whose heart beat quick,
    With fear of Gramarye,
Fast by his side, as he did ride,
    A foul phantom did espy.

Uprose the fell of his head, uprose
    The hood which his head did shroud ;
And all his teeth did chatter and girn,
    And he cried both long and loud ;
And his horse's flank with his spur he struck,
    As he never had struck before ;
And away he galloped, with might and main,
    Across the barren moor.

But ever as fast as the Butcher rode,
    The Ghost did grimly glide :
Now down on the earth before his horse,
    Then fast his rein beside :

---

* Chamber Knoll is about half a mile from Peak-Forest.

O'er stock and rock, and stone and pit,
    O'er hill and dale and down,
'Till Robin the Butcher gained his door-stone,
    In Tiddeswall's good old town.

"Oh, what thee ails, thou drunken Butcher?"
    Said his Wife, as he sank down ;
"And what thee ails, thou drunken Butcher?"
    Cried one-half of the Town.
"I have seen a Ghost, it hath raced my horse,
    For three good miles and more ;
And it vanished within the Churchyard wall,
    As I sank down at the door."

"Beshrew thy heart, for a drunken beast !"
    Cried his Wife, as she held him there ;
"Beshrew thy heart, for a drunken beast,
    And a coward, with heart of hare.
No Ghost hath raced thy horse to-night,
    Nor evened his wit with thine :
The Ghost was thy shadow, thou drunken wretch !
    I would the Ghost were mine."

A New Ballad of Robin Hood:

Shewing his Birth, Breeding, Valour and Marriage, at Titbury Bull-running: Calculated for the Meridian of Staffordshire but may serve for Derbyshire or Kent.

THERE are no series of ballads in our language so extensive or so popular as those relating to the noble outlaw, Robin Hood, and his "merry doings" in Sherwood Forest and its neighbourhood. Some of these relate immediately to Derbyshire; and many others might, from their allusions and the persons named in them, be claimed by that county. Some of his exploits are related to have been performed in Derbyshire; numerous places in that county are named after him; some of the relatives of his family resided within its confines; and last, though not least, his faithful friend and follower, *Little John*, is said not only to have been one of the sons of its soil, but to have died and been buried in the place of his birth.

That Robin Hood was a real and veritable personage seems to have been satisfactorily settled by the late Rev. Joseph Hunter, who discovered among the state papers some records wherein, besides the name being correctly given as "Robyn Hood," showed that that personage was in the King's service, and that he left it to travel;—doubtless into his favourite haunts in Yorkshire, Nottinghamshire, and Derbyshire. Among the entries relating to Robin Hood, Mr. Hunter gleaned several which tallied curiously and conclusively with the circumstances of his early life as given in the "Lytell Geste of Robyn Hode," printed about the year 1489, by Wynken de Worde.[*]

The ballad which I here give, showing "his birth, breeding, valour,

---

[*] For an account of this discovery see "The Reliquary," vol. I., page 129 et seq, where, in a paper entitled "The Ballad Hero, Robin Hood," an excellent resumé of his life is given by Mr. Gutch.

and marriage at Titbury Bull-running," I give from a curious old broadsheet in my own collection. It is printed broad-way on the paper, and has a rude wood-cut of Robin Hood with his buckler and quarter staff, and Clorinda,—another name for Maid Marian,—with a tall hat, or like the Welsh fashion, and a bow in her hand, the entrance to the church in the back-ground. It bears the imprint, "Northampton: Printed by R. Raikes and W. Dicey." A black-letter copy is in the Roxburgh Collection in the British Museum, and it has also been reprinted by Evans and by Gutch. The ballad is "supposed to be related by the fiddler who played at their wedding."

KIND Gentlemen will you be patient a while,
    Ay, and then you shall hear anon,
A very good Ballad of bold *Robin Hood*,
    and of his Man, brave little *John*.

In *Locksly* Town,* in merry *Nottinghamshire*,
    in merry sweet *Locksly* Town;
There bold *Robin Hood*, he was born and was bred,
    bold *Robin* of famous Renown.

The Father of *Robin* a Forester was,
    and he shot in a lusty long Bow,
Two North Country Miles and a Inch at a shot,
    as the *Pinder of Wakefield*† does know.

---

* "Locksley in Nottinghamshire." It seems pretty certain that the real birthplace of Robin Hood, although often attributed to Nottinghamshire, was at Loxley Chase, in Yorkshire, not far from Sheffield, and near the borders of Derbyshire.

† The *Pinder of Wakefield*, in Yorkshire, is often alluded to in Robin Hood ballads—

    "In Wakefield there lives a *jolly pinder*,
    In Wakefield all on a green."

The Pinder was, of course, an impounder of stray cattle.

For he brought *Adam Bell*,* and *Clim of the Glugh*,†
    and *William a Clowdel-le* : ‡
To shoot with our Forester, for forty Marks,
    and the Forester beat them all three.

His Mother was Niece to a *Coventry* Knight,
    which *Warwickshire* Men call Sir *Guy* ; §
For he slew the Blew Bore that hangs up at the Gate,
    or mine Host of the Bull tells a lie.

Her Brother was *Gamwell* ‖ of great *Gamwell-Hall*,
    and a noble House-keeper was he,
Ay, as ever broke Bread in sweet *Nottinghamshire*,
    and a Squire of famous Degree.

---

* *Adam Bell* was a northern outlaw, so celebrated for archery and other matters as to become proverbial, and

    "To shoot as well
      As Adam Bell"

became a common expression. He was also the subject of various ballads, and is thus alluded to by D'Avenant in 1673 :—

    "With loynes in canvass bow-case tyde,
      Where arrowes stick with mickle pride ;
      Like ghosts of *Adam Bell* and *Clymme*,
      Sol sets for fear theyl shoot at hym."

† *Clim of the Clough* was another famous archer, and is also alluded to in the extract given above. "Clough" signifies a ravine, or narrow glen, or close wooded dale.

‡ *William of Cloudeslee* was also a noted archer.

§ Guy, Earl of Warwick.

‖ Gamwell of Gamwell Hall. The family of Gamwell to which this lady belonged, was, I believe, of Cheshire, not of Nottinghamshire.

The Mother of *Robin* said to her Husband,
    my Honey, my Love and my Dear ;
Let *Robin* and I, ride this Morning to *Gamwel*,
    to take of my Brother's good Cheer.

And he said, I grant thee boon, gentle *Joan*,
    take one of my Horses I pray :
The Sun is a rising, and therefore make Haste,
    for to morrow is Christmas Day.

Then *Robin Hood's* Father's grey Gelding was brought
    and sadled and bridled was he,
God-wot, a blew Bonnet, his new Suit of Cloaths,
    and a Cloak that did reach to his Knee.

She got on her Holy-day Girdle and Gown,
    they were of a light *Lincoln* Green,
The Cloath was home spun, but for Colour and make
    it might a beseem'd our Queen.

And then *Robin* got on his Basket-hilt Sword,
    and a Dagger on his tother side :
And said, my dear Mother, let's haste to be gone,
    we have forty long Miles to ride.

When *Robin* had mounted his Gelding so grey,
    his Father without any Trouble,
Got her up behind him, and bid her not fear,
    for his Gelding had oft carried double.

And when she was settled, they rode to their Neighbours,
    and drank and shook Hands with them all :
And then *Robin* galop'd and never gave o're,
    till they lighted at *Gamwel-Hall*.

And now you may think the right worshipful Squire,
    was joyful his Sister to see ;
For he kist her and kist her, and swore a great Oath,
    thou art welcome, kind Sister, to me.

The morrow when Mass had been said in the Chappel
    six Tables were cover'd in the Hall ;
And in comes the 'Squire and makes a short Speech,
    it was, Neighbours you are welcome all.

But not a Man here, shall tast my *March* Beer,
    till Christmas Carrol be sung ;
Then all clapt their Hands, & they shouted & sung,
    till the Hall and the Parlour did ring.

Now Mustard, Braun, roast-Beef and Plumb-Pies,
    were set upon every Table :
And noble *George Gamwel* said, eat and be merry,
    and drink so as long as you're able.

When Dinner was ended his Chaplain said Grace,
    and be merry my Friends, said the 'Squire,
It rains and it blows, but call for more Ale,
    and lay some more Wood on the Fire.

And now call ye little *John* hither to me,
    for little *John* is a fine Lad,
At Gambols and Juggling, and twenty such Tricks,
    as shall make you both merry and glad.

When little *John* came, to Gambols they went,
    both Gentlemen, Yeomen and Cloun ;
And what do you think ? Why as true as I live,
    bold *Robin Hood* put them all down.

And now you may think the right worshipful Squire,
    was joyful this Sight for to see,
For he said Cousin *Robin*, thou'st go no more home,
    but tarry and dwell with me.

Thou shalt have my Land when I die, and till then
    thou shalt be the Staff of my Age:
Then grant me my boon, dear Uncle, said *Robin*,
    that little *John* may by my Page.

And he said kind Cousin I grant thee thy boon,
    with all my heart to let it be,
Then come hither little *John*, said *Robin Hood*,
    come hither my Page, unto me.

Go fetch me my Bow, my longest long Bow,
    and broad Arrows one two or three;
For when it is fair Weather, we'll into *Sherwood*,
    some merry Pastime to see.

When *Robin Hood* came into merry *Sherwood*,
    he winded his bugle so clear:
And twice five and twenty good Yeomen and bold,
    before *Robin Hood* did appear.

Where are your Companions all? (said *Robin Hood*)
    for still I want forty and three.
Then said a bold Yeoman, Lo yonder they stand,
    all under a green Wood Tree.

As that Word was spoke, *Clorinda** came by,
    the Queen of the Shepherds was she:

---

* Clorinda is, I presume, the same personage as the one so often alluded to as "Maid Marion."

And her Gown was of Velvet, as green as the Grass,
    and her Buskin did reach to her Knee.

Her Gate it was graceful, her Body was strait
    and her Countenance free from Pride :
A Bow in her Hand, and Quiver and Arrows,
    hung dangling by her sweet Side.

Her Eye-brows were black, ay, and so was her Hair,
    and her Chin was as smooth as Glass ;
Her Visage spoke Wisdom and Modesty too,
    sets with *Robin Hood* such a Lass.

Said *Robin Hood*, Lady fair, whether away,
    oh whither fair Lady away ?
And she made him Answer, to kill a fat Buck,
    for to-morrow is *Titbury*[*] Day.

---

[*] " Titbury day :" the day on which the " Minstrels' Court," with its " Bull-running," and other wild amusements, was held. The Minstrels Court at Tutbury, to which all minstrels living in the counties of Stafford and Derby did service, was presided over by a " King of the Minstrels," who was selected yearly by the four stewards, two of whom were chosen from the minstrels of Derbyshire, and the other two from those of Staffordshire. The court was held before the Stewards of the honour of Tutbury, on the morrow after the Assumption. A deed of " John of Gaunt, King of Castile and Leon, Duke of Lancaster," dated in the fourth of Richard II., confers certain powers on the " King of the Minstrels in our honour of Tutbury," and speaks of service and homage which even then had been performed by the Minstrels " from ancient times." By a later instrument it was ordered " that no person shall use or exercise the art and science of music within the said counties, as a common musician or minstrel, for benefit and gains, except he have served and been brought up in the same art and science by the space of seven years, and be allowed and admitted so to do at

Said *Robin Hood*, Lady fair wander with me,
    a little to yonder green Bower,
There sit down to rest you, and you shall be sure,
    of a brace or a lease in an Hour.

And as we were going towards the green Bower,
    two hundred good Bucks we espy'd:
She chose out the fattest that was in the Herd,
    and she shot him through side and side.

---

the said court by the jury thereof," under certain fines; that he shall not teach or instruct any one for a less time than seven years; and that he shall, under pain of forfeit, appear yearly at the "Minstrels' Court." On the day of holding the court,—"Tutbury Day," as it is called in the ballad,—all the minstrels within the honour came to the Bailiff of the Manor and proceeded in procession to the parish church, the "King" walking between the Bailiff of the Manor and the Steward of the Minstrel's Court, and attended by his own four stewards, bearing white wands. From church they proceeded in the same order to the Castle hall, where the "King" took his seat, with the Bailiff and steward on either side. The court was then opened by proclamation ordering that every minstrel dwelling within the honour of Tutbury, either in the counties of Derby, Stafford, Nottingham, Warwick, or Lancaster, should draw near and give his attendance, and that all pleas would be heard, and fines and amercements made. The musicians having been called over by court roll, two juries were empanelled and charged. The jurors then proceeded to the selection of officers for the ensuing year. The jurors having left the court for the purpose, the King and Stewards partook of a banquet, while the musicians played their best on their respective instruments. On the return of the Jurors they presented the new King whom they had chosen from the four Stewards, upon which the old King, rising, delivered to him his wand of office, and drank a cup of wine to his health and prosperity. In like manner the old Stewards saluted, and resigned their offices to their successors. This ended, the court rose, and adjourned to a general banquet, in another part of the castle. The sports of the day

By the Faith of my Body, said bold *Robin Hood*,
   I never saw Woman like thee,
And com'st thou from East, ay, or com'st thou from West
   thou needst not beg Venison of me.

However along to the Bower you shall go,
   and taste of a Forester's Meat ;
And when we came thither, we found as good cheer,
   as any man needs for to eat.

For there was hot Venison, and Warden pies cold,
   Cream coloured with Honey-Combs plenty,
And the Sarvitors they were besides little *John*,
   good yeomen at least four and twenty.

then commenced by a wild and infuriated bull being turned loose for the minstrels to catch. The bull was thus prepared : his horns were sawed off close to the head ; his tail cut off to the stump ; his ears cropped ; his body rubbed all over with grease ; and his nostrils, to madden him still further, blown full of pepper. While these preparations were being made, the Steward made proclamation that all manner of persons should give way to the bull, no person coming nearer to it than forty feet, except the minstrels, but that all should attend to their own safety, every one at his peril. The bull being then turned out, was to be caught by some one of the minstrels, and no one else, between that hour and sunset on the same day, within the county of Stafford. If he escaped, he remained the property of the person who gave it (formerly the Prior of Tutbury) ; but if any of the minstrels could lay hold of him so as to cut off a portion of his hair and bring it to the Market Cross, he was caught and taken to the Bailiff, by whom he was fastened with a rope, &c., and then brought to the bull-ring in the High Street, where he was baited by dogs. After this, the minstrels could either sell him or divide him amongst themselves. This custom appears to have prevailed from 1377 to 1778, when it was very properly discontinued. The day was one of feasting, revelry, and great excitement, for the whole district.

Clorinda said, Tell me your Name gentle Sir?
    and he said, 'Tis bold *Robin Hood;*
'Squire *Gamwel's* my Uncle, but all my delight,
    is to dwell in the merry *Sherwood:*

For 'tis a fine Life, and 'tis void of all Strife,
    so 'tis Sir, *Clorinda* reply'd;
But oh, said bold *Robin*, how sweet would it be,
    if *Clorinda* would be my Bride?

She blush'd at the Motion, yet after a Pause,
    said, yes Sir, and with all my Heart,
Then let us send for a Priest, said *Robin Hood,*
    and marry before we do part.

But she said, it may not be so gentle Sir,
    for I must be at *Titbury* Feast:
And if *Robin Hood* will go thither with me,
    I'll make him the most welcome Guest.

Said *Robin Hood*, reach me that Buck, little *John,*
    for I'll go along with my Dear;
And bid my Yeomen kill six brace of Bucks,
    go meet me to-morrow just here.

Before we had ridden five *Staffordshire* miles,
    eight Yoemen that were too bold,
Bid *Robin Hood* stand, and deliver his Buck,
    a truer tale never was told.

I will not faith, said bold *Robin;* come *John,*
    stand to me and we'll beat 'em all;
Then both drew their Swords, and cut 'em and slash'd 'em,
    that five of them did fall.

The three that remain'd call'd to *Robin* for quarter,
    and pitiful *John* beg'd their Lives ;
When *John's* boon was granted, he gave them good Counsel
    and so sent them home to their Wives.

This Battle was fought near *Titbury* Town,
    when the Bagpipes bated the Bull :
I am King of the Fields, and swear 'tis a Truth,
    and I call him that doubts it a Gull.

For I saw him Fighting and Fidling the while,
    and *Clorinda* sung, Hey derry down :
The Bumpkins are beaten put up thy Sword *Bob*,
    and let's dance into the Town.

Before we came to it, we heard a strange shouting,
    and all that were in it look'd madly,
For some were a Bull-back, some Dancing a Morris,
    and some singing *Arthur a Bradly.**

And there we see *Thomas* our Justices Clark,
    and *Mary* to whom he was kind :
For *Tom* rod before her, and call'd *Mary* Madam,
    and kist her full sweetly behind.

And so may your Worship's but we went to Dinner,
    with *Thomas,* and *Mary,* and *Nan :*
They all drank a Health to *Clorinda,* and told her,
    bold *Robin Hood* was a fine Man.

---

* "Arthur a Bradly." This curious ballad, I have reason to believe, is a purely Derbyshire one, the locality being Bradley near Ashborne, within only a few miles of Tutbury. Of this ballad I shall probably have more to say in another part of the present volume.

When Dinner was ended, Sir *Roger* the Parson
    of *Dubbridge** was sent for in haste :
He brought his Mass-Book, & he bid them take hands,
    and he join'd them in Marriage full fast.

And then as bold *Robin Hood*, and his sweet Bride,
    went Hand in Hand to the green Bower,
The Birds sung with Pleasure in merry *Sherwood*,
    and 'twas a most joyful hour.

And when *Robin* came in the sight of the Bower,
    where are my Yeomen? said he,
And little *John* answered, Lo yonder they stand,
    all under the green Wood Tree.

Then a Garland they brought her by two & by two
    and placed them at the Bride's Bed :
The Musick struck up, and we fell to dance,
    till the Bride and the Groom were in Bed.

And what they did there, must be Counsel to me,
    because they lay long the next Day :
And I had haste home, but I got a good Piece
    of the Bride-Cake and so came away.

Now out alas, I had forgot to tell ye,
    that marry'd they were with a Ring :
And so will *Nan Knight*, or be buried a Maiden,
    and now let us pray for the King.

---

* "Dubberidge." This is Doveridge, a village in Derbyshire, about seven miles from Tutbury.

That he may get Children, and they may get more,
   to govern and do us some good,
And then I'll make Ballads in *Robin Hood's* Bower,
   and sing 'em in merry *Sherwood*.

Robin Hood and Little John.

LITTLE JOHN, the friend and sturdy companion of Robin Hood, was made almost as popular in ballads as his noble master. He is said to have been a man of immense size, and of almost unequalled prowess and strength. His name of *Little* John was, it appears, given to him ironically, because of his extraordinary stature. He is believed to have been born at Hathersage, in the Peak of Derbyshire; a place not many miles distant from Loxley Chase, where Robin Hood first drew breath. The place of his birth is, however, claimed by other localities. The ballad I here give is interesting, as detailing his first meeting and encounter with Robin Hood, which ended in the defeat of the outlaw, and in their becoming sworn friends for life.

It will be seen that in the ballad Little John is said to have been seven feet in height. This, curiously enough, accords with the tradition current in Hathersage, where his bones were exhumed some years ago, and where his grave is still shown.

WHEN Robin Hood was about twenty years old,
   He happened to meet Little John,
A jolly brisk blade, right fit for the trade,
   For he was a lusty young man.

Tho' he was call'd little, his limbs they were large,
   And his stature was seven foot high;
Where ever he came, they quak'd at his name,
   For soon he would make them to fly.

How they came acquainted I'll tell you in brief,
   If you would but listen awhile;
For this very jest, among all the rest,
   I think, may cause you to smile.

For Robin Hood said to his jolly bowmen,
   Pray tarry you here in this grove,
And see that you all observe well my call,
   While thorough the forest I rove.

We have had no sport these fourteen long days,
   Therefore now abroad will I go;
Now should I be beat, and cannot retreat,
   My horn I will presently blow.

Then did he shake hands with his merry men all,
   And bid them at present good-bye:
Then as near a brook his journey he took,
   A stranger he chanc'd to espy.

They happen'd to meet on a long narrow bridge,
   And neither of them would give way;
Quoth bold Robin Hood, and sturdily stood,
   I'll shew you right Nottingham play.

With that from his quiver an arrow he drew,
   A broad arrow with a goose wing;
The stranger replied, I'll liquor thy hide,
   If thou offer to touch the string.

Quoth bold Robin Hood, thou dost prate like an ass,
   For, were I to bend but my bow,
I could send a dart quite through thy proud heart,
   Before thou could'st strike me one blow.

Thou talk'st like a coward, the stranger replied,
    Well arm'd with a long bow you stand,
To shoot at my breast, while I, I protest,
    Have nought but a staff in my hand.

The name of a coward, quoth Robin, I scorn,
    Therefore my long bow I'll lay by;
And now, for thy sake, a staff will I take,
    The truth of thy manhood to try.

Then Robin Hood stept to a thicket of trees,
    And chose him a staff of ground oak;
Now this being done, away he did run
    To the stranger, and merrily spoke:

Lo! see my staff is lusty and tough:
    Now, here on the bridge we will play;
Whoever falls in, the other shall win
    The battle, and so we'll away.

With all my whole heart, the stranger replied,
    I scorn in the least to give out.
This said, they fell to't without more dispute,
    And their staffs they did flourish about.

At first Robin gave the stranger a bang,
    So hard that he made his bones ring:
The stranger he said, this must be repaid,
    I'll give you as good as you bring.

So long as I'm able to handle a staff,
    To die in your debt, friend, I scorn:
Then to it each goes, and follow'd their blows,
    As if they had been threshing of corn.

The stranger gave Robin a crack on the crown,
    Which caused the blood to appear ;
Then Robin enrag'd more fiercely engag'd,
    And follow'd his blows more severe.

So thick and so fast did he lay it on him,
    With a passionate fury and ire ;
At every stroke he made him to smoke,
    As if he had been all on fire.

O then in a fury the stranger he grew,
    And gave him a damnable look ;
And with a blow, which laid him full low,
    And tumbled him into the brook.

I prithee, good fellow, O where art thou now ?
    The stranger, in laughter, he cried :
Quoth bold Robin Hood, Good faith, in the flood,
    And floating along with the tide :

I needs must acknowledge thou art a brave soul,
    With thee I'll no longer contend ;
For needs must I say thou hast got the day,
    Our battle shall be at an end.

Then unto the bank he did presently wade,
    And pull'd him out by a thorn ;
Which done, at the last he blew a loud blast
    Straightway on his fine bugle horn :

The echo of which thro' the vallies did fly,
    At which his stout bowmen appear'd,
All cloathed in green, most gay to be seen ;
    So up to their master they steer'd.

O what is the matter? quoth Will. Stutely.
    Good master, you are wet to the skin:
No matter, quoth he, the lad which you see,
    In fighting hath tumbled me in.

He shall not go scot-free, the others replied;
    So straight they were seizing him there,
To duck him likewise: but Robin Hood cries,
    He is a stout fellow, forbear.

There's no one shall wrong thee, friend, be not afraid;
    These bowmen upon me do wait:
There's threescore and nine; if thou will be mine,
    Thou shalt have my livery straight,

And other accoutrements fit for a man:
    Speak up, jolly blade, never fear:
I'll teach you also the use of the bow,
    To shoot at the fat fallow deer.

O here is my hand, the stranger replied,
    I'll serve you with all my whole heart:
My name is John Little, a man of good mettle;
    Ne'er doubt me, for I'll play my part.

His name shall be alter'd, quoth Will. Stutely,
    And I will his godfather be;
Prepare then a feast, and none of the least,
    For we will be merry, quoth he.

They presently fetch'd him a brace of fat does,
    With humming strong liquor likewise:
They lov'd what was good; so in the green wood
    This pretty sweet babe they baptiz'd.

He was, I must tell you, but seven feet high,
    And may be an ell in the waist :
A sweet pretty lad : much feasting they had,
    Bold Robin the christening grac'd,

With all his bowmen, which stood in a ring,
    And were of the Nottingham breed.
Brave Stutely came then with seven yeomen,
    And did in this manner proceed :

This infant was called John Little, quoth he,
    Which name shall be changed anon :
The words we'll transpose ; so wherever he goes,
    His name shall be call'd Little John.

They all with a shout made the elements ring,
    So soon as the office was o'er ;
To feasting they went, with true merriment,
    And tippled strong liquor gillore.

Then Robin he took the pretty sweet babe,
    And cloath'd him from top to the toe
In garments of green most gay to be seen,
    And gave him a curious long bow.

Thou shalt be an archer as well as the best,
    And range in the green wood with us,
Where we'll not want gold nor silver, behold,
    While bishops have ought in their purse.

We live here like squires or lords of renown,
    Without e'er a foot of free land ;
We feast on good cheer, with wine, ale, and beer,
    And every thing at our command.

Then music and dancing did finish the day:
　At length, when the sun waxed low,
Then all the whole train their grove did refrain,
　And unto their caves they did go.

And so ever after, as long as they liv'd,
　Although he was proper and tall,
Yet nevertheless, the truth to express,
　Still Little John they did him call.

Little John's End.

THE current tradition in Derbyshire concerning Little John is that he was born at Hathersage, in that county; that he was a man of immense stature, and of wonderful strength and prowess; that he was withal of mild and gentle temperament, of affectionate disposition, and faithful in his attachments; that after the death of Robin Hood at Kirklees, which he took deeply to heart, he was so dispirited that he sank under the loss, and having by great exertion succeeded in reaching the place of his birth, (Hathersage,) he was welcomed by his friends and old associates, who begged him to tarry with them for the rest of his life; that he had just strength enough left to point out the place in the churchyard where he wished to be buried, and to give them instructions for his burial; that he told them in three days he should die, and desired that his bow and cap should be hung up in the church; that on the third day he died, in a small cottage still standing, where, it is said, his length was so great when dead and "laid out," that his feet came outside the door; that he was buried where he had directed, his cap and bow being hung in the chancel of the church; that the people drave his last arrow into the ground near his grave, and that it took root and grew up into a tree. It is asserted that until within the last sixty or seventy years, his cap—a green cloth one—still hung high in the chancel, but was then taken away by some people from

Yorkshire, who also despoiled his grave, and took away the thigh bones, which were found to be of immense length. The grave, which is marked by two small upright stones, one at the head and the other at the foot, measures about ten feet in length. In 1728 it was opened, and bones of an enormous size found in it. Some years ago it was again opened, and a thigh bone measuring thirty-two inches taken away from it.

In reference to this tradition it will no doubt be interesting to give the accompanying fac-simile of the writing of Elias Ashmole, copied from his MSS. at Oxford, (who was born in 1617.) and who there says:—

"Little John lyes buried in Hatherseech Church yard within 3 miles fro Castleton in High Peake with one Stone set up at his head and another at his Feete, but a large distance betweene them. They say a part of his bow hangs up in the said Church Neere Grindleford Bridge are Robin Hoods 2 Pricks."

The following ballad, founded on a part of this tradition, was written by Mr. William Haines, and appeared in "The Reliquary," vol. II., page 11. Several other ballads relating to

Little John might well be given in this volume, but the two I have selected—his first acquaintance with Robin Hood, and his death and burial—will be sufficient to show their character. The others must be deferred for a future work.

WHEN Robin Hood, by guile betrayed,
   In Kirklees' cloister died,
Silent his merry men dispersed,
   And never more allied.

Some passed unknown, or pardon got,
   And peaceful callings sought,
Beyond the seas while others fled,
   And 'gainst the Paynim fought.

And Little John, as lonely through
   Their vacant haunts he strode,
Repented sadness in his soul
   Had e'er of old abode.

As there beneath an oak his limbs
   Repose long failing found,
A shape thrice warned him in a dream,
   To shun St. Michael's ground.

Affrighted, from the sward he starts—
   Deep shone the guardian night!
The moon the woods bowed motionless
   With plenitude of light.

St. Michael's road, presaging nought,
   Leal John yestreen had ta'en;
But now another way he chose,
   Lest there he should be slain.

Northward, compelling soon his steps,
    Across the Tweed he hied ;
Thence sea and land to traverse far,
    A long and cheerless tide.

For aye his heart in greenwood was,
    Wherever he might be ;
Till pleasing rose resolve once more
    The forests fair to see.

Yet bootless he retraced deject
    Each loved resort at last ;
The birds were mute, the leafless wold
    Held drearily the blast.

And as again John wandered wide,
    A fog so dense did fall,
He could not see nor hill nor tree ;
    It clos'd him like a wall.

That dismal night he roamed lost,
    Exhausted, sick, and cold :
The morn was long ere it was light,
    And long the vapour rolled.

On every side came mighty stones
    About a barren moor ;
No roof nor pale might be descried,
    As spread that waste forlore.

At length 'mid wreathing fog-smoke swam
    The sun's blanch'd disc on high ;
Mantled the ashy mists around ;
    Grew wide the rover's eye.

When, singing blithe as he approached,
    A shepherd boy met John:
"Pray tell to me," the outlaw cried,
    "What ground I here am on?"

"St. Michael's, gallant yeomen, this,"
    The boy made prompt reply;
"From yonder, Hathersage church-spire,
    May'st plainly now espy."

"There hast thou knelled," said Little John,
    "The solemn bell for me;
But Christ thee save, my bonny lad;
    Aye lucky shalt thou be!"

He had not many steps advanced,
    When in the vale appeared
The Church, and eke the village sweet,
    His foot had vainly feared.

Descending, welcome straight he finds
    The ruddy hearth before:
Cried young and old, "Among us dwell,
    And weary roam no more!"

Said Little John, "No, never hence
    Shall I fare forth again;
But that abode is yet to found,
    Wherein I must remain."

He led them to the churchyard frore,
    And digg'd therein a grave:
"Three days," said he, "and neighbours, this
    The little inn I crave.

> Without a coffin or a shroud
>   Inter me, I you pray,
> And o'er my corse, as now yclad,
>   The greensward lightly lay."

The morn ensued, as John foretold,
    He never rose to greet;
His bread upon the board was brought,
    Beside it stayed his seat.

They laid him in the grave which he
    With his own hands had made,
And overspread the fragrant sod,
    As he had wished and said.

His bow was in the chancel hung;
    His last good bolt they drave
Down to the nocke, its measured length,
    Westward fro' the grave.

And root and bud this shaft put forth,
    When Spring returned anon;
It grew a tree, and threw a shade
    Where slept staunch Little John.

The Lay of the Buckstone.

THE following excellent ballad has been collected from the *disjecta membra* of the forest minstrelsy of the High Peak, and arranged in its present form, by my friend Mr. William Bennett, of Chapel-en-le-Frith. Mr. Bennett considers, and with good reason, that it has originally formed two distinct ballads, one relating to a contention and fight between Robin Hood and the keepers of Peak Forest, and the other to a match with the long-bow between him and the Foresters. This ballad has been printed in "The Reliquary," vol. I., page 101.

'Tis merry in the high Peak Forest,
    Out upon the lea;
'Tis merry in the shady frith,
    Where birds are whistling free:
The heather blooms on Lady low;
    O'er Combs* the wind blows dree;
And the dappled deer are feeding there,
    Under the Greenwood tree.

"Now why amort, bold Robin Hood!
    And a buck so near at hand:
'Tis easier far to cleave his crown
    Than a peeled willow wand.
A nobler herd ne'er saw I run,
    Three hundred head and mo:
The King won't miss a hart o' grease,
    If thou use thy good yew bow."

"My bow's unstrung, Brian the Bearward!
    So much the worse for thee:
Thou elder likest the twang of the string,
    Than the deftest minstrelsy:
Thou prizest the swish of an arrow keen,
    When the mark is a buck of head;
And liefer than tripping o'er the sward,
    Thou wouldst see the Quarry dead."

---

* Combs Moss, one of the highest hills in the neighbourhood, between Chapel-en-le-Frith and Buxton.

"Ay, dead and buried," quoth the Bearward,
    "In the grave of a venison pie :
And so wouldst thou, or men thee wrong ;
    For all thou talk'st so high :
But if thou durst not fly a shaft,
    As well as I would fly mine,
Tend thou my bear, and lend thy bow ;
    I'll swop my trade for thine."

The Bearward strung the bow and shot
    Four hundred feet him fro :
And hit a good fat buck, which fell,
    Nor lack'd a second blow.
"Well shot, shot well," bold Robin cried,
    "Thou'rt of the greenwood free ;
At stable stand, or wanlass drift,
    Thou need'st no lere from me."

Then they were ware of six wight yeomen,
    That lusty were, and tall,
Come marching up from Fairfield* side,
    Beneath the archer's wall ;
All clad in Lincoln green were they ;
    And on their right arms wore
A silver shield, which, in its field,
    A lion passant bore.

"Good morrow, good fellows !" the foremost said,
    "You are got to work eftsoon,
I pray do you hold of the crown in chief,
    Or follow the Lady Moon ?

---

* A large village closely adjoining Buxton.

Of stout King Richard the lion's heart
    Ye should be liegemen good,
To break his laws, and kill his deer,
    Within his own greenwood."

"Thou liest now, thou proud spoken keeper!
    Forever I say thou dost lie:
Neither forest walk, nor deer are the King's,
    As I will well abye.
To John of Mortaigne, the deer belong;
    To John of Mortaigne and *me*;
And my share I'll take, when it me lists,
    Despite of him or thee."

"Why who art thou, thou bold tongued traitor!
    That durst thus mate with me;
And claim one half of the Prince's deer,
    Despite of his sovereignty?
I trou thou'rt one of the Bearward's men,
    By keeping his company;
And I'll make thee dance like a bear from France,
    If thy tongue not the kinder be."

Then on he rushed, with his staff uprais'd,
    And dealt bold Robin a blow;
But he was ware, and stopped him there,
    With his long and tough yew bow.
And Robin put his Horn to his mouth,
    And blew both loud and shrill;
And soon appeared five wight yeomen
    Come running down the hill.

The first was a man hight Little John,
    A yeoman good and tall;
The next Will Scarlet of gentle blood,
    Bred up in bower and hall;
The third, the minstrel, Alan a Dale,
    So well with the harp sang he;
The fourth was stalwart Clym o' the Clough,
    And William of Cloudeslie.

"Now, hold your hands," bold Robin cried,
    "Stand by and see fair play;
And the keeper and I will try this bout,
    And see who'll win the day.
The Bearward shall lay the dainty buck
    On this mossy boulder stone;
And he that fairly knocks down his foe,
    The fat buck shall have won."

"A match, a match," cried the yeomen all,
    "Whoever shall say it nay,
'Tis better ye two should fight it out,
    Than all should join in the fray:
So handle your staves, and to it like men,
    As it may no better be;
And he that first brings his man to ground,
    Shall gain the victory."

Then Ralph the Ranger squared his staff,
    And gloured on Robin the while;
The outlaw's staff lay loose in his hands,
    And he scarce forbore to smile.

They stood together like Brothers twain,
    Good men at their hands and tall;
But each seemed loth to begin the strife,
    Lest he first should have the fall.

And round and round each pressed his man,
    Before he could get a blow;
So well on guard, each kept his ward,
    As they traversed to and fro.
With feint and dodge each tried to draw,
    His wary foeman forth;
But both were cool, and cautious too;
    Like the good men of the north.

Bold Robin first his staff let fly,
    (The challenger was he,)
And for the honor of his craft,
    He must not dastard be.
Woe worth the while he dealt the blow,
    His staff had scarcely flown;
When Ralph's came dead athwart his head,
    And well nigh cracked his crown.

He backward gave a step or two,
    But not one whit dismayed;
Though now the Keeper's quarter staff
    About his shoulders played:
His eye was keen, his hand was true,
    As well the Keeper found;
For his staff did knap the Keeper's cap,
    And bring him to the ground.

"The buck is mine," the outlaw said,
  "Unless thou lik'st to try
Which of us twain upon the ground,
  Can best make arrow fly.
For kingly blood ye tend the frith ;
  Ye ought to shoot right well :
For mine own hand will I draw a bow,
  And see who bears the bell."

"A match, a match !" cried the yeomen all,
  "Whoever shall say it nay ;
Good men ye are if ye shoot a shaft,
  As ye've handled the staff this day.
So fix your mark, and choose your ground,
  And it may no better be ;
And he that first cleaves the willow wand,
  Shall gain the victory."

"No willow wand will we have," quoth Robin,
  "But the Buck's dead glassy eye ;
And we'll shoot the length of the archer's wall,*
  Seven hundred feet or nigh.
So Bearward lay the deer adown
  On yon mossy boulder stone ;
And he who lodges a shaft in his eye,
  The fat buck shall have won."

---

* In a copy of an ancient map made at the time of the enclosure of the wastes and commons in the parish of Chapel-en-le-Frith, (part of the ancient Forest of the High Peak,) in the year 1707, an old wall is traced, which is still a boundary fence of the wild moor called Combs Moss. This wall is named on the map "the Archer's Wall," and the length of it is traditionally called "Robin Hood's Marks."

The buck was laid on the boulder stone,
    With his head towards the east;
And the yeomen tall, with their bows in hand,
    To win the guerdon press'd;
The Keeper first with wary eye,
    Took long and careful aim;
And hit the buck right yeomanly
    In the middle of his wame.

"Well shot, well shot," bold Robin cried,
    (But the outlaw laughed the while,)
"Right woodmanly that shaft is placed;
    But a miss is as good as a mile."
With careless aim he drew his bow,
    And let his arrow fly;
And lodged the shaft, both hard and fast,
    In the dead buck's glassy eye.

So Robin he won the dainty Buck,
    By the side of the archer's wall;
And left the tale to be sung or said
    In Tower, and Bower, and Hall.
The old gray wall still stands on the hill,
    Though the archer's marks are gone;
And the Boulder Rock is still kept in mind,
    By the name of old Buckstone.

Sir Richard Whittington's Advancement:

Being an Historical Account of his Education, Unexpected Fortune, Charity, &c.

THE rhyme and the story of "Whittington and his Cat" are perhaps as well known as any ballads in the language. Sir Richard Whittington, or "Dick Whittington," as he is commonly called, was of the same family as the De Whittingtons, Lords of Whittington, near Chesterfield, Derbyshire. He was, it is stated, youngest son of a Sir William Whittington. In 1393, when he must have been about forty years of age, he became a member of the Mercers' Company, and was, it is said, besides being a Mercer, a Merchant Adventurer. He was also about this year an Alderman, and also Sheriff, of London. In 1397 he was appointed Lord Mayor of London, by writ from Richard II., to serve in place of the deceased Lord Mayor. In 1398, in 1406, and again in 1419, he was elected to and served the office of Lord Mayor. Whittington married Alice, daughter of Sir Hugh Fitzwarren and Maude his wife. He died in 1423. Besides being "*thrice Lord Mayor of London*," his body was, it seems, *thrice* buried in the church he had himself erected,—St. Michael Paternoster: first, by his executors, who erected a monument over his remains; secondly, in the reign of Edward VI., when the minister, thinking that probably some great riches had been buried with him, had his body taken up and despoiled of its leaden covering; and, thirdly, in the reign of Mary, when the parishioners were compelled to again take him up, re-enclose him in lead, and re-erect the monument over his remains. At the great fire of London, in 1666, both church and monument were destroyed. His memory has been well preserved in the popular mind by ballad and story and tradition; and his noble charities and his munificent acts, of which so many evidences remain in London, form a prouder and more enduring monument than the one which the fire destroyed.

The following version of the ballad is perhaps the one most generally known:—

> HERE must I tell the praise
>   Of worthy Whittington,
> Known to be in his days
>   Thrice lord-mayor of London.
>
> But of poor parentage
>   Born was he, as we hear,
> And in his tender age
>   Bred up in Lancashire.
>
> Poorly to London then
>   Came up this simple lad;
> Where, with a merchant-man,
>   Soon he a dwelling had;
>
> And in a kitchen plac'd,
>   A scullion for to be;
> Where a long time he pass'd
>   In labour drudgingly.
>
> His daily service was
>   Turning at the fire;
> And to scour pots of brass,
>   For a poor scullion's hire:
>
> Meat and drink all his pay,
>   Of coin he had no store;
> Therefore to run away,
>   In secret thought he bore.

So from the merchant-man
    Whittington secretly
Towards his country ran,
    To purchase liberty.

But as he went along,
    In a fair summer's morn,
London's bells sweetly rung
    " Whittington back return :"

Evermore sounding so,
    " Turn, again, Whittington ;
For thou, in time, shalt grow
    Lord-mayor of London."

Whereupon, back again
    Whittington came with speed,
A servant to remain,
    As the Lord had decreed.

Still blessed be the bells,
    This was his daily song ;
" This my good fortune tells,
    Most sweetly have they rung.

If God so favour me,
    I will not prove unkind ;
London my love shall see,
    And my large bounties find."

But, see his happy chance !
    This scullion had a cat,
Which did his state advance,
    And by it wealth he gat.

His master ventur'd forth,
    To a land far unknown,
With merchandize of worth,
    As is in stories shown:

Whittington had no more
    But this poor cat as then,
Which to the ship he bore,
    Like a brave valiant man.

"Vent'ring the same," quoth he,
    "I may get store of gold,
And mayor of London be,
    As the bells have me told."

Whittington's merchandise,
    Carried to a land
Troubled with rats and mice,
    As they did understand;

The king of the country there,
    As he at dinner sat,
Daily remain'd in fear
    Of many a mouse and rat.

Meat that on trenchers lay,
    No way they could keep safe;
But by rats bore away,
    Fearing no wand or staff;

Whereupon, soon they brought
    Whittington's nimble cat;
Which by the king was bought,
    Heaps of gold given for that.

Home again came these men,
    With their ship laden so;
Whittington's wealth began
    By this cat thus to grow:

Scullion's life he forsook,
    To be a merchant good,
And soon began to look
    How well his credit stood.

After that, he was chose
    Sheriff of the city here,
And then full quickly rose
    Higher, as did appear:

For, to the city's praise,
    Sir Richard Whittington
Came to be in his days,
    Thrice mayor of London.

More his fame to advance,
    Thousands he lent the king,
To maintain war in France,
    Glory from thence to bring.

And after, at a feast
    Which he the king did make,
He burnt the bonds all in jest,
    And would no money take.

Ten thousand pounds he gave
    To his prince willingly;
And would no penny have
    For this kind courtesy.

As God thus made him great,
   So he would daily see
Poor people fed with meat,
   To shew his charity:

Prisoners poor cherish'd were,
   Widows sweet comfort found:
Good deeds, both far and near,
   Of him do still resound.

Whittington's College is
   One of his charities;
Record reporteth this
   To lasting memories.

Newgate he builded fair,
   For prisoners to lie in;
Christ-church he did repair,
   Christian love for to win.

Many more such like deeds
   Were done by Whittington;
Which joy and comfort breeds,
   To such as look thereon.

The Derbyshire Miller.

I HAVE not as yet been able to recover the whole of the words of this ballad. The following fragment was written by Mr. Chappell, from the singing of Mr. Charles Sloman, and is all I have respecting it :—

The mil-ler he caught the maid by the toe; What d'ye call this, my dear-est? The mil-ler he caught the maid by the toe; What d'ye call this, my dear-est? Oh! this is my toe, near to my shoe sole. Thy toe on my ter-ri-to-ry. I'm the maid of the mill, and the corn grinds well.

Tideswell in an Uproar,

Or the Prince in the Town, and the Devil in the Church.

ONE Sunday in 1806 the Prince of Wales, afterwards George IV., passed through Tideswell, in the High Peak, and stopped to change horses at the principal inn of the place. The circumstance caused, as was only natural, considerable excitement in the place, which culminated in not only the whole of the congregation of the parish church, but also the clergyman himself, and his clerk, forsaking the service to see him pass. This circumstance gave rise to much merriment, and more than one ballad was the result. The following is the best :—

>DECLARE, O Muse, what demon 'twas
>   Crept into Tideswell Church,
>And tempted pious folk to leave
>   Their parson in the lurch.
>
>What caused this strange disaster, say,
>   What did the scene provoke?
>At which the men unborn will laugh,
>   At which the living joke!
>
>The Prince of Wales, great George's Heir,
>   To roam once took a freak;
>And as the fates did so decree,
>   He journey'd through the Peak.
>
>But, ah! my Prince, thy journey turn'd
>   The Sabbath into fun day;
>And Tideswell Lads will ne'er forget,
>   Thy trav'ling on a Sunday.

The Ringers somehow gain'd a hint,
    Their loyalty be praised !
That George would come that way, so got
    The Bells already rais'd.

The Prince arrived, then loudest shouts
    Thro' Tideswell streets soon rang ;
The loyal clappers strait fell down,
    With many a merry bang.

To Pulpit high, just then the Priest,
    His sacred gown had thrust ;
And, strange coincidence ! his Text
    " In Princes put no trust."

With Man of God they all agreed,
    Till bells went clitter clatter ;
When expectation did them feed,
    But not with heavenly matter.

The congregation, demon rous'd,
    Arose with one accord ;
And, shameful, put their trust in Prince,
    And left the living Lord.

They helter skelter sought the door,
    The Church did them disgorge ;
With fiercest fury, then they flew,
    Like Dragons to the "George."

As through Churchyard with tumult dire
    And wild uproar they fled ;
Confusion was so great, some thought
    They would have rais'd the Dead.

The Parson cried, with loudest lungs,
   "For love of God, pray stay!"
But love of Prince more prevalent,
   Soon hied them fast away.

The Demon hov'ring o'er their heads,
   Exulted as they pass'd;
"Friend Belzebub," the Parson cried,
   "Thou'st got a Prize at last."

The Clerk then to his master said,
   "We're left behind complete;
What harm if we start off for Prince,
   And run the second heat?"

The Parson with good Capon lin'd,
   Then ran with middling haste;
Spare Clerk, was at his rear, who knew,
   "Amen," should come the last.

Amidst the mob, they soon descried
   The Prince, Great Britain's Heir;
Then with the Mob they both did join,
   And play'd at gape and stare.

Their wish the sovereign People show,
   Impress'd with one accord;
It was to turn themselves to beasts,
   And draw their future Lord.

The Prince put forth what's filled with sense,
   It was his Royal sconce:
Insisted they should act like men,
   And break their rules for once.

Steeds more appropriate being brought,
    Huzzas formed parting speech ;
The Prince drove on and people went
    To swig with Mrs. Leech.

Thy Flock's frail error, Reverend Sir,
    Did serve a loyal dish up ;
For which, if Prince has any grace,
    He'll surely make thee Bishop.

Another short piece on this same subject may be added :

Ye Tideswellites, can this be true,
    Which Fame's loud Trumpet brings ;
That ye the Cambrian Prince to view,
    Forsook the King of kings?

That ye, when swiftly rattling wheels
    Proclaimed his Highness near ;
Trode almost on each other's heels,
    To leave the House of Prayer?

Another time adopt this plan,
    Lest ye be left i' th' lurch ;
Place at the end o' th' Town a man
    To ask him into th' church !

The Derby Ram.

THE origin of this popular old ballad has yet to be ascertained. At present it has puzzled more heads than one, and its elucidation must be left to future research. Its principal characteristic is its bold extravagance. Derby and Derby people have, however, I know by references to allusions to it, been fond of their Ram for more than a century. How much older it is than that time is difficult to say. There are several versions of the ballad : the one I here give is, however, the most complete I have met with. The "Derby Ram" has been set as a glee by Dr. Callcott, and is still sung with much applause at public dinners in the town. So popular, indeed, is the Ram in the district, that a few years ago—in 1855—the First Regiment of Derbyshire Militia, whose barracks and head quarters are at Derby, carrying out the idea of the Welsh Fusileers with their goat, attached a fine Ram to the staff of the regiment. So well trained was he, and so evidently proud of his post, that he marched with a stately step in front of the band as they marched day by day through the town while up for training, and attracted quite as much notice as any drum-major ever did. More than this, a political periodical, a kind of provincial *Charivarri*, has been issued under the title of the "Derby Ram," which is supposed to butt at party doings, and at local abuses of various kinds ; and I write this note with a steel pen which bears the extraordinary name stamped upon it of the "Derby Ram pen !"

  As I was going to Darby, Sir,
   All on a market day,
  I met the finest Ram, Sir,
   That ever was fed on hay.
    Daddle-i-day, daddle-i-day,
    Fal-de-ral, fal-de-ral, daddle i day.

  This Ram was fat behind, Sir,
   This Ram was fat before,

This Ram was ten yards high, Sir,
    Indeed he was no more.
        Daddle-i-day, &c.

The Wool upon his back, Sir,
    Reached up unto the sky,
The Eagles made their nests there, Sir,
    For I heard the young ones cry.
        Daddle-i-day, &c.

The Wool upon his belly, Sir,
    It dragged upon the ground,
It was sold in Darby town, Sir,
    For forty thousand pound.*
        Daddle-i-day, &c.

The space between his horns, Sir,
    Was as far as a man could reach,
And there they built a pulpit
    For the Parson there to preach.
        Daddle-i-day, &c.

The teeth that were in his mouth, Sir,
    Were like a regiment of men ;
And the tongue that hung between them, Sir,
    Would have dined them twice and again.
        Daddle-i-day, &c.

---

* Another version has—
    "The Wool upon his back, Sir,
        Was worth a thousand pound,
    The Wool upon his belly, Sir,
        It trailed upon the ground."

This Ram jumped o'er a wall, Sir,
   His tail caught on a briar,
It reached from Darby town, Sir,
   All into Leicestershire.
      Daddle-i-day, &c.

And of this tail so long, Sir,
   'Twas ten miles and an ell,
They made a goodly rope, Sir,
   To toll the market bell.
      Daddle-i-day, &c.

This Ram had four legs to walk on, Sir,
   This Ram had four legs to stand,
And every leg he had, Sir,
   Stood on an acre of land.*
      Daddle-i-day, &c.

The Butcher that killed this Ram, Sir,
   Was drownded in the blood,
And the boy that held the pail, Sir,
   Was carried away in the flood.†
      Daddle-i-day, &c.

All the maids in Darby, Sir,
   Came begging for his horns,

---

* Another version says—
    "And every time he shifted them,
      He covered an acre of land."

† Another version has—
    "And all the people of Darby
      Were carried away in the flood."

  To take them to coopers,
   To make them milking gawns.*
    Daddle-i-day, &c.

  The little boys of Darby, Sir.
   They came to beg his eyes,
  To kick about the streets, Sir,
   For they were football† size.
    Daddle-i-day, &c.

  The tanner that tanned its hide, Sir,
   Would never be poor any more,
  For when he had tanned and retched‡ it,
   It covered all Sinfin Moor. ‖
    Daddle-i-day, &c.

  The Jaws that were in his head, Sir,
   They were so fine and thin,

---

* "Gawn" is a provincialism for pail,—a milk pail.

† Football was essentially a Derby game, and was played every year, frequently with highly disastrous consequences, until put down by the authorities a few years back. On Shrove Tuesday business was entirely suspended, and the townspeople being divided into two parties,— All Saints and St. Peters,—the ball was, at noon, thrown from the Town Hall to the densely packed masses in the market-place, the two parties each trying to "goal" it at their respective places. The fight— for it was nothing less—continued for many hours, and sewers, brook-courses, and even rivers, were invaded, and scores of people who were fortunate enough not to get killed or lamed, were stripped of their clothing in the fray.

‡ Stretched,—*i.e.*, fastened it down with pegs to dry.

‖ Sinfin Moor is a few miles from Derby. It is a place where, in former times, Derby races were held. Another version says "Swinscoe Moor," which is in the neighbourhood of Ashborne.

They were sold to a Methodist Parson,
    For a pulpit to preach in.*
        Daddle-i-day, &c.

Indeed, Sir, this is true, Sir,
    I never was taught to lie,
And had you been to Darby, Sir,
    You'd have seen it as well as I.†
        Daddle-i-day, daddle-i-day,
        Fal-de-ral, fal-de-ral, daddle-i-day.

The Blink-Ey'd Cobler.

THE plot of the ballad of "The Blink Eyed Cobler," is the old story of a young gentleman falling in love with a servant, seducing her, promising to marry her, the marriage prevented by the "cruel father," a disguise adopted, the father giving a dowry to the supposed Cobbler so as to induce him to marry her, and in the end the happy reconciliation of all the parties. The ballad is here given from a broad-sheet in my own collection. It is printed broad-way of the paper, in four columns, and has a wood-cut at the head, of a lady and her waiting-woman before a looking-glass, and a gentleman standing in the room with them. It occurs also in other forms.

ALL you that delight in merriment,
    Come listen to my song,

---

* I take it that this verse is a later addition to the song, put in, probably, by some singer who was antagonistic to Methodism. It does not appear in most of the versions I have collected.

† Another version says—
    "And if you go to Darby, Sir,
        You may eat a bit of the pie."

It is very new and certain true,
    You need not tarry long,
Before you laugh your belly full,
    Therefore be pleas'd to stay,
I hope that you will be pleased,
    Before you go away.
It's of a knight in Derbyshire,
    Who had a handsome son,
He kept a handsome chambermaid,
    Who had his favour won;
They dearly lov'd each other,
    Being full of sport and play,

Having seduced this "handsome chambermaid," and she having told him that she is likely to become a mother, the ballad goes on—

He cries love be contented,
    (This is what must be said,)
And do not let my father know,
    For on Sunday we will wed.
But mind how cruel fortune,
    Their fate did seem to force,
The old man stood in the corner,
    And heard the whole discourse.
Next morn he call'd the maid,
    Likewise the youth his son,
And with a smiling sneering look,
    The story thus begun.
He said I wish you both much joy,
    You are to wed on Sunday,
But I'd have you be rul'd by me,
    And put it off till Monday.

'Twill be but one day longer,
    With that he laugh'd outright,
But I'm resolv'd to part you both,
    For fear it should be to-night.
He paid the girl her wages,
    And home he then her sent,
And confin'd him to his chamber,
    In tears for to lament.
Next morning unto London,
    Along with a sturdy guide,
To his uncle's house on Cornhill,
    He sent him to abide.
But as they rode along the way,
    He said unto the guide
I'll give thee twenty guineas
    To let me step aside.
Because this very morning,
    One word my father said,
The same I do remember,
    And keep it in my head.
The guide straightway gave consent,
    And he went to his sweetheart Sue,
Then told to her the story,
    And what he design'd to do.
Disguis'd like a poor cobler,
    With a long rusty beard,
With a leather coat not worth a groat,
    To his father's house he steer'd.
He knocked boldly at the door,
    And when his father came,

He said, sir, be you such a one?
    He answered, yes, the same,
He cry'd, I understand your son,
    Wanton tricks has play'd,
Unknown to your worship,
    Along with your chambermaid.
I understand some money
    With her you are freely to give,
To help to keep the child and she,
    So long as they do live.
Now I am an honest cobler,
    Who do live here just by,
For fifty pounds I'll marry her,
    If that will but satisfy.
The old man answer'd, before
    The money I do pay,
I'll see her fairly marry'd,
    And give her myself away.
With all my heart, the cobler
    Unto the old man did say,
With that he fetch'd the fifty pounds,
    And the bargain he made straightway.
And when they came unto the church,
    As we do understand,
The old man strutted boldly,
    Then took her by the hand,
Crying, heavens bless you from above,
    And send you long to live,
And as a token of my love,
    This fifty pounds I give.

They parted very friendly,
    The old man home he went,
The bride and bridegroom rode away,
    To London by consent.
Where she was fairly brought to bed,
    With joy and much content,
A letter into the country,
    To his father then he sent,
Sir, I think it is my duty,
    And am bound to acquaint thee,
That there is a lady in this city,
    Who has fallen in love with me.
Five thousand pounds a year she,
    All in good house and land,
That if you're willing for the match,
    Come to London out of hand.
The old man got his coach ready,
    And up to London came,
For to view this charming lady,
    Who was of birth and fame.
Then coming to his brother's house,
    This beauty for to view,
He little thought this beauty bright,
    Was his old servant Sue.
With gold and silver spangles,
    She was bedeck'd all round,
The noise of her portion being told,
    For so many thousand pounds.
The old man took his son aside,
    And thus to him did say,

Take my advice and marry her,
    My dearest child this day.
That morning they were marry'd,
    And dinner being done,
The old man being mellow,
    The story thus begun.
He said dear son I'll tell you,
    And nothing but what is true,
A poor blinking one ey'd cobler,
    Has wedded thy sweetheart Sue.
The young man went a little aside.
    As I to you confess,
And then within a short time,
    He put on his cobler's dress.
Then taking Susan by the hand,
    They fell on their bended knees,
Saying, pardon, honoured father,
    Pardon if you please.
For I am John the cobler,
    And this is my sweetheart Sue,
O pardon us, dear father,
    Because we tell you true.
If you are the cobler, said the old man,
    Who had the blinking eye,
Thou'st cobl'd me of a thousand pounds
    And a pox on thy policy.
The uncle he persuaded him,
    So did all the guests,
The old man fell a laughing,
    Saying, " 'tis but a merry jest,"

>   That I cannot be angry.
>   Then straight these words did say,
>   I pray fetch me the fiddlers,
>   And so let's dance away.
>   Now we may see the old and rich,
>   Are bit by policy,
>   For beauty, wit, and good manners,
>   Beyond all riches be.
>   So here's a good health to the cobler,
>   With another to handsome Sue,
>   Let every one drink off his glass,
>   Without any more ado.

A Strange Banquet;

Or the Devil's Entertainment by Cook Laurel, at the Peak in Derby-shire; with an Account of the several Dishes served to Table.

To the tune of *Cook Laurel*, &c.

COOK LAUREL, or Cock Lorel, as he is variously called, was a notorious rogue in the thirteenth or fourteenth century, and is not unfrequently alluded to by the old writers. Lorel, or Laurel, was a word signifying a rascal,—a bad, low, worthless fellow; and *Cock* Lorel would therefore denote an arch-rogue, a very prince of rascals! *Lorel's den* was a place of resort, no doubt, for thieves and sharpers, and "lazy lorel," which is an expression even now not unfrequently heard, means an idle, worthless fellow. A curious little tract, entitled "Cocke Lorrell's Bote," was printed by Wynken de Worde; and this "Cock Lorel's Boat" is mentioned in a MS. poem of *Doctor Double Ale*, in the Bodleian Library, and in other writings. In it persons of various classes, including the minstrels, are summoned to go on board his ship of Fools. In Rowland's "Martin Markhall, his Defence and Answer to the Bellman of London," (1610,) Cock Lorrell stands second only in the list of rogues there given, and is thus described: "After him succeeded, by the generall council, one Cock Lorrell, the most notorious knave that ever lived. By trade he was a tinker, often carrying a pan and hammer for show; but when he came to a good booty he would cast his profession in a ditch, and play the padder." *

The ballad of Cock Lorrell is introduced in Ben Jonson's masque of the "Gipsies Metamorphosed," and in "Pills to purge Melancholy." The copy I here give I have copied from the original broad-sheet in the Roxburghe Collection in the British Museum. It is in some parts exceedingly coarse in its wording, and is therefore unfit to be given entire. It will be seen that Cock Lorrell, the prince of rogues, invites his Satanic Majesty to Castleton, in the High Peak of Derbyshire, to dinner, and the dishes served up for the occasion are people of various disreputable callings and hypocritical habits, against whom the shafts of the writer are levelled.

The broad-sheet from which the ballad is here copied, is printed in black letter, and has an engraving of the banquet at the head. It is "Licensed and entered according to order. London: Printed by and for W. O. and A. M. ....to be sold by J. Deacon, at the Angel in Guiltspur Street." It begins :—

  COOK LAWREL would have the Devil his guest,
   and bid him home to Peak to dinner,
  Where fiend never had such a feast,
   prepared at the charge of a sinner.
    With a hey down, down adown, down.

---

* A foot-pad.

His stomach was quesie, he came thither coached,
    the joggings had caused his cruets to rise,
To help which he call'd for a Puritan poach'd,
    that used to turn up the white of his eyes.
        With a hey down, &c.

And so he recovered unto his wish;
    he sat him down and began to eat:
A Promooter* in plumb broth was the first dish,
    his own privy-kitchen had no such meat.
        With a hey down, &c.

Yet though with (it) he much was taken,
    upon a sudden he shifted his trencher
As soon as he spied the Bawd † and bacon,
    by which you may know the Devil's a wencher.
        With a hey down, &c.

Six pickled Taylors sliced and cut
    with Semsters ‡ and Tire-woman, || fit for his pallet,
With Feather-men and Perfumers, put
    some twelve in a charger, to make a grand sallet. §
        With a hey down, &c.

A rich fat Usurer stewed in his marrow,
    with him a Lawyer's head and green sawce

were the next dishes; usurers and lawyers, in those days, being common subjects for satire.

---

  * A *promooter*, was an informer.   † A provincialism for hare.
  ‡ A sempstress. || A milliner.
  § This verse is evidently altogether a shaft levelled against the follies of fashion and foppery of the time, and against those who made it their trade to promote them.

Then carbanado'd* and cook'd with pains
    was brought up a Serjent's cloven face,
The sawce was made of a Yeoman's brains
    that had been beaten out with his mace.
        With a hey down, &c.

Two roasted Sheriffs came whole to the Board,
    the feast had nothing been without them,
Both living and dead were foxed and fur'd,
    and their chains like Sassages hung about them.
        With a hey down, &c.

The next dish was the Mayor of the Town,
    with pudding of maintenance† put in his belly,
Like a goose in her feathers, in his gown
    with a couple of Hinch boys‡ boyl'd to jelly.
        With a hey down, &c.

Then came the over-worn Justice of Peace,
    with Clerks like gizzards stuck under each arm,
And warrants like Sippets,|| lay in his own grease,
    set over a chafing dish to be kept warm.
        With a hey down, &c.

In the next four verses, other "dainty dishes" were served up. Then followed—

The jewel of a time-server for a fish,
    a Constable sowced, with vinegar by

---

  * *Carbanado*, a steak cut crossways for broiling.
  † The "Cap of Maintenance" was a mark of dignity: the "Pudding of Maintenance" is evidently a severe satirical allusion to the fondness for good living of corporate functionaries.
  ‡ Hench boy.—a page ; an attendant on a nobleman or dignitary.
  || Small thin pieces of bread soaked in gravy or broth.

Two Alderman-lobsters laid in a dish
    a Deputy-tart and Church-warden pye.*
      With a hey down, &c.

All which devoured, then for a close
    he did for a draught of *Derby*† call,
He heaved the vessel up to his nose,
    and never left till he'd drank up all.
      With a hey down, &c.

Then from the table he gave a start
    where banquet and whine was not to seek—

And thus the banquet ended. The ballad closes with the assertion that from this feast the common name of the cavern at Castleton, where it is said to have taken place, is derived.

The Taylor's Ramble,

Or the Blue's Valour Displayed.

THIS ballad I print from a MS. copy of full fifty years old, in my own collection. I am not aware that it has ever before been printed. To another copy in the Bateman Collection, (which differs in the wording, though not in the sense, in many places, and in which the sixth verse is wanting,) is appended this note : "The Tailor's name was Eyre, and this curious exploit was performed on the 19th January, 1797."

COME all you gallant heroes of courage stout and bold,
And I'll tell you of a Taylor that would not be controled ;

---

   * *Warden* was a large baking pear. "Warden pies" were very favourite dishes, and are frequently to be found alluded to by the old writers. The wit of " *Church*-warden pie " is very obvious.
   † Derby ale.

K

It happened in Derbyshire, as you may understand,
Five troops of the cavelry to take this noble man.

So now I do begin to tell you of the fun,
Full twenty miles that morning this Taylor he had run,
And when he came to Ashford,* the people they did cry,
Make haste, my jovel lad, for your enimies are nigh.

This Taylor was a mighty man, a man of wonderous size,
And when he came to Entcliff† hill, you would have thought
    he would have reached the skies;
And when he did climb those rocks that was so wonderous
    high,
The cavelry came all round, and the Taylor they did spy.

They loaded their Pistols with Powder and with Ball,
All for to take this Taylor that was both stout and tall;
He was near four feet high, and a mighty man indeed,
You'd a laugh'd to have seen the cavelry ride after him
    full speed.

In lighting from their horses, their valour for to shew,
Five of them upon the ground this Taylor he did throw;
They being sore afrighted, saying, we would shoot him if
    we durst,
But their Carbines would not fire, for their Balls they had
    put in first.

---

   * Ashford-in-the-Water, a considerable village and parish, three
miles from Bakewell, in the High Peak of Derbyshire.
   † Endcliff, or Entcliffe, is about a mile from Bakewell, on the way
to Ashford.

Their Captain, as Commander, he ordered ranks to form,
All for to take this Taylor, and Entcliff rocks to storm ;
Prime and load then was the word their captain he did cry,
Chear up, my jovel lads, let us conquerors be or die.

These valiants being reinforced, they took the Taylor bold,
And guarded him to Bakewell,* the truth I will unfold :
At the White Horse Inn in Bakewell, as you may understand,
Full fifty of their troops to guard this noble man.

The Battle being over, the Taylor they have won,
And this is the first prank our cavelry has done ;
I'll tell you the truth, they cannot refuse,
They are ten times worse than the run away blues.

Here's a health unto the Taylor, of courage stout and bold,
And by our noble cavelry he scorns to be controld ;
If he'd but had his goose, his bodkin, and his shears,
He would soon have cleared Bakewell of those Derby
    Volunteers.

Squire Vernon's Fox-Chace.

THIS ballad, one of the most popular of our hunting songs, relates to the noble old Derbyshire family of Vernon, in olden times of Haddon Hall, but for several generations of Sudbury Hall, in the same county, which family is now represented by the Right Hon. Lord Vernon, whose seat Sudbury Hall is. " Squire

---

* Bakewell is a town of considerable importance in the High Peak, about twenty-five miles from Derby, and twelve from Buxton.

Vernon," of this ballad, was George Vernon, an ancestor of Lord Vernon, and was, like his namesake and ancestor of old, George Vernon of Haddon, (father of the celebrated Dorothy Vernon,) who acquired and deserved the name of the "King of the Peak," remarkably fond of hunting, and kept a capital pack of hounds. The copy I here give I print from a very scarce broad-sheet in my own collection. It is in two columns, with two curious little wood-cuts at the head.

ONE morning last winter to Shirley Park* came,
A noble brave Sportsman George Vernon by name
Resolved over hedges and ditches to fly,
Came a hunting the Fox—bold Reynard must die.

It was early in the morning before it was light,
Where a great many Gentlemen appointed to meet,
To meet 'Squire Vernon of honour and fame,
His Hounds they bring glory and honour to his name.

Hoke cross him and wind him: Tom Mullins he cry'd,
I warrant we shall unkennel him by the South side,
Let us draw to the cover that lies on the South,
Bold Reynard lies there, Trouler doubles his Mouth.

Cries, loo, hark to Trouler that never fails,
Do you hear how young Snowball does challenge the train
There are Fowler and Royal two brave hounds,
They'll find out bold Reynard if he lies above ground.

---

* Shirley Park.—Shirley, a village and parish, lies about ten miles from Derby, and three and a half from Ashborne. From it the noble family of Shirley, Viscount Tamworth and Earl of Ferrars, takes its name. It has, however, long ceased to be the seat of the Shirleys.

Hark, rogues, together, while Juno comes in,
There's Lady and Lambert likewise little Trim,
There's Pleasant and Careless, a bitch that runs fleet,
But loo, hark to little Justice, for she sets you to right.

There is Jovial and Frolick, and Vigour besides,
There is Dido the best bitch that ever was try'd,
There is Tospot and Bumper and Virgin I say,
There is fifty-four couple that run every day.

Mr. Walker then over the cover did stand,
He hollow'd most clearly with horn in his hand,
Cries, loo, hark together, we'll storm Reynard's fort,
And if cover he breaks, we'll tear his old coat.

Loo, hark rogues together, the scent it lies warm,
Mr. Walker and Tom Mullins both concert with horn,
Tantwivee, tantwivee, the horn they did sound,
They alarmed the country for above a mile round.

Tom Mullins the huntsman his whip he did crack,
Cries, loo, hark to little Careless, that leedeth the pack,
These words made Jack Wooley, that was whipper in,
To hollow most clearly, loo, hark rogues, hark in.

The hounds they did rally and flourish about,
Bold Reynard broke cover, Tom Mullins did shout,
Over Wheyersome* common away he did trim,
Then so merrily run by the Tinker's inn.†

---

* Wyaston.
† Tinker's Inn is a hamlet about a mile and a half from Osmaston-by-Ashborne.

Then for Blakeley Oldhurst but the door was stop'd there
Then bold Reynard was forc'd to take Staffordshire,
Then he crossed the river Dove I declare,
And straight for Durintwoods, for great cover was there.

But the hounds they pursu'd him so hot in the chace,
Which Reynard perceiving would not take the place,
Then he took Weaver hill,* which was a pleasant thing,
To hear the wood echo, and the College hall ring.

Tom Mullins was mounted on a trusty bay,
Over hedges and ditches the devil would play,
Up rocks and high mountains so merrily did climb,
Cries, hark to little Careless she runs him like wind.

Then for the New Buildings away he did steer,
I thought we should run him all round Staffordshire,
But we briskly pursu'd him with Hound and with Horn,
And we forced him back again by the Tyth Barn.

'Squire Vernon was mounted upon Golden Dun,
He leaped with courage and like fury did run,
Mr. Walker was on a gelding so free,
He maintained the Chace and kept him company.

'Squire Vernon's a Sportsman 'tis very well known,
He rid swiftly all day, you'd have thought he had flown,
'Squire Brown rid a gelding that run very fleet,
He may challenge the country to carry his weight.

---

* The Weaver Hills are among the highest in Staffordshire, lying about midway between Alton Towers and Ilam Hall.

'Squire Boothby of Ashbourn* rid over the plain,
Expecting every minute bold Reynard was slain,
He rid with great courage all the day through,
He was rarely well mounted upon his True Blue.

Mr. Boothby of Bradford who never was cast,
But in all the whole course he rallied at last,
Mr. Gretion, of Langford,† he bravely came in,
He was rarely well mounted on Tearing Robin.

Mr. Walker did hollow cry'd sentence is past,
Here is Trouler and Snowball puts up at the last,
Come, Gentlemen, ride, for the game is our own,
Now the old hounds puts up I find Reynard is blown.

The Sportsmen they rid at a desperate rate,
As if they had run for a Thousand pound plate,
No hedges could turn them, nor wall could them set,
For the choicest of Sportsmen in England were met.

The hounds they did rally and briskly pursue,
Do you hear little Careless, she runs him in view,
Fifty miles in four hours which is a great ride.
But in Wooton‡ old park bold Reynard he died.

---

* "Squire Boothby of Ashborne" and "Mr. Boothby of Bradford," were of the family of the Boothbys of Ashborne Hall, a family connected by marriage with the Vernons. The present Dowager Lady Vernon was a Miss Boothby.

† Longford, about two miles from Shirley. Longford Hall is now the residence of the Hon. E. K. Coke.

‡ Wooton is under the Weaver Hills, on the side next Alton.
> "Wooton-under-Weaver,
> Where God comes never."

is a common, though not very complimentary, saying regarding this place.

And for Jack Wooley we'll not him forget,
He rid with great courage and ne'er fear'd his neck,
No hedges or walls could turn him again,
He came in that same minute that Reynard was slain.

The Sportsmen came in every one at the last,
The hounds they run briskly not one that was cast,
Let's Ring Reynard's farewell with a horn that sounds
    clear
You've not heard such an hollow this hundred year.

All pastime in hunting here doth command,
There's the Otter by water the Deer upon land,
Here hunting is pleasant the Stag's noble Chace,
To the animal Reynard all ought to give place.

Come Gentlemen Sportsmen, where'er you be,
All you that love hunting draw near unto me,
The Chace is now ended, you've heard Reynards fall,
So here's a health to 'Squire Vernon of Sidbury Hall.

The Trusley Hunting Song.

THIS interesting ballad, which has been more than once printed, recounts the events of a famous day's "sport,"—a run with the hounds,--at Trusley, in Derbyshire; Trusley Hall being one of the seats of the Coke family for many generations. The ballad was written by Tom Handford, a blacksmith at Trusley, who also acted in the capacity of "Whipper-in" to "Squire Coke," who was the last William Coke of Trusley, and who died in 1716. A portrait of Tom Handford was painted by order of Squire Coke, and hung up in the servants' hall at Trusley, with this inscription, written by Mr. Coke —

> "This is Tom Handford—Don't you know it?
> He was both Smith and Poet!"

A version of this ballad, preserved in MS. by the late D'Ewes Coke, Esq., was furnished to me by that gentleman. It differs in many essential points from the one I now print, both in the names as well as in the construction of the stanzas. The different versions of this and other ballads have doubtless arisen from their having been written down from memory; and the different singers would also, probably, take some little license in altering the words to suit their own particular tastes. I prefer giving the *printed* version, which is evidently the original one. My copy, which I here give, was "Printed by W. O. in Leadenhall Street," and is of an almost contemporaneous period with the song itself. It is printed broadway on the sheet, in four columns, and has at the head of the first two columns a rude engraving of two huntsmen galloping past a tree, and following a stag and a couple of hounds. It is headed "*Princely Diversion: or The Jovial Hunting-Match.*"

Trusley is a village and parish nearly seven miles from Derby, and about midway between Radbourne and Longford, a seat of the Coke family.

> ONE *Valentine's* Day in the Morning
> Bright Phœbus began to appear
> Sir *William Cook* winded his horn
> And was going a Hunting the Hare
> Says *Handford** uncouple your Beagles
> And let them go Questing along
> For lose her or win her, I must go to Dinner
> Or else they will think me long.
>
> Says *Handford*, I pray now forbear, Sir
> And talk not of Dinner so soon

---

* Handford acted as Whipper-in.

For I've not been a Hunting this Year
And how can you give over by Noon.
Black *Sloven* shall warm your Bay *Robin*
And make him go smoaking along
Bonny *Dick* shall not Gallop so quick
If we light of a Hare that is Strong.

 Well, *Handford*, then said the good Squire
I mean for to show you a Trick
I value no Hedges nor Ditches,
But I'll let you know Bonny *Dick* :
Then hye for the *Clossam Bowfield*
We shall get her Ten Thousand to One
There's *Wonder*, lays hard *Thunder*
Away, o're away, she is gone.

 The Morning was pleasant all o're
So bright and so clear was the Air
We made all the Woods for to Roar
With the Noise of our sweet Harmony.
It was for the space of Three Hours
We held all our Horses to speed
Black *Slovin* held hard to Bay *Robin*
But yet could not do the Deed.

 It was about Nine in the Morning
We sounded our first Passing Bell
Sir *William*, pray put up your Horn
For another fresh Hare will do well.
Well, *Handford*, then said the good Squire
What think you of my Bonny *Dick*
Do's think thou can make him to retire
Or not for to Gallop so quick ?

Faith, Master, I needs must Confess
That I fear I was boasting too soon
But I for another fresh Hare
And you *Dick* shall have Din'd by Noon.
Well *Handford*, have at your black *Sloven*
I'll make him in Purple to Ride
And if he does offer to Tire
I'll certainly Liquor thy Hide.

You'd serve him right well, says *Jack Wilson*[*]
For he has been taunting at me
I never was beat in the Field
So for a fresh Hare let us see,
For here is some Closses of Corn
See well to your Place e'ry one,
Then Master, pray pull out your Horn
For away, o're away she is gone.

Young *Blew-Bell*, she cry'd it before
And she cry'd it all over the Lane
And after her twelve Couple more
Thus they Rattled it o're the Plain,
Bonny *Dick* play'd with his Bridle
And went at a desperate Rate
Come *Handford*, Pox take you, your Idle,
Must I open you the Gate.

O, Your humble Servant good Master
But I will not Die in your debt,

---

[*] Jack Wilson. The Coke version of the ballad says "Wheeldon," and Mr. Coke adds a note, "Wheeldon the huntsman." I am inclined, however, to think "Jack Wilson" is the correct name.

You shall find Black *Sloven* go faster
For now he begins for to Sweat.
There's *Wonder*, and *Thunder*, and *Dido*
And *Merry Lass* sweetly runs on,
There's *Younger*, Old *Ranter*, and *Rain-Bow*
But *Beauty*, she leads the Van.

She headed them Stoutly and Bravely
Just up into *Sutton's* * Cross Field
Black *Sloven* began to go heavy
And made a fair Offer to yield.
Jack Wilson came swinging before
So well did Bay *Robin* maintain
And after him Bonny *Dick* scour'd,
Black *Sloven* was Spur'd in Vain.

But he had the Luck and good Chance
For to go now and then by the String,
She led us a dilicate Dance
But as we came the last Ring
A fresh Hare, Duce take her, we Started,
We ne'er was so vexed before,
And e're we could make em forsake her
We run her two Miles or more.

And then we left Sir *William Cook*
For to ponder upon the Old Hare
Who presently leap'd o're a Brook
And a desperate leap I declare.

---

* Sutton-on-the-Hill, the adjoining village to Trusley.

He had not got past half a Mile
But this cunning Old Gypsie he spy'd
Was making back to her old File
Then away, o're away, he cry'd,

Away, o're away, my brave Boys,
And he merrily Winded his Horn
Our Beagles all toss'd up their Heads
And they soon made a speedy return,
And drawing just up to a Point
Where this cunning Old Gypsie had gone,
You never saw better Dogs Hunt
For Life underneath the Sun.

Now there was *Tantive* and *Ranter*,
They sounded her last Passing Bell,
And *Wilson* made Moan unto *Handford*
A Cup of Old Hock will do well
And *Handford* cry'd Master, ride faster
For now I begin to Cool
With Sweat, all my Cloaths are as wet
As if I had been in some Pool.

Where not these two dainty fine Pusses
They held us from Seven till One,
We scour'd thro Hedges and Bushes
So Merrily they run on.
And as for the Praise of these Hounds
And Horses that Gallops so free,
My Pen would not bring to Bounds
If Time would allow it to be.

Now Gallants, I bid you Farewel
For I fear I your Patience have try'd,
And hie for a Glass of good Ale
That Poetry may be admir'd.
And heres a good Health to the Sportsman
That Hunts with the Horn and Hound,
I hope you'll all pledge for the future
And so let this Health go round.*

Squire Frith's Hunting Song.

ANOTHER good old Derbyshire hunting song is the following, which relates to a celebrated run with the hounds of "Squire Frith, of Bank Hall," near Chapel-en-le-Frith, in the High Peak. Mr. Samuel Frith was a keen sportsman, and for more than fifty years was one of the most daring and best hunters in the district—one of the roughest and most awkward that could be found anywhere. With regard to the run celebrated in this song, it appears that one December morning, some eighty or ninety years ago, in a keen frost, Mr. Frith turned out his own pack of harriers at Castle Naze Rocks, on

---

* In the Trusley version this verse occurs:—

"Then coming home by the Ash Holt,
   Close under the Royal oak tree,
There *Blood** and old *Willett*† were fall'n
   Asleep as it happen'd to be.
Come *Handford* and give them a Larum,
   My lips are grown sore with the horn,
And round about they did be-stare 'em
   Like Babies that were newly born."

* Blood, one of the beaters.   † Willett, the Squire's gardener, on foot and tired.

the moors near his residence. To the surprise of the Squire, instead of
a hare putting off, a fine fox broke covert, and made away to the Moors.
The dogs got away after him, and Mr. Frith and his huntsman, Jack
Owen, followed over some of the most tremendous ground even of
Derbyshire. The fox made off across the moors, skirting Axe-edge,—
the highest mountain in the Peak,—to Macclesfield forest; thence by
Langley and Gracely woods to Swithingley. From thence he went by
Housley and Gawsworth, and at length, after a run of more than forty
miles, was killed at Clouds Hill, near Congleton, Mr. Frith and his
huntsman being up at the time. Mr. Frith rode a favourite black cob
of his called "Black Jack," one of the best fencers in the county,—a
quality of essential importance in that district of stone walls and rocks.
Bank Hall is about two and a half miles from Chapel-en-le-Frith.

Hark! hark! brother Sportsmen, what a melodious sound,
How the valleys doth echo with the merry-mouthed hound;
There's none in this world with Squire Frith can compare,
When chasing bold Reynard, or hunting the Hare.

Bright Phœbus peeps over yon Eastern hills,
And darted his rays through the meadows and fields;
On the eighth of December, that memorable morn,
We chased bold Reynard with hound and with horn.

Then over young Cumrocks like lightning he flew,
What a melodious chorus when Reynard's in view;
There's nothing like hunting we mortals do know,
Then follow, boys, follow, tally-ho! tally-ho!

With a staunch and fleet pack, most sagacious and true,
What a melodious chorus when Reynard's in view;
The hills and the valleys do echo around,
With the shouts of the hunter, and cries of the hound.

Squire Frith being mounted upon a swift steed,
Black Jack, there's but few that can match him for speed;
The Squire and his Huntsman no horse-flesh will spare,
When chasing bold Reynard, or hunting the Hare.

There's Grinder, and Saddler, two dogs of great fame,
Hark to Primrose, and Bonny Lass, and Conqueror by name;
There's Killman, and Bowman, Ringwood, and Dido,
With Lily, and Lady, and Rolly, also.

O'er Macclesfield Forest old Reynard did fly,
By Tragnell, and Runcorn, and unto Langly;
By Shalcross, and Greswark, and unto Swithinly,
At his brush close did follow the hounds in full cry.

By Shalcross and Greswark we came back again,
It was speed that prolonged his life it was plain;
Full forty long miles that old creature did return,
And he holed in Clown Hills, near to Congleton.

Of geese, ducks, and hens, great havoc he's made,
And innocent lambs, he has worried the said;
There's no barn-door fowls old Reynard did spare,
Take care, all ye farmers, of your poultry, take care.

Here's a health to all Hunters, wherever they be,
To all honest sportsmen of every degree;
With a full flowing bowl, we'll drink a health all,
To that great and true Sportsman, Squire Frith, of Bank Hall.

Derbyshire Men.

HERE is an old saying connected with Derbyshire, which is not very complimentary to the sons of its soil:—

"Derbyshire born and Derbyshire bred,
Strong in the arm, but weak in the head."

This saying forms the text of the following excellent lines, written by Mr. Walter Kirkland, which first appeared in print in "The Reliquary" for October, 1864.

"I' Darbyshire who're born an' bred,
Are strong i' th' arm, bu' weak i' th' head:"
    So th' lying Proverb says.
Strength o' th' arm, who doubts shall feel:
Strength o' th' head, its power can seal
    The lips that scoff, always.

The rich vein'd Mine, the Mountain hoar,
We sink, an' blast, an' pierce, 'an bore
    By th' might o' Darby brawn.
An' Darby brain con think an' plon,
As well as that o' ony mon;
    An' clearly as the morn.

"Strong i' th' arm, an' strong i' th' head,"
The fou' fause Proverb should ha' said,
    If th' truth she meant to tell.
Bu' th' union, so wise an' rare
O *brawn* an' *brain*, she didna care
    To see or speak of well.

The jealous jade, nor Darby born,
Where praise wor due, pour'd forth bu' scorn,
  An' lying words let fau.
Bu' far above the Proverb stands
The Truth, that God's Almighty hands
Ha' welded strength an' mind i' one ;
An' pour'd it down i' plenty on
  Born Darbyshire men au.

An Elegy

Upon the Death of all the greatest Gentry in Darley-Dalle, who loved Hunting and Hawking, and several other Games. The Poet's view, well known to you, to be too true, and so adieu, by me LEO. W. 1672.

THE following extremely curious poem, containing many interesting allusions to families long since departed, was written in 1672, by Leonard Wheatcroft, some time clerk of the parish, poet, tailor, and schoolmaster, at Ashover, in Derbyshire. He was a man of talent, and wrote many things which are worth collecting together. It is here printed from the original MS. The last verse was evidently added after the accession of George the First.

The title of the ballad is particularly quaint, and characteristic of the man and of the county of which he was a native. In the dialect of the district the rhymes would be perfect, and would read thus :—

    The Poet's view
    Well known to yew,
    To be too trew,
    And so adieu
    By me Leo Double Vew.
    Sixteen seventy tew.

1.

As I on Oaker-hill* one-day did stand,
Viewing the world which I could not command,
I turn'd my face tou'rd Berchore† partly west,
To view where Greaveses us'd to have their nest;
But out, alas! I found they were all gone,
Not one was left to rest against a stone.

2.

Then looking forward, the coast being very cleare,
At Rowther,‡ there I found one Adam Eayre;
But now he's gone, left house and land behind him,
So to be short I know not where to find him;
But if any counceller can make it out,
He'st have his land and I will go without.

3.

I'll up to Hassap‖ to hear them sing a mass,
There I shall know who made the old man pass;
Death made it wrong, I send him to purgatory,
Where he must stay till he be fit for glory;
But if there be such a place 'twixt this and heaven,
I fear he cannot pass, 'tis so uneven.

4.

Then did I to my panting muses say,
Haste and begone, you shall no longer stay
    (within this place);

---

* Oker Hill, near Darley Dale.   † Birchover.
‡ Roo Tor, or Row Tor, by Birchover, an old seat of the Eyre family.
‖ Hassop, a principal residence of the family of Eyre.

Haste and begone, upon Calton top your banners,
And call at Haddon, where lived ould John Manners,
O use him kindly I strictly you command,
For he was kind to th' poore of Ingland.

5.

But now he's gone, like others hence away,
Then for another Earle like him ever pray,
That will be kind both unto Rich and Poore,
Then God Almighty will increase his store,
And bless him here upon this earthly throne,
And at the last call him one of his owne.

6.

Walking by the River, Stanton* I did spye,
But neither Calton† nor a Bage‡ saw I:
They are all gone and none left but old Boards,
Alas! alas! what doth this world affordes.
There's severall more that are slipt out o' th' way,
But not one word of them I here will say.

7.

Then calling back my muses, mee thought I
Spyed Little Stancliffe‖ standing pleasantly,

---

* Stanton, the present residence of W. P. Thornhill, Esq.

† The Caltons were an old Derbyshire family, long settled in this district and at Chesterfield.

‡ Bache, this family resided for two centuries at Stanton Hall, and from them the name of Bache-Thornhill was derived.

‖ Stancliffe, now the seat of Joseph Whitworth, Esq., the inventor of the celebrated Whitworth rifles and rifled canons.

But not one Steare* i' th' stall shall yet be seene;
Well fed win springs and deck'd with Lorrells green,
But one old Backer Bourning of the owne,
Till Steare retourne, there' no one knows how sowne.

8.

Then on the hills I came to Darley Hall,
To hear that music in those Ashes tall.
Listening awhile, I not being pleased well,
Thought I where is my pretty Cullen-bell,†
Whose name and fame made all this vale once sound,
But now that honour's buried under ground.

9.

Besides your Parsons of Divinity
As Pain, and Pot, Edwards, and Mosley,
All four divines and men of noble birth,
All dead and gone and buried in the earth;
How can I chuse but must lament to see
My friends all gone who did make much of me.

10.

Tho' all in haste one place I have past by,
That's Cowley Hall, where oft I heard the cry
Of great-mouthed doggs who did not feare to kill
What was their master's pleasure, word, and will;

---

* Steere. Stancliffe Hall passed to the Steeres by purchase in 1655, from whom it passed to Jenkinson, and from them, in 1715, to Greensmith.

† Columbell. Nether Hall, Darley Dale, was for many years the chief seat of the Columbell family, who held it till the death, in 1673, of John Columbell, whose heiress married Marbury.

His name was Sinner, who ever did him know,
He's dead and gone now many years ago.

11.

Then turning round, all gone, thus did I thinke,
Where shall I make my friend or muses drinke;
Then looking down below I did espy
A pretty hall which stood me very ney,
Where lived the Father, Son, and Wives of either,
Both in my time, all-tho' not both together.

12.

A Knight the Father, and a Squire the Son,
One heir is left, if dead that name is done;
This heir being young, with Ladies durst not play,
So he in sorrow quickly went away,
Leaving no heir o' th' name, no, not one,
So farewell Milwards* now of Snitterton.

13.

Then rushing forward down by Darwen side,
My muses presently through Matlock hied,
And finding there the good ould pastur gone,
I hide to Riber† there to make my mone;
But out, alas! my sorrows to increase,
That name is gone now buried under hears.

---

* The Milwards held Snitterton for a long time. The last of the family, John Milward, died *circa* 1670, when the estate passed by marriage of his heiress with Adderley.

† Riber Hall, in Matlock parish, was for many generations the property and seat of the Wolley family. Anthony Wolley, the last of that branch, died a bachelor in 1688, when his co-heiresses sold the estate to Statham.

14.

Wolley, Wolley, Woolley, farewell to thee,
A noble Esquire, thou was both kind and free
To all that come, I say, both rich and poore,
There's few went empty that came to his doore.
Walker's fair Hous is almost wore away,
With several more now going to decay.

15.

To speak of Dedick* what shall I do there,
Babbington's† Treason hateful doth appear;
Their house is down, and they are gone to nought,
So will all those which ere rebellion sought.
Then pray to God for peace and unity,
That King and nobles all may well agree.

16.

Then I to Ogston,‡ there to break my fast,
They all in mourning stood at me agast,
To think my friend and lover was departed,
And so I left them almost broken hearted;
What shall I doe thought I to hide my head,
Seeing so many gallants now are dead.

17.

Then up by Amber I did quickly hey,
None of my ancient friends I could espey,

---

* Dethick.
† Anthony Babington, the unfortunate conspirator, was of Dethick.
‡ Now the seat of Gladwin Turbutt, Esq.

In Asher* parish I could find not one,
Old Crich,† and Dakin,‡ and ould Hobskinson,‖
They are departed and gone hence away,
As er self, I have not long to stay.

18.

I will retourne unto my hill againe,
And cause my muses to sing out a straine,
And that in mourning too she shall be drest,
To sing new anthems of the very best.
And thus you see in a few dayes how they
Are all gone hence and tourned to dirt and clay.

19.

Farewell you Huntsmen that did hunt the hare,
Farewell you Hounds that tired both horse and mare,
Farewell you gallant Falkners every one,
The chief of all did live at Snitterton.
So to conclude both greate and small,
Those that are left the Lord preserve them all.

By me LEONARD WHEATCROFT.

---

* Ashover.

† The family of Crich was one of considerable note in this parish, and at one time owned the Stubbing Edge estate.

‡ The Dakeynes were of Ashover and of Darley Dale, and were people of much note.

‖ Hodgkinson. Part of the Old Hall Manor, as well as Overton Manor, in this parish, belonged to this family. Overton passed from them, by marriage, to Sir Joseph Banks.

20.

The conclusion.

This verse is written in a blacker ink, and at a much later time.

. If any one of this same truth do doubt,
From Oker Hill Ide have them walk about
From house to house to prove the truth of this,
And then they'll say there's nothing in't amiss.
I have no more to say but this my charge,
Let all that's heare say pray God bless King George.

FINIS.

Cocktail Reel.

THE "Merriment" recounted in this singular ballad, which I am not aware has ever before been printed, is said to have taken place at Dronfield, in Derbyshire, and I have heard the sixth line sung as

"From Chesterfield, Beighton, and Masber."

It is, however, uncertain whether this is correct, or whether it may not more probably have taken place at Rotherham, which is near both Kimberworth, Brightside, and Masber (Masborough). The copy I here give is from a MS. of more than half a century old.

SOON as old Ball was got better,
   A merriment there was appointed,
Creditor as well as debtor,
   Both met to be better acquainted.
Number of lads there were present
   From Kimberworth, Brightside, and Masper,
Each with a countenance pleasant,
   His true love did cuddle and clasp her.

Stephen turn'd out with his fiddle,
Each lad took his lass by the middle,
Went reeling about like a riddle,
   As if they had been enchanted.
Care, the forerunner of sorrow,
Was kick'd out of door till to-morrow,
Not one in his spirit was narrow;
   Then, boh! cry'd Tyger, undaunted.

2.

Tyger connected with Jemmy,
   Conducted Ball out of the stable,
Join'd in the yard by old Sammy,
   Who alefied came from the table.
Ball being well prim'd with ginger,
   Was fit to jump over the fences,
Neighbour as well as each stranger
   All thought they were out of their senses.
Sammy, who hates to be idle,
Seized Ball fast by the Bridle,
Then gave him a kick made him sidle,
   So went far round as they wanted,
Right hand and left they did clever,
Made Jem to squint harder than ever,
He promis'd his partner som liver;
   Then, boh! cried Tyger, undaunted.

3.

Out jump'd the calf, elevated;
   The cow broke her sole and ran after;
Shout upon shout it created,
   And filled the spectators with laughter.

Tideswell the cow was so nam'd,
    Because at that fair they had bought her,
She ran at Tyger untam'd,
    To fork him as nature had taught her.
Tyger at that was displeas'd,
Which caus'd a fresh dust to be rais'd;
Her nose in a instant he seiz'd,
    At which old Samuel ranted.
Tideswell took off like be madded,
O'er mother and daughter she gadded,
Huzzas in abundance were added,
    Then, boh! cried Tyger, undaunted.

4.

Stephen, though blind as a beetle,
    Laughed hard at old Hannah's disaster,
He lost no time with his fiddle,
    His elbow went quicker and faster:
Ball cut such a new fashion'd caper,
    Which really by-standers amazed,
All his four feet were at tapers,
    The pavement it perfectly blazed;
Samuel nor no one that join'd him
Durst venture their carcase behind him,
Tho' age in a manner did blind him.
    No colt could win him 'twas granted,
Tideswell caught Tyger and tost him
Quite out of the ring till she lost him,
Though many a bruise it did cost him;
    Still, boh! cried Tyger, undaunted.

5.

Oceans to drink being call'd for,
   Hot cuddle-me-buff was the liquor,
Wife of my own Jemmy called for,
   Old Hannah, cried Stephen, play quicker.
Off they went after each other,
   As if they had quicksilver in them,
Join'd by first one, then another,
   You never see nothing could win them
Setting down sides, and then up again,
Crossing in couples, to sup again,
Sam'el, inspir'd with his cup, again
   Of his activity vaunted.
Ball being prim'd with the best of them,
Pranced and kick'd with the rest of them,
Seeing he made a mere jest of them ;
   Boh ! cried Tyger, undaunted.

6.

Tyger ran under Ball's belly,
   All danger, like Rodney, kept scorning,
Some thought he was rather silly,
   As Ball was new frosted that morning.
Sam'el got hurt in the scuffle,
   As Ball his fore feet was advancing,
That seem'd his temper to ruffle,
   And quite put an end to their dancing.
So they dismiss'd in civility,
Talking of Ball's great agility,
Tideswell and Tyger's fidelity,
   Which kind nature implanted.

How the four brutes in particular
Danc'd with their tails perpendicular,
Straight forwards, sideways, and circular :
Boh ! cries Tyger, undaunted.

LINES OCCASIONED BY

A Yorkshire Pye,*

Sent as a Present from Sir William St. Quintin, to His Grace the Duke of Devonshire, at Bath, on Christmas-Day, 1762. *Written by Mr. Derrick.*

THIS curious effusion of Samuel Derrick's, who was Master of the Ceremonies at Bath at the time, I here reprint from a slip broad-sheet of the period in my own collection. The peer to whom this famous Yorkshire pie was sent, was William, fourth Duke of Devonshire, who died in 1764. Sir William St. Quintin, Bart., of Harpham, in the county of York, who died in 1771, was Member of Parliament for Thirsk, and High Sheriff in 1733. He married Rebecca, daughter of Sir John Thompson, Lord Mayor of London, and by her was father of the last baronet of the name of St. Quintin.

WERE but my Muse inspir'd by *Fludyer's*† Taste,
Or with *Quin's* Skill and lively Poignance grac'd ;

---

* This Pye was composed of Pheasants, Turkeys, Plovers, Snipes, Woodcocks, Partridges, Ox Tongue, and Hare, &c.

† When their present Majesties honoured the City of London with their Presence, Sir Samuel Fludyer, Bart., late Lord Mayor, entertained them with more Elegance than ever was known.

Th' *Apician* Muse, who bade *Lucullus* treat,
And taught the gay *Mark Anthony* to eat ;
I'd venture then *St. Quintin* to commend,
Whose faithful Memory ne'er forgets his Friend ;
Of placid Temper, and of gen'rous Blood,
Whose only Vanity is doing Good ;
Whose open Looks imply an honest Heart,
Courtly in Manners, yet unspoil'd by Art ;
The Emblem of whose liberal Soul I see
In yonder pile of Hospitality ;
An Edifice for *Cavendish* to view,
All English Fabric, and that Fabric true.

   Such plenteous Sights were known in Times of old,
When Christmas by th' expiring Year was told ;
Long e'er our hardy Sires, un-nerv'd by Sloth,
Had dwindled down into a Pigmy Growth.
Within this Pile Varieties unite,
To please at once the Taste, the Smell, the Sight.
Robb'd of his vivid Green, and glossy Dyes,
His golden Plumage, and his Scarlet Eyes,
Here rests the *Attic* Pheasant,*—never more,
Narcissus like, his Image to adore ;

   Here lies the Turkey,† who with redd'ning Pride
Once all the Farmer's feather'd Brood defy'd ;
True Emblem of *Bœotia*, whence he came,
A noisy Blockhead, emulous of Fame.

---

  * According to Aldrovandus, the Pheasant is very fond of viewing his own image.

  † According to the same writer, the Turkey is originally a Bœotian bird.

The wheeling Plover, and the timid Hare,
Here mix;—the generous Ox bestows a Share—
His Tongue—at jovial Tables always found:
And Indian Spice enriches the Compound;
The rare Compound! where various Parts conspire
To form one Mass, which all who taste admire.

   Thus out of Chaos did the World first rise,
And from Confusion sprung th' illumin'd Skies.
Life's Pleasures on Variety depend,
Her various Views make Hope so much our Friend.

   Thus while the Bard by *Avon's* winding Stream
Unfolded to the *Naiades* his Theme,
While from the humid Rocks, and cavern'd Hills,
He mark'd them, guiding the salubrious Rills
To Bladud's Baths, where rosey Health presides,
Shedding her Influence o'er the steaming Tides;
Wondering he saw Britannia's Genius nigh,
Aiding the Nymphs, and blessing their Supply.

   If near my Springs, she cry'd, you chance to view
My Son, to Honour and to Virtue true;
My fav'rite Devonshire, of antient Line,
Where Loyalty and Truth united shine,
The faithful Guardian of his Country's Fate,
The Friend of Freedom and the British State,
Exert the Panacea of your Art,
Hygeia fair, your sovereign Powers impart;
Unlock the sacred Treasures of your Store,
And give the Patriot to my Arms once more;
Esteem'd in Public, as in Private lov'd,
And ev'n by Foes unwillingly approv'd.

The Agricultural Meeting.

Tune—"*The King of the Cannibal Islands.*"

THIS excellent song was written on occasion of the meeting of the Royal Agricultural Society of England at Derby, in the year 1843, under the Presidency of the Earl of Hardwicke, and was a general favourite.

  Come gather round and form a throng,
  And trust me I'll not keep you long,
  I'll entertain you with a Song
    On the Agricultural Meeting!
A subject I have good and pat,
To make you smile, I'll answer that;
They say that laughing makes one fat,
And if you don't laugh I'll eat my hat!
I'll not give pain by any jokes,—
Tho' of the Derby 'tis, good folks,
About it there's not any "*hoax*,"
    The Agricultural Meeting!
  Away with sorrow, care, and strife,
  All the world will, and his wife,
  Muster there, upon my life,
    At the Agricultural Meeting.

  The wish'd-for time is very nigh,
  And all to do their best will try,
  On the Eleventh of July,
    At the Agricultural Meeting!

Come forward, lads, your best make haste,
You that plough, and you that rake ;—
Let 'em see that you're awake,
For you've a chance a prize to take !
Forward bring the ox and sheaf,
Show Foreigners unto their grief,
The meaning of *real* corn and beef,
   At the Agricultural Meeting !
 Away with sorrow, &c.

The thing will just be as it should,
For there'll be there, 'tis understood,
The rich, the titled, and the good,
   At the Agricultural Meeting !
Of those who in the good cause stand,
And help with purse, and heart, and hand,
Are SPENCER, HARDWICK, COLVILE,* and
THE DUKE OF RICHMOND—what a band !
Joy will beam in heart and face,
To know that surely 'tis the case,
That their gay presence here will grace
   The Agricultural Meeting !
 Away with sorrow, &c.

'Twill be a glorious holiday—
All the week for fun and play—
No one then at home will stay
   From the Agricultural Meeting !
Every one some sport will catch—
For there will be of fun a batch :—

---

* Earl Spencer, Earl of Hardwicke, and C. R. Colvile, Esq., M.P.

TUESDAY they'll come to the scratch,
And try the famous Ploughing Match!
Of Implements there will be a show,—
Of things that reap, and things that mow,
Things to dig, and things that sow,
    At the Agricultural Meeting!
  Away with sorrow &c.

When this is o'er, at close of day,
Again for fun they'll start away—
Gents. and Ladies, such display—
    At the Agricultural Meeting!
They'll to the Grand Hotel repair,
For JOHN BELL CROMPTON, who's the MAYOR,
Will give a dinner of rare fare,
And all the Council will be there!
Then after this, they'll dancing go,
And trip it gaily to and fro,
Upon "the light fantastic toe,"
    At the Agricultural Meeting!
  Away with sorrow, &c.

On WEDNESDAY there's another spree—
The Implements again we'll see,
And prove what's done in Husbandry,
    At the Agricultural Meeting!
Come Dick and Thomas, Ralph and Giles,
In your best clothes, and your smiles,
Over hedges, ditches, stiles—
Across the country—many miles!

Then on *that* night it will fall—
The Council are invited all
To dinner at the County-Hall,
      From the Agricultural Meeting!
  Away with sorrow, &c.

On THURSDAY there'll be more than this—
And such enjoyment who would miss?
On that day there'll be double bliss
      At the Agricultural Meeting!
Won't there be a fine to do?
Pigs and sheep, and oxen, too ;—
Four-legged calves—and, 'tween I and you,
A few, no doubt, that *walk on two!*
Lots of cattle will be there,
DERBY horses, I declare,
As well as our good *Derby Mayor*,
      At the Agricultural Meeting!
  Away with sorrow, &c.

On THURSDAY there's another feed—
When they've shown their live-stock breed ;
For after work they'll something need,
      At the Agricultural Meeting!
The Grand Pavilion, deck'd out fine,
Will be—and there'll two thousand dine :—
And they'll astonish, I opine,
Above a bit—the food and wine!
And even then the sport ne'er stops,
For they'll for dancing leave their drops,
And take to *capers* and to *hops*,
      At the Agricultural Meeting!

Away with sorrow, care, and strife,
All the world will, and his wife,
Muster there, upon my life,
At the Agricultural Meeting !

THE
Complainte of Anthonie Babington.

THE following deeply interesting "complaynt" was written by Richard Williams, and dedicated, in MS., to King James the First. It remained unpublished until 1862, when it was communicated to "The Reliquary" by Mr. W. Durrant Cooper, F.S.A. Anthony Babington was born in 1561, and on the death of his father, succeeded to the family estates at Dethick, in Derbyshire, which had been acquired by the Babingtons through marriage with the heiress of Dethick. He was executed, along with thirteen others, under circumstances of peculiar barbarity, on the 20th of September, 1586, for a conspiracy to liberate the truly unfortunate and much to be commiserated Mary Queen of Scots. His petition to Queen Elizabeth is simple and touching in the extreme, and the heart must indeed have been callous to good and womanly feeling that could withstand it and spurn its prayer. It is as follows :—*

"Most gratious Souvarigne yf either bitter teares a pensisve contrite harte ore any dutyfull sighte of the wretched Synner might work any pitty in your royall brest, I would wringe out of my drayned eyes as much bloode as in bemoaninge my drery tragedye shold, lamentably bewayll my faulte, and somewhat (no dought) move you to compassion, but synnce there is no proportione betwixte the qualitye of my crimes and any human commiseration, Showe sweet Queene some mirakle on

* The original is in the Bateman Collection at Lomberdale House.

a wretch that lyethe prostrate in yr prison, most grivously bewaylinge his offence and imploringe such comforte at your anoynted hande as my poore wives misfortunes doth begge, my childe innocence doth crave, my gyltless family doth wishe, and my heynous trecherye dothe leaste deserve, So shall your divine mersy make your glorye shyne as far above all princes, as my most horrible practices are more detestable amongst your beste subiectes, whom lovinglye and happielye to governe.

I humbly beseche the mercye Master himself to grante for his sweete Sonnes sake, Jesus Christe.

L. JEWITT. SC

The following is the "Complaynte of Anthonie Babington by Richard Williams:"—

> To the kinges most excellent maiestie with all other kinglie titles and dignities whatsoever to whome your poore humble subject RICHARD WILLIAMS wishethe healthe long life and many happy yeares to reigne over us to the glory of God and your Maiesties comforte.

My dreade and royall sovereigne,

This ANTHONIE BABINGTON was borne at a mansion house of his father called Dethicke in the Countie of Darbye in the parishe of Critche; whose father was a man of good accompte and lived well and orderlie in his contrie, kept a good house, and releived the poore. But he was inclined to papistrie as the times then required; who had a brother that was doctor of divinitie in queene Maryes dayes, of whome some mention is made in this storye. This Anthonye, the son, was a yonge man, well featured, and of good proportion in all the lyneamentes of his bodie, of a most pregnante fyne witt and great capacitie, had a watchinge head, ande a moste prowde aspiringe mynde; and by nature a papist, whereinn hee was borne and brought upp; where if he had bene trayned otherwise hee might have proved a good member of the common wealthe, where nowe be became a reproche and scandall to the same.

In whose course of life many accidents hapned even from his birthe to his deathe as appeares in this his complainte wherein I have followed the methode of a booke intituled, the "Mirrour of Magistrates" wherein everye man semes to complayne of his owne misfortunes, humbly beseeching your royall maiestie to pardon all defectes as well in my writinge as in the baseness of the verses. In the one I have done as well as my learninge did serve me, for the other as well as my olde eyes woulde permitt me, which I beseech your royall Maiestie to censure with clemencye, and I will trulye praise to the almightie for the long continuance of your healthe and happie Estate bothe to Godes glorye and your Maiesties comforte.

Your poore distressed subjecte
RICHARD WILLIAMS.

The Complainte of Anthonie Babington, sometyme of Lyncolns Inne Esquier, who with others weare executed for highe treason in the feildes nere Lyncolns Inne the xixth of September A° 1586.*

---

* An error for 20th.

A DREAME OR INDUCTION.
ANTHONIE BABINGTON HIS COMPLAYNT.

What will it avayle on fortune to exclayme
  When a due desarte is chiefest cause of all ;
Myself and none but myselfe justlie can I blame,
  That thus have procured myne untymelie fall ;
  And turned have my honnye swete unto bitter gall.
    Wherefore good frende take thie penne and write,
    And in mournful verse my Tragedie recite.

Long mighte I have lived a contented happie state,
  And have borne a porte and countnance with the beste,
If fortune should me cheicke, I could her mate ;
  Thus none like me more happie was and bleste,
  Till that discontente procured myne unreste ;
    And the pompe of pride so glared in myne eyen,
    That I rejected vertue moste devyne.

But firste I will tell thee myne estate, and name,
  And contrie soile, where I was bredd and borne ;
Anthonie Babington I hight ; of a worthy house I came,
  Till my mysdemeanours made me forlorne,
  Givinge cause to my foes to laugh me to scorne.
    Whoe have stayned my state and blemisht my name,
    In clymbing by follie have falne to my shame.

At Dethwicke in Darbye shire I was both borne and bredd ;
  My father was an esquier of good reputation ;
A good house he kepte, a virtuose life he ledd ;
  My selfe beinge a childe was helde in estimation ;
  But havinge gott the rayne I changed my facion ;

Then privatlie I sought my owne will and pleasure,
  Livinge to my liking, but never kepte a measure.

Doctour Babington myne eame* did pronosticate
  That harde was the happe whereto I was borne,
He sayde that "pride by glorye shoulde abate
  And destenye decreede I shoulde be folorne;"
Whose wordes my father then helde in scorne,
    "O trayne him up well," mine unkell did saye,
    "Unlesse hee repente the same a nother daye."

"Give hym not brother his libertie in youthe,
  For then olde dayes hee never shall see,
Hee is my nephewe the more is my rewthe,
  To think of his happe and harde destinie,
  If skill beguyle me not hanged he shalbe."
    This was the foresight of my father's brother,
    For which lote of his hee was hated by my mother.

I know not where hee spoke by hassarde or skill,
  For such divinations I doe not comende;
Yet his counsell was good to flie future ill;
  For whoe so in vertue there dayes doe not spende
  Shalbe sure with me repente them in th' ende.
    The proofe of myne unkells worde I founde so trewe
    As by the sequell hereafter you may viewe.

Not longe after my father resyned upp his breathe,
  And lefte my wofull mother with a great charge;
Whiche proved for us all to tymelie a deathe;

---

* This word signifies uncle. *Vide* Ash. Dict.

For then good gentelwoman her purse ranne at large,
Havinge of debts and legacies great somes to discharge ;
   But in the state of widowhode not long she tarried
     For with that good gentleman Henry Foljambe she married.

Whoe loved us all tenderlie as wee had benne his owne,
  And was verye carefull of oure education,
Whose love so mee was diverse wayes showne,
  And I of the saime had daylie probation,
  And by this maye appeare of whiche I make narration.
   Withe his owne chaine of golde hee would mee oftene decke
    Whiche made me a proud boye to weare about my necke.

As on a tyme this chayne about my necke I did weare,
  And going to an orcharde some apples to gett,
When clymbing a high tree, as one without feare,
  The boughe then brake, whereon my foote I sett,
  And downwarde I slipt, but was caught in a nett.
   In the tree I was hanged faste by the chayne,
    So desyre of my pride was cause of my payne.

But was not suffered there longe to hang,
  But was nere strangled or I was taken downe,
For there I strugled with suche a deadlie pange ;
  My mother shee frighted and fell in a sowne,
  And griefe made my father likewise to frowne.
   But my reviving, there sorrowes over caste ;
    Then they rejoyeste sayinge, "my destinie was paste."

Thus carelesse a tyme with them I lived at pleasure,
  Surfetted with self will and with fonde delite ;

I knew no golden meane, nor never kepte a measure,
  But like a kyndlie beare gan tymelie to byte.
  Even then I harborde envye and sucked despite ;
    And pride at that instante tooke so deepe a roote,
    That humilitie for ever was troden under foote.

In myne noneage I was when my father dyde,
  Philip Draycott, of Paynslie hee did me obtayne,
Whoe had appoynted me his doughter for my bryde,
  And in whose house a space I did remayne ;
    There suckte I pleasure that proved to my payne ;
      There was I misled in papistre my soul to wounde ;
      There was I corrupted made rotten and unsounde.

There, even there awhile, I spente my youthfull tyme,
  There was I lulled in securitie faste asleepe,
Then was I frollicke, there was I in my pryme,
  In jollitie then I laught, but never thought to weepe ;
    My witts were moste fynne and conceits verye depe.
      But oh Paynslie ! Paynslie ! I may thee curse ;
      Where nature made me ill, education made me worse.

For by nature I was with papistrie infected,
  But might have beene restrayned, had it pleased God ;
My father and myne eame they weare suspected ;
  They lived with there censcience wherein I was odd,
    Therefore was beaten with a more sharper rodd ;
      There conscience they kepte, & ruled it by reason ;
      Livinge like subjectes, and still detested treason.

My father-in-lawe still ledd me to what I was inclined ;
  I meane for my conscience, no farther he coulde deale ;

My mayntnance sufficient to content my mynde,
  So that all this, whiche I tasted, nought but weale,
  But could not be contente, which I muste nowe reveale.
    My fynne head was desyrouse to studye the lawe,
    In attainge whereof I proved my selfe a dawe.

And for that cause forthwith I to London wente,
  Where in Lyncolns Inne a student I became;
And there some part of my flittinge tyme I spente,
  But to bee a good lawyer my mynde coulde not frame;
  I addicted was to pleasure and given so to game;
    But to the theater and curtayne woulde often resorte,
    Where I mett companyons fittinge my disporte.

Companyons, quothe you, I had companyons in deede,
  Suche as in youthe with me weare well content to drawe;
Lyncked so in myscheife, wherein wee did excede,
  We cared not for order nor paste of reasons lawe;
  Of God, nor of good man, wee stoode in little awe.
    Wee paste the bounds of modestie, and lived without shame,
    Wee spotted our conscience, and spoiled our good name.

We cared not for the church, that place we not frequented;
  The tavernes weere better our humors to fitt.
The companye of dayntie dames, wee chieflie invented;
  With whom in dalliance wee desyred ofte to sitt.
  Theise weare the fruytes of yonge hedds and witt;
    Thus in lustlie libertie I led a loose life,
    And thoughe I weare maried I cared not for my wife.

Yett to the sermons wee woulde oftene resorte,
  Not in hope edification by them to obtayne;

But rather to jeste and make of them a sporte ;
   Whiche nowe I feele to my sorrowe griefe and payne ;
   These bee the fruytes that sicophantes doe gayne,
     Cheiflie when they mocke, and skorne God's worde,
     Disdaining the servantts and prophetts of the Lorde.

With Catholicks still conversant I coveted to be,
   That weare alwayes in hope and looked for a daye ;
Gapinge for a change which wee trusted to see.
   Ambition so stonge me my selfe I could not staye,
   Whiche makes me sighes to sighe well a waye.
     Then I had my will and playde with pleasure's ball,
     Then I was alofte and feared not this fall.

Yett so covertlie all this tyme I did my selfe behave,
   And so closelie wrought in subtell *syners* faime,
What so ere I thought my selfe I sought to save,
   Livinge all this while without suspecte or blame ;
   And more to wynne mee credditt a courtier I becaime ;
     Where the syrens song so swetelie I did synge,
     I never was suspected to worke such a thinge.

The nobles of the courte of me thoughte so well,
   That often to their tables they would me invite ;
Where in gesture and talke I did the common sorte excell ;
   Thereby wynninge favor in my company to delite,
   Whiche with a Judas kisse I soughte to requyte.
     As in a sequell of my storye will after appeare,
     Which I shame to tell it toucheth me so nere.

And daylie more and more my credditt did increase,
   And so in like manner did pride still abounde ;

Beloved I was bothe of more and lesse ;
  When my inwarde motions were all unsounde ;
  My parsonage was comelie which favour eache where founde ;
    But pryde had so blynded me I could not see.
    That with Iccarus aloft, I mynded was to flee.

The grounde, that I troade on, my feet could not holde,
  Nor I bee contente in a happie state to reste,
Like Bayarde that blushed not, then was I more bolde ;
  When rancor inwardlie still boyled in my breste,
  That like an unnaturall birde I filed my neste ;
    In parlinge with parasites that looked for a daye,
    By the counsell of Caterpillers, I wrought my decaye.

Then I beganne to prie into matters of the state,
  And with what I liked nott I secrett faulte did fynde ;
Where I fawned openlie, I inwardlie did hate,
  And to my confederates would closelie breake my mynde ;
  I mean to suche as to my love weare inclynde ;
    Betweene whome and mee suche mischiefe intented,
    That we thoughte to have made all England repented.

Where upon in to France a jorney I did frame,
  To parle with *Padgett*, *Morgan*, and others of that crewe ;
What wee had but decrede, they resolved on the same ;
  Whose pretended purpose at large, when I knewe,
  I willinglie consented too, which makes mee nowe to rewe ;
    And to sett the same forwarde a solleme oathe did take ;
    O cursed conscience that a traytor didst me make !

Then into Englande I retorned agayne with spede,
  And gott conferrence hereof with some of greate fame.
Manye weare the plotts, whereon we agreed ;
  And greate the attemptes, whereat wee did aime ;
  Which afterwarde proved oure ruynose shaime ;
    And aspiringe pride so fyred my harte,
    I was content to playe a traytors parte.

HIS ARTICLES OF ARRAYGNMENT.

Yea to bee a most savage monster agaynste all kynde,
  In seking the deathe of my Queene, the Lord's anoynted,
Ambition so stonge me, that I was stroke blynde,
  In pluckinge her downe that God had appoynted,
  And the unitie of the realme in sonder to have joynted ;
    To have made kings and rulers at our pleasure ;
    To have exceeded in vyllanye without rule or measure.

To have made suche lawes as wee thought beste ;
  To have turned the state quyte upside downe ;
The nobles to have slayne and clene dispossest ;
  And on a stranger hedd have placed the crowne ;
  Herein we weare resolute, but fortune did frowne,
    No twas God woulde not suffer our villanyes take place ;
    But unlookte for retornde them to our shamefull disgrace.

Farther our intente was to poyson the ordinance of the realme ;
  A most haynouse matter as ever was invented,
Whoe ever hath harde of trecheries so extreame,
  Concluded, agreed upon, and fullye consented ?
  An wofull matter of all to be lamented.

All court rolls and records we mente to have raced,
And them to have burned spoyled and defaced.

The faire cittie of London wee also mente to rifell,
　To have rob'de the rich, and killed eke the poore ;
Theis thinges in effecte we counted but a trifell ;
　In all places of the lande have sett an uprore ;
The wealthie to have bereavde both of life and store,
　　No state nor degree we weare mente to spare,
　　But if hee would resiste deathe should be his share.

Theise weare our intents, with mischiefs many more,
　Even confusion to the whole realme to have brought,
Confederates we had, and that no small store ;
　　Which ruyne and destruction weare readie to have wrought ;
　　We either mente to make or bringe all to noughte.
　　　Nought ne nought indeede, for nought weare our happs,
　　　For desperate myndes doe feare no after clapps:

So forwarde weare that the verye daye was sett
　To murther our good queene, that God had preserved ;
Barnewell and Savage should have done the feate ;
　But justice rewarded them as they well deserved,
　Being twoe monstrose traytors that from duty swerved ;
　　The daggs and all things weare redye preparde,
　　But in the nett they layde, they themselves weare snared.

And Ballarde, that beast, hee into England was come,
　A Jesuite, a prieste, and a semynarie vilde ;
Hee brought with him our absolution from Roome,

Promysinge good successe, wherein he was beguyled;
So that from our hartes all pitye hee exilde;
   And still he incoraged us in my myscheife to procede,
   Egging us forwarde wherein there was no neede.

But God woulde not suffer us so closelie to worke,
   But that all our doyngs laye open in his sight:
Revealinge those myscheifs, that in our hartes did lurke,
   When wee suspected not, he brought the same to light.
   Then must wee hyde our hedds, or scape awaye by flight;
     But when wee had inklinge our treasons were descryde,
     Away awaye in haste twas then no tyme to byde.

Then watche and warde was made in everye coaste,
   Then weare wee taken, eache houre of the daye:
My selfe was once taken, but whie shoulde I boaste,
   Howe that I made a scape and so gott awaye,
   Not knowinge where to goe nor have perfitt staye;
     But to Harrow on the Hill my selfe I convayde,
     There in *Bellamyes* howse a little tyme I stayde.

But there was made for me suche previe watche and warde,
   And the contrie so besett, I no where coulde flye,
All hope of my escape was utterlie debarde;
   And searche in eache corner was made no nye,
   That I was compelde this polecye to trye;
     To forsake the house and my self disguyse,
     Lyke an Inkeper of London, to bleare the people's eyes.

But a rewarde was promyst hym that coulde me take,
   Which made the people looke so much the nere;
And beinge constrayned the house to forsake;

Walked throughe the pastures as men without feer;
My man, like an hostler, was cladd in simple geare;
   But this woulde not serve if truthe I shall tell,
   My favor I could not change, my face was knowen well.

There was a poore man, a weaver, was one of the watch,
By whome the gate laye, as of force I must walke;
Hee came to mee boldly, by the arme did me catche,
" Staye, good frende," quothe he, " with you I must talke :"
My consciense beinge guyltie my tonge gane to balke.
   " Wee are not those you looke for," I foltringlie did say,
   " Our comyssion," quoth hee, " is all passengers to
     staye."

Then the people gan flocke aboute me a pace,
   And before the Master of the Rolls I forthwith was
     broughte;
When I came there, I was knowne by my face.
  To bee the same man that theye so longe had soughte;
  And chiefest of the crewe that all the sturr had wroughte;
    Sir *Gilberte Gerrarde* examynde, and sente me to the
     Towre,
    And stronglie was I guarded with a myghtie greate
     powre.

Then the Londoners rejoyced, and merrye did make,
   With ringinge of bells, givinge God the prayse;
All my olde comon frendes did me clene forsake,
   That before had flattred me dyverse and sondry wayes;
   But favor, friendshipp, and faithe by treason decayes,
    As appeares by me, whosse faime creditt and renowne,
    My traytrose attempts had sone plucked downe.

Then shortlie after to the Kings Benche wee were broughte,
  And a nomber of others confederates like case ;
There to make awnswer to the deeds wee had wroughte ;
  But then my glorye gan darkyne apace,
  Yett with a countnance I sett thereon a face ;
    Where beinge arraygned, I guyltie was found
    Of high treason, agaynste my kinge and crowne.

Barnewell and *Savage* had confest the same before ;
  Then bootlesse twas for us anye poynte to denaye ;
Our conscience beinge guiltie it irkt us the more ;
  So that fourteene of us weare condemned that daye.
  We carde not for deathe, wee stowtlie did saye ;
    Our judgment was to bee hanged & quartered like case ;
    Of whiche wee made no accounte deathe coulde not
      us disgrace.

And nowe the day of our execution drewe nere,
  In whiche wee did playe our laste tragicke parte ;
When seven of us on hurdles from the towre were drawne,
  Whiche was no small *corsive** to our heavie hartes,
  Yet a juste rewarde for our wicked desartes ;
    The people flockte aboute us with this heavie sounde,
    "God save the Queene, and all traytors confounde."

In the fieldes near Lyncolns Inne a stage was sett upp,
  And a mightie high gallose was rayled on the same,
Whiche was the verye instrument & our deadlie cuppe,
  Of whiche to taste our selves wee must frame ;
  And beastlye *Ballarde* twas hee beganne the game,

---

* *Sic.* query corrosive ?

Whoe was hanged and quartered in all the peoples sight,
And his head on a poule on the gallose sett upright.

Nexte muste I make readie to treade the same dance;
 Wherto I prepared myselfe, as a man without feare,
Thousands lamented I had so harde a chance,
 And for mee there was shedd many a salte teare;
They lookte for confession, but weare never the nere,
 Sir *Francis Knolls* with others offered with me to praye.
 "None but Catholick's prayers will profitt thus" did
  I saye.

Thus died I stoutlie and did not trulie repente,
 My wicked life paste and moste haynouse treason;
If in a good cause my life had been spente,
 To have avouchte the same there had bene some reason:
But wickedlie I lived and died at that season.
 Havinge hanged a while, and my head cut off in haste,
 On the right hande of *Ballards* it was placed.*

* These executions were also commemorated by Thomas Deloney, in a ballad edited by Mr. J. P. Collier, for the Percy Society, in 1840.—*Old Ballads*, p. 104.

The lines on Babington are
> Next *Babington*, that caitife vilde,
> Was hanged for his hier;
> His carcase likewise quartered,
> And hart cast in the fire.

And of those executed on the 21st, he makes *Donne* and *Jones* both complain of Babington.
> The first of them was *Salsburie*,
> And next to him was *Dun*,
> Who did complaine most earnestly
> Of *proud rong* Babington.

Then died *Barnwell;* *Savage;* and yonge *Tuchborne:*
  With *Tilnie;* and *Abington,* in order as they came ;
But O Tuchborne ! Tuchborne ! thou makest me follorn !
  For I was the firste that allurde thee to the same,
    Thie witts beinge yonge likewaye I did frame,
      Thou beinge well inclined through mee didst consente
      To conceale the thinge that made us all repente.

The nexte daye dyed *Salsburye;* *Henrye Dunne;* & *Jones;*
  And *John Travice* of Preskott, which is in Lancashire ;
So did *John Charnocke,* a traytor for the nonce ;
  Robert Gage of Croydon muste then on stage appeare ;
  And lastlie *Bellamye* our hoste that made us all the chere.
    Theise seven weare apointed on *Sainte Matthewes* daye,
    The twentithe of September their partes they did playe.

Oure quarters weare boyled like the flesh of swyne,
  And on the cittie gates in open veiwe doe stande :
Our conceited hedds, that once wee thought so fyne,

> Both Lords and Knights of hye renowne
>   He meant for to displace,
> And likewise all the towers and townes
>   And cities for to raze :
>
> So likewise *Jones* did much complaine
>   Of his detested pride,
> And shewed how lewdly he did live
>   Before the time he died.

Richard Jones had been licensed on 27th August, to print a Ballad authorised by the Archbishop of Canterbury, " beinge a joyfull songe made by a citizen of London in the behalfe of Her Mat^{ies} subjectes touchinge the Joye for the taking of the Traytors." *Registers of the Stationers' Company,* vol. II., p. 214 ; but no copy is known to be extant.

On London bridge be spectakles to subjectes of the lande,
Warning them to shunne to take like things in hande.
   Our selves in the censure of God's judgments doe reste ;
   This was the rewarde for the treasons wee profeste.

Thus have I tolde thee my traggedie at large,
  In everye particular as the same was wroughte ;
Reporte it to my contrie men, I thee straytlie charge,
  To shunn those things, that my destruction brought,
  For traytrose attempts at all tyme prove noughte,
   Serche our Englishe Chronikells thou shalte fynde the same,
    That, whoe beginns in trecherie, hee endeth still in shame.

At my request therefore admonyshe then all men,
  To spende well the tallente, that God hathe them lente ;
And hee that hathe but one lett hym not toyle for tenne,
  For one is to muche unlesse it be well spente ;
  I meane by ambition leaste he to sone repente.
   To conclude happie is the man and threefold bleste is he,
   That can be contente to live with his degree.

    FELIX QUAM FACIUNT ALIENA PERICULA CANTUM.

                                            FINIS.

A NEW SONG IN PRAISE OF

The Derbyshire Militia.

THIS song is of the period from 1780 to 1790, and is here given from a broad-sheet in my own collection. It is the only copy I have as yet met with. At the head of the song is a wood-cut of three soldiers seated round a table, smoking. On the table is a punch-bowl and glasses. On the same sheet is "*The Pressed Man's Lamentation*," a song of four verses, beginning, "Farewell our Daddies and our Mammies." At the head is a wood-cut of two ships at sea, one of which has struck on a rock.

SHOULD the French but presume on our coast to appear,
We'll meet them as freely as we would drink beer
    With courage undaunted
    Or glory enhance,
Nor let our roast Beef be a dainty to France,
    Be this our ambition
    In chorus to sing,
He's just to himself who is true to his king.

So brave our Commanders so generous and kind,
To love and obey them we are all inclin'd,
    No Terror nor Dread
    In our conduct is shewn,
Their good and our King we prefer to our own.
    Be this our ambition
    In chorus to sing
He's just to himself who is true to his King.

Those false-hearted fellows who fall from their lot,
And others procure as they think to be shot,
        Deserve with a badge
        To be branded with Shame,
They are not of Britains deserving the name,
        But make us quite angry
        Whilst that we sing,
They're untrue to themselves their Country and King.

We are willing and free now the Order is come,
From Derby to march with the fife and the drum.
        Come fill up your glasses
        Boys up to the brim,
That they mayn't overflow let us chalk round the rim,
        Let each take his bumper
        And drive away care,
With a Toast to the King and the Duke of Devonshire.

To our Wives and our Sweethearts that we must leave behind,
We hope all true britons to them will be kind,
        Altho that we go
        For the term of three years,
And as we expect to face proud Monsieurs,
        If we live to return
        Then we'll merrily sing,
And we'll drink a good health unto George our King.

The Florist's Song.

THE Florists' Society of Derby flourished in the latter part of last century. Its meetings were held at the Angel Inn, in the Corn-market; and it held exhibitions, at which prizes were awarded. The following song was sung at the convivial meetings of its members, and is here reprinted from a broad-sheet in my own possession.

 ATTEND ye jolly GARDENERS
  of every Degree,
 From the Setter of a *Flower*,
  to the Planter of a *Tree:*
   And a Planting we will go, will go,
   and a Planting we will go.

 Our first Great Father ADAM,
  was a GARDENER by Trade;
 And likewise EVE our Mother,
  did use the pruning Blade:
   And a Planting, &c.

 Since GARDENING so Ancient,
  it's Praises let Us sing;
 For in his own Enclosure,
  he's as happy as a King:
   And a planting we will go, &c.

 Observe th' lowly *Shrub*,
  and lofty spreading *Trees:*
 That form the pleasant Shade,
  fann'd by th' pleasant Breeze:
   And a Planting, &c.

The FLORIST claims the Precedence,
   in this delightful Art ;
In ranging of his *Flowers*,
   and setting each a-part :
     And a planting, &c.

Take Notice of their Beauties,
   and all their various Hues ;
Set by his skillful Hand,
   and rais'd by gentle Dews :
     And a Planting, &c.

It wou'd be much too tedious,
   to tell each *Flower's* Name ;
Or, which for Smell or Beauty,
   th' Preference can claim :
     And a Planting, &c.

Yet all allow the AURICULA
   has the greatest Share :
Since FEASTS are held in Honour
   of the *Flower* ev'ry Year :
     And a Planting, &c.

It is of Ancient standing,
   and well conducted too :
When each in Emulation,
   their finest *Flowers* show :
     And a Planting, &c.

There is a *Prize* allotted,
   to him that gains the Day :

And 'tis the noblest *Flower*,
   that bears the Prize away:
      And a Planting, &c.

Likewise the Second best,
   for so we all agree;
Has both his Ordinary
   and Extraordinary free:
      And a Planting, &c.

These *Flowers* rais'd from Seed,
   which we preserve with Care;
For if the Seed be bad,
   the *Flowers* they are not Fair:
      And a Planting, &c.

We have STEWARDS at our *Feasts*,
   to see that all be right;
In Joy we spend the Day,
   and Pleasure crowns the Night:
      And a Planting, &c.

Our *Feasts* are full of Mirth,
   we have no windy Wars;
We never raise Disputes,
   and are very free from Jars:
      And a Planting, &c.

Our Judges are impartial,
   both faithful Men and true;
They never take a Bribe,
   but gives each Man his due:
      And a Planting, &c.

Then to Conclude, since *FLORISTS*
 enjoy so sweet a Life:
Here's a Health to the SOCIETY
 all Foes to *Care* and *Strife:*
  And a Planting we will go, will go,
  and a Planting we will go.

THE SORROWFUL LAMENTATION, LAST DYING SPEECH AND CONFESSION OF

Old Nun's Green,

Who after upwards of 460 Years (being a great and good Gift, by JOHN of GAUNT, Duke of Lancaster, and Earl of Leicester) was tried, cast and condemned, on the 14th of February, 1791, for being serviceable to the Poor People of this Town, as well as a Stranger, but a great Eye Sore to some particular Gentlemen; but the Execution is left till the Pleasure of Parliament be known.

NUN'S GREEN was a large piece of ground, containing about fifty acres of land, in the town of Derby, on which the inhabitants of the borough had right of common. On this common many encroachments were made by persons digging for gravel, erecting small buildings, etc.; and in 1768 an act was passed for selling a portion of the Green, so as to erect dwelling-houses for the increasing population of the town, and for the removal of nuisances and encroachments.

In 1791 the remaining portion of the Green was determined to be sold for the like purpose, and application for the necessary powers was made to Parliament, the scheme being that the proceeds should in part, at all events, go towards defraying the cost of paving and lighting, and otherwise improving, the town of Derby. This movement provoked the utmost opposition, and I have in my own collection some thirty or forty, at least, different hand-bills, squibs, pamphlets, and songs to which the excitement gave birth. Despite the opposition and the petitions which were got up, Nun's Green was disposed of, and the tract of land is now covered with thickly inhabited streets. The following pieces will serve to show the style of the songs and ballads to which I have alluded. The first, which is printed in two columns, has a wood-cut, at its head, of a man being led to execution in a cart, with hangman, parson, javelin-men, and others around—

A TRAVELLER'S DREAM.

Last Night as slumbering on my Bed I lay,
Good People pray now mind but what I say,
I thought as I was walking over cross Nun's Green,
I saw the fairest Goddess that was ever seen:
Her Head reclining o'er the purling Stream,
At first I thought this could not be a Dream,
I ask'd her Name, and weeping thus said she.
I once was call'd, that Jewel LIBERTY.
I ask'd her, why she in that Posture lay,
She rais'd Her head, and softly thus did say,
With broken Accents and with flowing Tears,
" I have liv'd here, Four Hundred and Sixty Years;
Was station'd here by Glorious JOHN of GAUNT,
Who never thought the poor should ever want,

But now I'm doom'd to die a cruel Death,
By Gentlemen, who never knew my Birth;
Because I gave Assistance to the Poor,
And oft times kept the Wolf, Sir, from the Door,
Because I'll not be sold the Streets to light,
That is the Reason, Sir they owe me spite;
If Gentlemen could only once agree,
They need not hang nor sell poor LIBERTY,
But let me live as I was first design'd,
To be a Comfort to the poorest Kind:
Tho' I'm the smallest of that Family,
I'm not the only Child of LIBERTY.
If you will tamely stand and see me die,
You'll soon repent the Loss of LIBERTY:
My other Sisters soon, must fall a Prey,
To those who falsely take my Life away;
Now Tyranny does put the Town in Fear,
Don't wonder why I drop this melting Tear,
Tread on a Worm, that Insect cannot bite,
But turns in Anguish to revenge its Spite:
So let them know such Usage you'll not brook
Whilst such a Man does live as PARKER COKE;"
At this I shouted, but found it a Joke,
A Dream it was, so instantly awoke.

A Poem,

*Found by Mr. * * * and Dedicated to Major Trowel.*—MDCCXCII.

When Heav'n from Earth had shut out day,
   And all was wrapt in darkest night,
On Nuns Green Bridge in proud array
   There stood a venerable sprite.

Pale was his face, and, marked with scars,
   His burnished steel was all complete;
The same with which in rueful wars,
   He did our ancient foes defeat.

A goodly Knight, forsooth, was he,
   (As in old story may be seen)
For he to Derby gave in Fee,
   That airy, healthful, pleasant Green.

Across the plain the spectre went,
   (He stalked with all the pomp of yore)
Then calling loud, "I'm John of Ghent,"
   He tapt at Sammy's chamber door.

Now pow'r of speech from Samuel flew,
   His pride and courage were quite gone,
Full sorely now he did him rue,
   Of all the guilty deeds he'd done.

The door upon the hinges creak'd,
   In came the Envoy from the dead,
Poor Sammy, sweating, frighted, sneaked
   Under the cov'ring of his bed.

"Crompton," the spectre said, "I come
  "Thy guilty conduct to arraign,
"From the close confines of the tomb
  "Where I for ages past have lain.

"Nuns Green was mine by martial lot,
  "The just acquirement of the brave:
"And what by prowess I had got,
  "To Charity I freely gave.

"How dar'st thou then with impious hand,
  "This public property invade?
"Nor shall thy mean and quibbling band
  "Defeat the generous grant I made.

"Why not a bright example give,
  "Why not espouse an honest cause,
"Why not support those men who strive,
  "T' inforce our good and ancient laws?

"Oh Sammy! quit the hireling crew
  "Which now the town so much disgrace,
"And be it said thou can'st be true,
  "To th' Rights of this thy native place.

"Renounce that nonconforming set,
  "Whose party zeal, and public hate,
"Would wildest anarchy beget,
  "And glory in a ruin'd state.

"Remember how they serv'd their King,
  "How serv'd the faithful Barons bold—
"They voted one an useless thing,
  "To unjust death the other sold.

"In all the wiles of Satan taught,
    " Despising order, God, and laws ;
" With bitter rage and envy fraught,
    " They plead the grand reforming cause.

" To that unhappy time look back,
    " When Britain, tottering from her base,
" Sent forth her chosen sons t' attack,
    " A haughty and rebellious race.

" Ah! think of Saratoga's day,
    " Or on that horrid murd'rous scene,
" When fainting legions bleeding lay
    " Unpitied on the rebel plain.

" And when repeated losses prov'd,
    " The brave embattled hosts betrayed ;
" The gloomy tale they heard unmov'd,
    " And, smiling, her defeats survey'd.

" No longer then such miscreants join,
    " To rob the poor of Common Right :
" Renounce this guilty scheme of thine,
    " By other means the town enlight.

" To meddling Majors leave the field,
    " Who, deeply skill'd in warlike art,
" The battle-sword can fiercely wield,
    " And march their armies 'gainst a Cart.*

---

* A great impediment to the manœuv'ring of the Militia, about 15 years ago.

"The Red Rose gift shall ne'er be seen
 "Immur'd in filth, and foul'd by crimes;
"Nor shall the Lancastrian Green,
 "Disgrac'd, descend to distant times."

Thus spoke the fierce offended sprite,
 Then vanishing, with sullen gloom,
Through the dark realms of dreary night,
 He hasten'd to the silent tomb.

The clock struck One, and Sam arose
 From off his damp and dewy bed,
And swore he'd ne'er again oppose
 What angry JOHN OF GHENT had said.

The Quadrupedes, &c.,

Or, Four-footed Petitioners, against the Sale of Nun's-Green. A Terrestrial Poem. Written by me The Celestial Bard!!

☞ I SING OF ASSES:———(A Motto of my own.)

Two *Jack-Asses*, (the *Father*, and his *Son*,)
Who, after work, on *Nun's-Green* us'd to run
Exactly like two *Bards*;—the other day
Stood in a *muse*;—and then began to bray
With human voice;—For *Balaam's* breed were they.

Quoth *old Ned*, to his *Lad*;—"I have been told,
Nun's-Green, my little dear, is to be sold

O

To pave, and light, old *Derby*; *(fulsome town!)*
And save the POOR from *laying money down.*
Now is it *fair*, that you and I should be
Depriv'd of our just *Rights*, and *Property?*
It is an *Insult* on the *Jack-Ass* kind,
Who have possess'd this *Green*, time out of mind;
And in Co-partnership with *Pigs* and *Geese*
(A truly ancient, honorable race!)
Enjoy'd a *bit o' mouth*, and Common run,
Quite down from *John of Ghent*, to you my son.

" Say little *David*, why the devil should *Asses*
Find fault with *dirty* ways, and *narrow* passes!
These wild *Projectors*, are the *Asses* foes,
For *pavements*, boy, will only hurt our *toes;*
And when the town's improv'd, in proud array
We poor *Jack-Asses*, shall be driven away!
No *panniers* then, forsooth, must there be seen,
So let us all *unite* to keep *Nun's-Green*."

The youthful *Ass*, brim full of *spiteful* Ire,
Prick'd up his ears; and answer'd *thus*, his *Sire*,
" This shall not be;—this shall not come to pass;
They shall not rob us of our *lawful grass!*
And if to Parliament the *Knaves* should stray,
We'll throw *Petitions* in the *Robbers'* way."

So saying, young *David*, on all fours bent,
To *Lawyer Goose*, for pious counsel went:
Quill took his *fee*, (the *life* and *soul* of Law)
Then heard the *Case;* and *thus*, unscrew'd his jaw:

"You must *petition*, Sir; and every creature
That is *aggriev'd*, must put his *pen* to *paper:*

"As hunters' *pudding*, we most toothsome find,
The more with *currants* or with *plumbs*, 'tis lin'd;
So your *Petition* will disturb their dreams,
The more 'tis stuff'd, with *any kind of names.*"

"Thank ye," quoth he; "my business now is done;
Back to my *Daddy*, and *Nun's-Green* I'll run;"
So saying, swift he flew; and *Edward* found
All at his ease; and rolling on the ground:
The *scrawl* he read; and all compos'dly then,
Stretch'd forth his hoofs; and 'twixt them held his pen,
The paper sign'd, and after him the *Geese*,
And *Pigs*, aggriev'd;—fill'd up each vacant space.
Yet not enough, to please his craving maw,
And answer all the good *intents* of Law,
Young *David* did a *glorious* thought reveal;
"That *Rats*, and *Mice*, would suffer by the *Sale!*
And by destroying *Swamps*, and *wholesome Bogs*,
It must invade the *property* of *Frogs!*
So *these* amongst the rest, as I divine
Should be solicited, forthwith to *sign.*"

"Right;" said old *Ned*, "you reason well, my son;
Directly to the *dikes*, and *gutters* run;
And if you cannot there, get *names* enough,
Employ some *Rat* to canvass every *sough.*"

Away he went; away, away, went he;
Out came my Lady *Froggy*, who but she!

Smirk'd at the *paper*, nibb'd her crow quill pen,
Then sign'd her *name* against these *naughty men*.

Next to the *Mice*, young *David* went with speed ;
Poor little souls, they could not *write* or *read !*
But well inclin'd, to stop, these *horrid scenes*,
Employ'd the *Jack-Ass*, to write down their names.

Now *David* got the whole, engross'd on skins,
Forming a pile, much higher than one's shins !
And when roll'd up, upon his back 'twas ty'd,
Who, then for *London* went, in *stately pride !*

But here's the *Rub :*—when Parliament, serene,
Consider'd *well*, the business of *Nun's-Green :*
And by *each* house, most clearly understood,
That 'twas a Plan, design'd for PUBLIC GOOD,
They curs'd the *names*, and laugh'd at all the *rigs*,
Contriv'd by Asses, Geese, Frogs, Mice, and Pigs.

Paving and Lighting,

A NEW SONG.

To the tune of Chivy Chase.

GOD prosper long fair DERBY Town,
    And may it still be free ;
From hellish plots of every kind,
    Against its liberty.

A juncto formed of wicked men,
    Though rich its true they be,
They'd rob the poor of Common-right,
    That they may go shot free.

The Prebyterians Jesuit like,
    The established Church took in;
To do the drudgery of their work,
    And trudged through thick and thin.

Poor silly men to be misled,
    By that deceitful race;
That would cut your throat behind your back,
    But smile before your face.

From the Town-hall they issue forth,
    With *Eunuch* at their head;
Lazarus the Banker followed him,
    You'd have thought they wanted bread.

Next one from beggar's blood that sprung,
    To opulence grown is he;
And *struts* along with iron rod,
    And swears you shan't be free.

A tawny *Smith* was of the gang,
    And others as well as he;
They've neither house nor land in town,
    Yet want your property.

A brazen face with empty skull,
    In Dibden's Tour well known;
That cares not what he does or says,
    So that the poor's o'erthrown.

Sly *Foxes* too with silly *hopes*,
  Expect to have their share;
Of all the Common-right you have,
  Their pockets for to spare.

Lo! deep in thought as Tragic Muse,
  With dagger to stab behind;
Lo! another as bad as he,
  And much of the same kind.

The Scribbling kind with parchment roll,
  For you to sign away,
The Right you have upon *Nun's-Green*,
  Their charges to defray.

There are many others of the gang,
  As bad as bad can be;
That lie, fawn, and threat, and use deceit,
  To get your property.

Old *Shot-bag* he has chang'd about,
  That his Mills may go shot-free;
Some others too have done the same,
  Such worthless men there be.

But all's a blank that they have done,
  If you but true will be;
To the first promise that was made,
  The friends to liberty.

Now Mundy's join'd with Parker Coke,
  And others of renown;
Those tyrants for to circumvent,
  To save this goodly town.

Those veterans that have stood the brunt,
    Of many a well fought day ;
Will always cheer you in the front,
    And shew you the right way.

For to be free as Britons ought,
    And have a right to be ;
In spite of these tyrannic fools,
    That want your liberty.

The Nun's-Green Rangers,

Or the Triple Alliance. Consisting of an Old Sergeant, a Tinker, and a Bear.

Tune—*Bow, Wow, Wow.**

COME listen to me, neighbours all, attend unto my story,
My song concerns not *Church* or *King*, neither *Whig* nor *Tory ;*
But my Ballad is to caution you, against the machinations,
Of those who mean t' impose on you by false insinuations.
    Bow, wow, wow.

There's JEMMY PAD, that *Irish Lad*, who heads the clan of faction,
Swears by the *Holy Poker* now, he'll make us all distraction,

---

* This tune is the same as "The Barking Barber" and "Date obolum Belisario."

To keep Nun's Green that *precious* Land, for his own *dear* advantage,
He means by lies to dupe you all, and GOBBLE up the Pasturage.
  Bow, wow, wow.

Good Twenty Pounds a year, this son of a Teague Sir,
Of lawful British money is regularly paid Sir,
For driving the Poor Geese, from the Land their inheritance,
Whereby he addeth Riches to *Irish Impertinence*.
  Bow, wow, wow.

There's TINKER JOE comes next, because next in colour,
He tells you all he'll make a speech, but alas, he's no Scholar ;
He'll talk of Lords and Baronets his Juvenile connections,
By mending all their Pots and Pans, he's gained their affections.
  Bow, wow, wow.

To claim your attention more, he'll talk about the Parliament,
And say how many Members, old *Ruby Face* has thither sent,
That his interest is great in affairs of the nation,
Though still *Baboon* of Nottingham, *Nun's Green* shall be his station.
  Bow, wow, wow.

OROONOKO next presents himself, t' engage your attention,
As oft' before the *Bear* has done, with many a vile intention,

By blasts and oaths to lead you all, against your common
 senses,
For tho' almost an Ideot, he'll forge some false Pretences.
 Bow, wow, wow.

But none of you've forgot, the *sixteenth* of *September*,
Th' exalted part he then perform'd, you all must well
 remember;
By such a wretch you'll ne'er be led, against your inclinations,
Who persecutes the poor man with *Game Informations.*
 Bow, wow, wow.

Then join neighbours all, without hesitation,
Resist these Imposters, without exceptation,
May all of us with one accord, oppose this host of evil,
And send Sergeant Pad and Co. to Canvas with the D—l.
 Bow, wow, wow.

A Birch Rod for the Presbytarians.

A NEW SONG.

Tune of "*Cherry Chace.*"

THIS ballad, printed from the original broad-sheet in my possession, is another of the series to which I have alluded as being connected with the sale of Nun's Green, Derby. It is printed in two columns, with a wood-cut at its head representing a Highlander playing on the bag-pipes.

GOOD neighbours all, both great and small,
 Of high and low degree;

Let's straight unite, ourselves to fight,
  Against this *presbytree*.

If you'll but trace this hellish race,
  Thro' every stage of life ;
Where e'er they be you'll plainly see,
  Nought but discord and strife.

If you'll history read your hearts will bleed,
  To hear of their transactions ;
For *king* and *church* have suffered much,
  By their damn hellish factions.

Must we be opprest by this vile nest,
  Who strives us to enslave ;
Such is their spleen to sell *Nun's Green*,
  The town to light and pave.

They do not care who the burden bear,
  Such is their tyranny ;
To enforce the tax on others' backs,
  Whilst they themselves go free.

I wish all such Aldermen and folks like them,
  Was forc'd to change their situation ;
And that Greenland hulks for their vile bulks,
  Might for ever be their station.

Proud oppulence with impudence,
  As he struts along the streets ;
Swears by his God with his iron rod,
  He'll beat down all he meets.

There's shufling Charles both grins and snarles,
    And where he can he'll bite ;
For this last mishap he'll surely snap,
    Except he's musseld tight.

There's Jemmy Twichit did both scrub and fidge it,
    His head he roll'd about ;
He stampt and swore he'd come there no more,
    When he found the bill thrown out.

They blam'd old George that did not discharge,
    His duty as he ought ;
And his addle pate that cou'd not relate,
    What kind of a bill he'd brought.

The wigs got a fall, I wish they ne'er may rise,
    But henceforth for the future, may learn to be more wise ;
And ne'er persume to sit in chairs, nor honoured be with Town affairs,
    But stay at home and say their prayers, & not over us tyrannize.

Pray God above from this earth remove,
    This vile deceitful crew,
And send them hence for their offence,
    Where they may receive their due.

God bless *Mundy* and *Cooke*, on them we look,
    As two from heaven sent ;
To set us free from tyranny,
    And serve in Parliament.

Lost and Dead.

IN the parish register of Chapel-en-le-Frith is the sad entry of the burial of a child which was found dead in the neighbourhood—" S. Sept. 20, 1656. A poor child found dead in ye Forest." The following ballad, from the pen of Mr. Henry Kirke, is founded on this circumstance. It has not before been printed.

THE fire burns brightly upon the hearth,
    And dances and crackles with glee ;
And the cottar's wife sits before the blaze,
    But the child—ah, where is she.

The cottar's hand is on the latch,
    And he stands by the opened door,
And his wife she kisses his sunburnt cheek,
    But his child he shall see no more.

" She is gone out to play," the dame replied,
    " And will soon be back again ;"
But their hearts felt heavy, they knew not why
    And ach'd sorely as if with pain.

And soon the gude wife on the ample board
    Has spread out the frugal fare,
But a mist rose up in the cottar's eyes
    As he gazed on that empty chair.

And he started up from his chair and cried,
    " I can stay no longer here,
I must go and find my own bonnie child,
    For my heart aches sore wi' fear."

And he wandered around from house to house,
    Across the weary wild ;
And his heart grew heavier every step,
    For no one had seen his child.

The night had drawn her curtains dark,
    And every star shone clear ;
But still he followed his fruitless search,
    Half dead with fatigue and fear.

Through brake and copse of the forest drear
    He followed his weary way,
Till the rosy light of the morning sun
    Told the dawn of another day.

It bathed his face in gladsome light
    With the stream of its glorious ray,
It seemed but to mock his saddened heart,
    And he turned with a sigh away ;

He turned away down a mossy dell,
    Where the sunbeams danced and smiled,
And there midst the fern and the mossy cups
    The father found his child.

One little arm beneath its head
    On the mossy bank was laid,
And the sunbeams lighted its little face,
    And the wind with its tresses played.

A smile still lingered on those sweet lips,
    Which seemed as by sleep untied,
But the father's heart grew cold as he looked,
    For he knew it had smiled—as it died.

Song.

Tune—"*Vicar and Moses.*"

S a satirical attack on some members of the choir of All Saints Church, Derby, in the last century, the following verses are clever. All Saints is the principal church in Derby, and its choir has generally had the reputation of being at least tolerably good. I prefer leaving the blanks in the names of the parties, still unfilled. The broad-sheet from which I here reprint it is in my own collection.

I.

WHEN Apollo thinks fit to handle his Lyre,
    The sweet Vocal Muses take place ;
The *Treble* and *Counter* repair to their Choir,
    Attended with *Tenor* and *Bass*.

II.

As Mortals below—the high Gods will be aping
    In all their sublime Occupations ;
They love to be *Singing* and *Piping* and *Scraping*
    To assist your devout Congregation.

III.

Thus to raise our Devotion and stop all Complaints,
    (As ev'ry Man knows it's his duty)
We've compleated our Choir at the Church of *All Saints ;*
    That God may be worship'd in *Beauty*.

IV.

Whoever comes in it can't help but admire
    A Worship so Solomn and goodly ;
Such Voices were sure never heard from a Choir,
    As those that are led by *Will. D—d—y*.

V.

Sam. D—d—y's sweet *Counter Will's Treble* excells,
    Well strengthen'd with *Roger's* strong *Bass*
Each softning each like a good Peal of Bells,
    Were *C—b—y's* fine *Tenor* takes place.

VI.

Neither *Paul's* nor *King's Chapel* can boast of such Voices,
    Nor can our grand *Op'ras* come near 'em ;
When on 'em I think, how my Spirit rejoices !
    Then what must it do when I hear 'em !

VII.

Tho' their Parts are all charming how much his Excels,
    Adorning the Vocal Profession !
Their *Treble* I mean, that so quavers and swells,
    Enchanting beyond all Expression !

VIII.

By the *Doctor's* fine *Treble* how well they are led,
    Whose Expression all hearers admire ;
O'er topping his Fellows at least by the *Head*,
    So well he ennobles the *Choir*.

IX.

Altho' in the *Choir* he so *Eminent* stands,
    Yet still ith' *Orchestra* he's greater:
With his *Fiddle* excelling the greatest of Hands,
    So bountiful to him is Nature!

X.

With this he can *irritate* all that is quick,
    (Such Pow'r have his Taste and his Tone!)
For he ev'ry thing moves but his long Fiddle-Stick,
    None like him before was yet known.

XI.

So useful a Hand (without Doubt) was ne'er born,
    For *Concerts*, *Assembly* and *Ball*;
He can turn to the *Fiddle*, *Bass Trumpet*, or *Horne*,
    Yet equally *great* upon all.

XII.

For *here* his Expressions so *full* I must own,
    We ne'er were so fiddled before;
But then his fine *Taste*, *Execution* and *Tone*,
    Delight us a Thousand Times more.

XIII.

Where lives that grave mortal so strangely supine,
    So Senseless and stupidly lazy;
In hearing such Hands himself to confine,
    And not like his Brother, grow *crazy?*

XIV.

To hear such sweet Hands who wou'd not but give,
  Or spend the best part of his Rental;
At so charming a Place as *Derby* to live,
  With such *Vocal* and such *Instrumental!*

XV.

And this is the Reason your strolling *Italians*,
  (As it happen'd, we know, to'ther Day)
At *Derby* are treated like Tatter—de Mallions,
  When *unheard* they went weeping away.

FINIS.

N.B. Speedily will be published, a Particular Account of the great Abilities of each of these Famous *Singers*, wherein will be shewn their Ignorance and Impudence in attempting such Things as Solo and Verse Anthems by Dr. *Greene*, *Boyce*, *Nares*, &c. Oratorio Songs and Chorusses by Mr. Handel, &c., &c., It being well known to every Person who has the least Ear to Music, that they are not capable of *decently* singing a Bar in any such Compositions. Mr. W—— some time since absolutely discharged them from making Use of any thing but the Old Psalm Tunes. The scandalous Behaviour of *D*——, and *C*——, on this occasion shall be particularly pointed out.

Sir Francis Leke;

OR THE POWER OF LOVE.

A Derbyshire Catholic Legend of Cromwell's time.

THE Lekes, or Leakes, of Sutton-in-Scarsdale, Derbyshire, derived their descent from Alan de Leka, of Leak in Nottinghamshire, who was living in 1141. The first of the family who settled at Sutton was William, a younger son of Sir John Leke of Gotham, in the early part of the fifteenth century; and the manor was acquired by a marriage with the heiress of the Hilarys, who took the name of Gray, and who inherited it from Robert de Hareston, Lord of Sutton. Sir Francis Leake, the fourth in descent from William abovenamed, married a co-heiress of Swift, and was succeeded by his son Francis, who in 1611 was created a baronet. In 1642 he was created Lord Deincourt of Sutton, and in 1645, Earl of Scarsdale. These titles became, however, extinct in 1736, by the death of Nicholas, the fourth Earl, and the last of the family. His lordship took an active part in the Civil Wars; and Lysons, speaking of him, says in 1643, (the beginning of April) "Lord Deincourt began to fortify his house at Sutton. Sir John Gell sent his brother, Colonel Thomas Gell, with five hundred men and three pieces of ordnance to besiege it. Lord Deincourt was summoned, but refused to surrender, and for some time obstinately defended himself. The house was taken, and Lord Deincourt and his men made prisoners. The works were demolished, and Lord Deincourt set at liberty, on giving his word that he would repair to Derby within eight days and submit himself to the Parliament. Sir John Gell observes that the forfeiture of his word on this occasion was revenged by the garrison at Bolsover, who some time afterwards, when that castle was in the hands of the Parliament, plundered Lord Deincourt's house at Sutton. In 1645 Lord Deincourt was created Earl of Scarsdale. Having rendered himself very obnoxious to the Parliament by his exertions in the royal cause during the Civil War, his estates were sequestered, and, as he refused to compound, they were sold. His son procured some friends to be the purchasers, he paying the sum of £18,000, fixed by the Parliamentary Commissioners as the composition." His lordship felt so deeply the execution of his royal master, Charles the First, that he clothed himself in sackcloth, and, causing his grave to be dug some years before his death, laid himself in it, it is said, every Friday for divine meditation and prayer.

The following ballad, embodying a tradition concerning Sir Francis Leke, is by Richard Howitt, one of the "worthies" of Derbyshire, of which county I am proud to say he is a native.

Part I.

"O, say not so, Sir Francis,
    Breathe not such woe to me :—
Broad and pleasant are your lands,
    And your Hall is fair to see.

Faithful servants have you many,
    Fortune fair on you attends ;
Nor hath Knight in all the Island,
    Braver followers or friends.

With the Court you are a favourite—
    Yet your King shall righted be :
In his hour of deadly peril
    Can you from your monarch flee ?

Look upon your blooming children,
    Flowers of Heaven newly blown !
Here renewed behold your Lucy,
    And that boy is all your own.

Shall we in these dread commotions,
    Neither need your arm nor mind,
Where shall I behold defender,
    Where shall these a Father find?

How I thought you loved us! Never
    Lightly could such love decline;
Nor could you to idly voyage,
    All the wealth of life resign!"

———" Lucy! this is only torture—
    Here I may no longer pause—
Long I for my King have battled—
    Now we've neither King nor laws.

With our shrewd exultant Victor,
    Bootless now were strife of steel;
Looking on my bleeding country
    Can I for her cease to feel?

All the land is grown outrageous:
    Honour, worth, are hunted down:
Demons mock at our religion—
    Idiots trample on the Crown.

Roaming o'er the billowy ocean,
    Peace may greet me here unknown;
And, returning, civil tempests
    May be fairly overblown.

Should aught menacing approach you,
    To your noble Brothers, look:
Danger! did they ever dread it?
    Insult! did they ever brook?

Guard your precious life, my Lucy!
    Need I say—not your's alone!
Present—absent—living—dying—
    I am—fear not—all your own!"

Starting from her arms, Sir Francis
    Quick his noble steed bestrode:
And, with manly face averted,
    Forward—seaward—fleetly rode.

Soon his vessell, anchor weighing,
    To the sails the winds were true:
And with sad, not weak, delaying,
    He bade his native land adieu!

Part II.

Far amidst the western ocean,
    Lies a small and pleasant isle;
Fair with everlasting verdure,
    Bright with summer's endless smile.

There o'er one, all sadly musing
    Sweets distil from spicy trees;
Yet, though all around is blooming,
    Nothing cheers him that he sees.

Lonely in sweet groves of myrtle,
    Sad amongst the orange bloom;
Nothing cheers his drooping spirit,
    Nothing dissipates his gloom.

Twice ten years he there has wandered,
    Nor one human face has seen ;
Moving like a silent shadow,
    Rocks have his companions been.

Clad in skins of beasts ; like serpents
    Wild, is his unheeded hair ;
Yet through lines of deep dejection,
    His once manly face is fair.

As from gathered flowers, the odour
    Never wholly dies away,—
Of the warrior, and the scholar,
    Intimations round him play.

Nurtured in the camp, the college,
    Never can his soul be void ;
In the busy past his spirit,
    Heart, and mind, must be employed.

Lists he yet the stirring battle,
    Lists he victory's rending shout ?
Tranquil is the isle, the ocean,
    Pain within him, peace without.

Yes ! he oft-times hears the trumpet,
    Captains' shouting, horses' neigh !
Till before the horrid stillness,
    All the tumult dies away.

And is this the courtly warrior,
    Gallant, gay Sir Francis Leke ?
He, the same !—who shunning discord,
    Found a peace he did not seek ?

Bravely sailed he from Old England,
  Boldly with adventurous prow;
From the horrors of that voyage
  He alone is living now.

To his bravery owes he being—
  Last to quit the groaning deck—
In his fight his comrades perished—
  Days he floated on the wreck.

Till this lone and lovely island,
  Cheered him with refreshing bloom;
Saved him from the ravening ocean,
  To a sad and lingering doom.

In a cave has he his dwelling,
  High, o'erlooking wide the main,
Where he feeds in painful being,
  Longings infinite and vain.

Nightly there he burns a beacon;
  Often there the day he spends;
And towards his native country
  Wistful gaze o'er ocean sends.

There a cross has he erected—
  Near to which an altar stands,
Humble growth of feelings holy
  Reared by his unaided hands.

Truly needs he prove a Christian,
  Thus cut off from all his kind;
Firmest faith he needs in Heaven;
  And boundless fortitude of mind.

Store he needs of endless knowledge,
    His unvaried hours to cheer ;
Furnished with sublime resources
    For this solitude austere.

Still the isle is very lovely—
    Never yet in Poet's mind,
Haunt of Peri, realm of faëry,
    Was more lavishly divined.

Lovely as the Primal Garden,
    In the light of Sabbath blest ;
Human love alone is wanting
    In this Eden of the West.

Leap from rocks the living waters :
    Hang delicious fruits around :
And all birds of gorgeous plumage
    Fill the air with happy sound.

Painful is to him its beauty—
    Sad the splendour of the sun ;
To the odorous air he utters
    Sorrow that is never done :—

" Blest was I beyond all blessing !
    " In my wife and children blest :
" In my friends and in my fortune—
    " Yet in peace I could not rest.

" Never in his prosperous greatness,
    " Can himself the wisest trust ;
" God has weighed and found me wanting—
    " And the punishment is just."

Oft before the cross, the altar,
    Murmuring prayer he sinks to rest ;
To his God, and to his Saviour—
    And the Virgin Mother blest.

And for love unto the Virgin
    Finds in Heaven his prayer chief grace !
" Mary, Mother, me deliver,
    " From the horrors of this place !

" Others crave more worldly guerdon—
    " Wealth, or fame, or station high ;
" Love I seek—to see my country—
    " My own people—and to die !"

Praying thus, old legends tell us,
    Scarce his eyes in sleep were sealed ;
When, O, happy inward vision,
    To him was his home revealed.

There his patrimonial mansion,
    He beheld in moonlight sleep,
Saw with joy though mystery veiled it—
    Sadness and a silence deep.

And, O miracle of gladness !
    More, those ancient legends say,
Was permitted him to witness,
    Waking, in the open day.

In his old church-porch awaking—
    Trance, or voyage all unknown ;
O'er his own domains he wandered—
    Saw, and knew them for his own.

Had chance Voyagers beheld him,
    In a trance, who slumbering bore,
By some heavenly impulse, guided
    Him unto his native shore?

Not so—says the holy legend—
    Force of penitential prayer—
And the love he bore the Virgin—
    Won for him that transit fair.

Spare the legend for its beauty—
    Carp not—what is it to you
If the letter is a fable?
    In its spirit it is true.

Leave we unto old tradition
    That which its dim mist sublimes,
Nor submit the ancient spirit
    To the light of later times!

See! before his welcome threshold!
    Once again, Sir Francis stand:
Oh! the transport,—it is real!—
    He is in his native land!

Part III.

Merry once again is England,
    Civil warfare is forgot;
Now another Charles is reigning
    Plenty smiles in hall and cot.

Spring is like a present angel :
  Loosened waters leap in light :
Flowers are springing, birds are singing,
  All the world is glad and bright.

May, the blue-eyed bloomy creature,
  From God's presence yearly sent,
Works with sweet ethereal fingers,
  Till both heaven and earth are blent.

Lovliest is a rural village
  In the May-time of the year;
With its hall, its woods and waters,
  Verdant slopes, and herds of deer.

And in one, joy is exultant—
  For this day the manly heir
Of Sir Francis Leke is wedded—
  Wedded too, his daughter fair.

Age rejoices ; in the Mansion
  Rural hinds find wassail cheer ;
And bright troops of Knights and Ladies,
  Crowd the Hall from far and near.

Who is this in weeds unseemly,
  Half a man that seems, half beast,
Who obtrudes himself unbidden
  On the merry marriage feast ?

Hermit is he, or some Pilgrim,
  Entering boldly his own cell ?
No,—he lacks those ancient symbols,
  Sandal-shoon, and scallop shell.

All the youngsters titter; anger
    Flushes cheeks austere and cold:
Whilst the aged look complacent
    On a beggar that is bold.

"Bear this Ring unto your Mistress,"
    To a Page Sir Francis cried;
And his words emphatic uttered
    Rung throughout the dwelling wide.

One there is—an age-blind servant—
    Who in darkness sits apart—
Carried forth to feel the sunshine—
    She has heard him in her heart;

And in agony of gladness,
    At that voice so long desired,
She has loudly named her Master—
    And then instantly expired.

Pensive in her room, the Matron
    Grieved—but distant from the crowd;
She would not with selfish sorrow
    Their bright countenances cloud.

There her Ring receiving; Lucy
    Knew the sender of her gift,
And, it seemed, by feet unaided,
    To him she descended swift.

There upon the rugged stranger,
    Gazed, with momentary check,
Gazed, but for a passing moment,
    And then fell upon his neck.

Twice ten weary summers absent;
  By his faithful wife deplored;
Like Ulysses to his Consort,
  Good Sir Francis is restored.

'Tis a time of double gladness—
  Never was a scene like this;
Joy o'erflows the Hall, the Village—
  'Tis a time of boundless bliss!

Clothed as instantly became him,
  Of Vile Skins all disarrayed,
In his old Paternal Mansion
  He is honoured and obeyed.

All he prayed for to the Virgin,
  She has granted him and more;
Not to die, his own beholding,
  First, when on his native shore.

Added years of happy ending,
  Are accorded him of right;
'Midst a cloud of friends descending,
  In a sunset warm and bright.

The True Lover's Knot Untied:

Being the right path whereby to advise princely Virgins how to behave themselves, by the example of the renowned Princess the Lady Arabella, and the second son of the Lord Seymour, late Earl of Hertford.

THE beautiful, much-injured, and ill-fated Lady Arabella of this touching ballad, whose sole crime was that she was born a Stuart, was the daughter of Elizabeth Cavendish of Chatsworth, in Derbyshire, by her husband Charles Stuart, Earl of Lennox, who was brother to Lord Darnley, the husband of the unfortunate Mary Queen of Scots. She was grand-daughter of Sir William Cavendish of Chatsworth, and of his wife, the celebrated "Bess of Hardwick," afterwards Countess of Shrewsbury.

The incidents of the life of this young, beautiful, and accomplished lady, which form one of the most touching episodes in our history,—the jealous eye with which Elizabeth looked upon her from her birth,—the careful watch set over her by Cecil,—the trials of Raleigh and his friends,—her troubles with her aunt (Mary, Countess of Shrewsbury),—her being placed under restraint,—her marriage with Seymour,—her seizure, imprisonment, sufferings, and death as a hopeless lunatic in the Tower of London, where she had been thrown by her cousin, James the First,—are all matters of history, and invest her life with a sad and melancholy interest.

As the autograph signature of this ill-starred but lovely and exemplary young lady is but little known, I append a fac-simile,

Arbella Stuart

which no doubt will add to the interest of the following ballad. The ballad was sung to the tune of "The Frog Galliard."

Derbyshire Ballads.

As I to Ireland did pass,
    I saw a ship at anchor lay,
Another ship likewise there was,
    Which from fair England took her way.

This ship that sail'd from fair England,
    Unknown unto our gracious king,
The lord chief justice did command,
    That they to London should her bring.

I then drew near and saw more plain,
    Lady Arabella in distress,
She wrung her hands, and wept amain,
    Bewailing of her heaviness.

When near fair London Tower she came,
    Whereas her landing place should be,
The king and queen with all their train,
    Did meet this lady gallantly.

"How now, Arabella," said our good king,
    Unto this lady straight did say,
"Who hath first try'd thee to this thing,
    That you from England took your way?"

"None but myself," my gracious liege,
    "These ten long years I have been in love,
With the lord Seymour's second son,
    The earl of Hertford, so we prove:

"Full many a hundred pound I had
    In goods and livings in the land,
Yet I have lands us to maintain,
    So much your grace doth understand.

"My lands and livings so well known
    Unto your books of majesty,
Amount to twelvescore pounds a week,
    Besides what I do give," quoth she.

"In gallant Derbyshire likewise,
    I ninescore beadsmen maintain there,
With hats and gowns and house-rent free,
    And every man five marks a year.

"I never raised rent," said she,
    "Nor yet oppress'd the tenant poor,
I never did take bribes for fines,
    For why, I had enough before.

"Whom of your nobles will do so,
    For to maintain the commonalty?
Such multitudes would never grow,
    Nor be such store of poverty.

"I would I had a milk-maid been,
    Or born of some more low degree,
Then I might have lov'd where I liked,
    And no man could have hinder'd me.

"Or would I were some yeoman's child,
    For to receive my portion now,
According unto my degree,
    As other virgins whom I know.

"The highest branch that soars aloft,
    Needs must beshade the myrtle-tree,
Needs must the shadow of them both,
    Shadow the third in his degree.

"But when the tree is cut and gone,
    And from the ground is bore away,
The lowest tree that there doth stand,
    In time may grow as high as they.

"Once too I might have been a queen,
    But that I ever did deny,
I knew your grace had right to th' crown,
    Before Elizabeth did die.

"You of the eldest sister came,
    I of the second in degree,
The earl of Hertford of the third,
    A man of royal blood was he.

"And so good night, my sovereign liege,
    Since in the Tower I must lie,
I hope your Grace will condescend,
    That I may have my liberty."

"Lady Arabella," said the king,
    "I to your freedom would consent,
If you would turn and go to church,
    There to receive the sacrament.

And so good night, Arabella fair,"
    Our king replied to her again,
"I will take council of my nobility,
    That you your freedom may obtain."

"Once more to prison must I go,"
    Lady Arabella then did say,
"To leave my love breeds all my woe,
    The which will bring my life's decay.

> "Love is a knot none can unknit,
>   Fancy a liking of the heart,
> Him whom I love I can't forget,
>   Tho' from his presence I must part.
>
> "The meanest people enjoy their mates,
>   But I was born unhappily,
> For being cross'd by cruel fates,
>   I want both love and liberty.
>
> "But death I hope will end the strife,"
>   "Farewel, farewel, my love," quoth she,
> "Once I had thought to have been thy wife,
>   But now am forc'd to part with thee."
>
> At this sad meeting she had cause,
>   In heart and mind to grieve full sore,
> After that time Arabella fair,
>   Did never see lord Seymour more.

An Address to "Dickie."

AT a farm-house at Tunstead, near Chapel-en-le-Frith, a human skull, about which hangs many a strange story, has for several generations—indeed "time out of mind"—been preserved. There are some curious traditions connected with this skull, which is popularly known as "Dickie," or "Dicky o' Tunsted." How it first came to the farm is a complete mystery. All that is known is that it has been there for many generations, and always occupies the same position in the window-seat of the house. No matter what changes take place in the other occupiers of the house, Dicky holds his own against all comers, and remains quietly ensconced in his favourite place. It is firmly and persistently believed that so long as Dick remains in the house, unburied, everything will go on well and prosperously, but that if he is buried, or "discommoded," unpleasant consequences will assuredly follow. On more than one occasion he has been put "out of sight," but tempests have arisen and injured the building, deaths have ensued, cattle have been diseased and died off, or crops have failed, until the people have been humbled, and restored him to his proper place. One of the crowning triumphs of Dickie's power is said to have been evinced over the formation of the new Buxton and Whaley Bridge line of railway. He seems to have held the project in thorough hatred, and let no opportunity pass of doing damage. Whenever there was a landslip or a sinking, or whenever any mishap to man, beast, or line happened, the credit was at once given to Dickie, and he was sought to be propitiated in a variety of ways.

Hutchinson, who wrote "A Tour through the High Peak" in 1807, thus speaks of the skull, and of the supernatural powers attributed to it:—"Having heard a singular account of a human skull being preserved in a house at Tunstead, near the above place, and which was said to be haunted, curiosity induced me to deviate a little, for the purpose of making some enquiries respecting these *natural* or *supernatural* appearances. That there are three parts of a human skull in the house is certain, and which I traced to have remained on the premises for near two centuries past, during all the revolutions of owners and tenants in that time. As to the truth of the supernatural appearance, it is not my design either to affirm or contradict, though I have been informed by a creditable person, a Mr. Adam Fox, who was brought up in the house, that he has not only repeatedly heard singular noises, and observed very singular circumstances, but can produce fifty persons, within the parish, who have seen an apparition at this place. He has often found the doors opening to his hand—the servants have been repeatedly called up in the morning—many good offices have been done by the apparition, at different times;—and, in fact, it is looked upon more as a guardian spirit than a terror to the family, never disturbing them but in case of an approaching death of a relation or neighbour, and showing its resentment only when spoken of with disrespect, or when its own awful memorial of mortality is removed. For twice within the memory of man the skull has been taken from the premises,—once on building the present house on the site of the old one, and another time when it was buried in Chapel churchyard;—but there was no peace! no rest! it must be replaced! Venerable time carries a report that one of two coheiresses residing here was murdered, and declared, in her last moments, that her bones should remain on the place for ever.* On this head the candid reader will think for himself; my duty is only faithfully to relate what I have been told. However, the circumstance of the skull being traced to have remained on the premises during the changes of different tenants and purchasers for near two centuries, must be a subject well worth the antiquarian's research, and often more than the investigation of a bust or a coin!"

The following clever *Address to "Dickie"* was written by Mr. Samuel Laycock, and first appeared in the *Buxton Advertiser*.

> Neaw, Dickie, be quiet wi' thee, lad,
> An' let navvies an' railways a be;
> Mon, tha shouldn't do soa,—it's to' bad,
> What harm are they doin' to thee?
> Deod folk shouldn't meddle at o',
> But leov o' these matters to th' wick;
> They'll see they're done gradeley, aw know,—
> Dos' t' yer what aw say to thee, Dick?
>
> Neaw dunna go spoil 'em i' th' dark
> What's cost so mich labber an' thowt;
> Iv tha'll let 'em go on wi' their wark,
> Tha shall ride deawn to Buxton for nowt;

---

* On examining the parts of the skull, they did not appear to be the least decayed.

An' be a " director " too, mon ;
    Get thi beef an' thi bottles o' wine,
An' mak' as much brass as tha con
    Eawt o' th' London an' North Western line.

Awm surproised, Dick, at thee bein' here ;
    Heaw is it tha'rt noan i' thi grave ?
Ar' t' come eawt o' gettin' thi beer,
    Or havin' a bit ov a shave ?
But *that's* noan thi business, aw deawt,
    For tha hasn't a hair o' thi yed ;
Hast a woife an' some childer abeawt ?
    When tha'rn living up here wurt wed ?

Neaw, spake, or else let it a be.
    An' dunna be lookin' soa shy :
Tha needn't be freeten'd o' me,
    Aw shall say nowt abeawt it, not I !
It'll noan matter mich iv aw do,
    I can do thee no harm iv aw tell,
Mon there's moor folk nor thee bin a foo',
    Aw've a woife an some childer misel'.

Heaw's business below ; is it slack ?
    Dos' t' yer ? aw'm noan chaffin thee, mon '
But aw reckon 'at when tha goes back
    Tha'll do me o' th' hurt as tha con.
Neaw dunna do, that's a good lad,
    For awm freeten'd to deoth very nee,
An' ewar Betty, poor lass, hoo'd go mad
    Iv aw wur to happen to dee !

When aw'n ceawer'd upo' th' hearston' awhoam,
    Aw'm inclined, very often, to boast ;
An' aw'n noan hawve as feart as some,
    But aw don't loike to talke to a ghost.
So, Dickie, aw've written this song,
    An' aw trust it'll find thee o' reet ;
Look it o'er when tha'rt noan very throng,
    An' tha'll greatly obleege me,—good neet.

P.S.—Iv tha'rt wantin' to send a reply,
    Aw can gi'e thee mi place ov abode,
It's reet under Dukinfilt sky,
    At thirty-nine, Cheetham Hill road.
Aw'm awfully freeten'd dos t' see,
    Or else aw'd invite thee to come,
An' ewar Betty, hoo's softer nor me,
    So aw'd *raythar* tha'd tarry awhoam.

The Driving of the Deer.

THIS admirable ballad, founded on an old Derbyshire tradition, is by my friend Mr. William Bennett, of whom I have before spoken. The Peverels were, as a part of the immense possessions given to them by William the Conqueror, owners of the tract of country comprising the Honour and Forest of the High Peak. Their stronghold was the castle at Castleton. The "Lord's seat" mentioned in the ballad is a mountain separating Rushop Edge from the valley of Edale. The view from here, where Peverel used to alight from his horse to watch the progress of the chace, says Mr. Bennett, "is magnificent; perhaps one of the finest in north Derbyshire, as from its summit you may see the Pennine chain of Cheshire,

Derbyshire, and Staffordshire, with many of the lovely valleys which lie among the hills. Westward, you look down upon the valley of Chapel-en-le-Frith, the eastern part of which contains the ancient manor of Bowdon. To realize the following ballad, my readers must imagine the Lord of the Peak, William Peverel, with a number of his knights and gentlemen, on the Lord's Seat, preparing for the chace, when they hear the bugle blast which informs the proud baron that some audacious sportsmen are in chase of the deer within his forest. We may picture to ourselves the astonishment and indignation of the Norman prince, and his fierce determination to pounce upon the trespassers and punish them with all the severity of the cruel forest law. Well was it for all parties that he was attended by his brother Payne Peverel, the lord of Whittington, who was one of the noblest sons of chivalry, and whose presence prevented an affray which in all probability would have been fatal to many. Payne Peverel had previous to this time exhibited a grand pageant at Castleton, accompanied by a tournament held in the meadows below the castle, when he gave away his daughter to the knight who most distinguished himself on that occasion."

> Lord Peverel stood on the Lordis Seat,
>   And an angry man was he ;
> For he heard the sound of a hunter's horn
>   Slow winding up the lea.
> He look'd to north, he look'd to south,
>   And east and west look'd he ;
> And "Holy Cross !" the fierce Norman cried,
>   "Who hunts in my country ?
>
> Belike they think the Peverel dead,
>   Or far from forest walk ;
> Woe worth their hunting, they shall find
>   Abroad is still the Hawk."

Again he looked where Helldon Hill
    Joins with the Konying's Dale ;
And then once more the bugle blast
    Came swelling along the gale.

"Mount, mount and ride!" the baron cried,
    "The sound comes o'er the Edge,
By Perry dale, or Gautriss side,
    My knightly spurs I pledge.
These outlaws, who now drive my deer,
    Shall sooth our quarry be ;
And he who reaches first the hounds
    Shall win a guerdon free."

Each knight and squire soon sat in selle,
    And urged his horse to speed,
And Peverel, first among the rout,
    Proved his horse good at need.
Adown the slope, along the flat,
    Against the hill they ride,
Nor pull a rein 'till every steed
    Stands fast on Gautriss side.

"Hold hard! They're here," the Peverel said,
    And upward held his hand,
While all his meany kept behind,
    Awaiting their lord's command ;
And westward, on the Bolt-edge Moor,
    Beyond the rocky height,
Both hounds and hunters, men and horse,
    And deer were all in sight.

Said then the baron, "Who are these
    Who fear not Peverel's sword
Nor forest laws." Outspoke a squire,
    "Of Bowdon he's the lord ;
Sir Bruno, hight, a Franklin brave,
    One of the Saxon swine
Who feasts each day on fat fed beef,
    And guzzles ale, not wine.

"What stirs the sodden headed knave
    To make his pastime here !"
Cried Peverel, "and thus dare to brave
    Him whom the king doth fear !
Ride down the villains, horse and man ;
    Would we were armed to-day,
No Saxon chine should bear its head
    Forth from the bloody fray."

Up spoke his frere, Payne Peverel, then,
    Of Whittington lord was he,
And said, "Fair Sir, for ruth and grace
    This slaughter may not be.
The Saxon's lands are widely spread,
    And he holds them in capité,
And claims three days with hawk and hound
    To wind his bugle free."

"Beshrew his horn, and beshrew his heart,
    In my forest he may not ride :
If he kills a deer, by the Conqueror's bow
    By forest law he shall bide.

Ride on, Sir Payne, and tell the churl
 He must cease his hunting cheer,
And come to the knee of his suzerain lord
 Awaiting his presence here.

Ride with him, sirs, some two or three,
 And bring him hither straight:
'Twere best for him to come at once
 Than cause his lord to wait.
There are trees in the forest strong enow
 To bear the madman's corse,
And he shall hang on the highest bough
 If hither he comes perforce."

Sir Payne rode swiftly cross the dale,
 Followed by gentles three,
Nor stayed his horse 'till he had reached
 The hunter's company:
And then he said, "Fair sirs, ye ride
 And drive our deer as free
As if the land were all your own
 And not in forestry.

Lord Peverel yonder waits your ease,
 To know how this may be;
Since he is lord of the forest wide,
 And will no trespass see.
He bids you, as your suzerain lord,
 Forthwith to come to his knee,
And as his liegeman humbly stand,
 And answer him truthfully."

"No man of his," cried the Franklin, "then
    Am I, as he knows full well,
Though within the bounds of his forest walk
    It likes me sooth to dwell.
My manor of Bowdon, I hold in chief
    From good King Harry I trow;
And to him alone will I homage pay
    And make my fealty vow."

"Beware, Sir Franklin," cried Sir Payne,
    "Beware how thou play the fool!
To brave the ire of thy suzerain lord
    Will lead to direful dule.
Come on with me, and make thy peace,
    Better do that than worse;
He'll hang thee on the forest tree
    If we take thee hence perforce."

"Take me you can't while I have thews,
    And these have bows and spears,"
Cried the brave Franklin. "Threaten him
    Who the Lord Peverel fears.
We've broke no forest law to-day;
    Our hunting here's my right;
And only ye can force me hence
    If strongest in the fight."

Each hunter then upraised his spear,
    Or twanged his good yew bow,
While cloth yard shafts from every sheaf
    Glinted a threatening shew.

And back Payne Peverel reined his horse,
    And, as he rode away,
Cried, " Fare ye well, this day of sport
    Will breed a bloody day."

Well was it for the Saxons then
    The Normans rode unarmed,
Or they had scantly left that field
    And homeward gone unharmed.
Lord Peverel viewed their bows and spears,
    And marked their strong array,
And grimly smiled, and softly said,
    " We'll right this wrong some day."

But e'er that day, for fearful crime,
    The Peverel fled the land,
And lost his pride of place, and eke
    His lordship and command.
For Ranulph Earl of Chester's death,
    By him most foully wrought,
He fled fair England's realm for aye,
    And other regions sought.

Where, so 'tis writ, a monk he turned,
    And penance dreed so sore,
That all the holy brotherhood
    Quailed at the pains he bore.
And yet the haughty Norman blood
    No sign of dolour showed ;
But bore all stoutly to the last,
    And died beneath the rood.

So Heaven receive his soul at last,
    He was a warrior brave ;
And Pope and priest were joined in mass
    His guilty soul to save.
For Holy Church and Kingly Crown
    He was ever a champion true ;
For chivalry and ladies' grace
    Chiváler foiál et preux.

The Ashupton Garland,

OR A DAY IN THE WOODLANDS;

Showing how a "righte merrie companie" went forth to seek a diversion in the Woodlands, and what befell them there.

To a pleasant Northern Tune.

ASHOPTON is a small village, but little known away from its own neighbourhood, in the vale of the river Ashop, in the chapelry of Derwent, in the High Peak. This very clever ballad was written on occasion of what was evidently an extremely happy pic-nic party, held there not many years ago. It is one of the best modern ballads I have seen.

    IN summer time when leaves were green,
        With a hey derry down, you shall see ;
    James Oakes he called his merry men all,
        Unto the green-wood tree.

James Oakes he was a worthy squire,
    Full six feet high he stood;
No braver chief the forest rang'd,
    Since the days of Robin Hood.

Then some came East, and some came West,
    And Southrons there came three;
Such a jovial band of fine fellows,
    You never more shall see.

Nor fairer Maidens ever tripp'd,
    Than bore them companie;
The wood-nymphs peep'd, in wonder all,
    As they were passing by.

There was Sally of Riddings with her wit so sly,
    That young men's hearts beguil'd;
And wilding Meg, with the hazel eye,
    And sweet maid-Marian mild.

Then came blithe Helen of Osgarthorpe,
    With her sister, as you shall know;
Two fairer maids in Sheffield town
    Did ne'er set foot I trow.

Maid-Marian's sister too was there,
    And a merry little minx was she;
And they were merry merry maidens all,
    When under the greenwood tree.

Then followed straight a matron dame,
    That summers more had seen;
Her kindly eye did sparkle bright,
    And she seemed the woodland queen.

James Oakes the elder he went first,
　　As captain of the band ;
Bill Graham of Skiers was by his side,
　　And they shouted, " For merry England !"

Sylvester next, that rover bold,
　　(Some called him little John,)
With Bob the tall, from London town,
　　As you shall hear anon.

Two stalworth blades, sworn friends, were there,
　　Jem Oakes, and Asho'er Will ;
They wanted only a good cross-bow,
　　The Queen's fat deer to kill.

Then came Nick Milnes, that smart young man,
　　Of fifteen winters old ;
With Charley Oakes, a proper young man,
　　Of courage stout and bold.

Next Tom of Riddings, the rural swain,
　　(Their Allen-a-dale was he,)
Came tripping o'er the heather bell,
　　As blithe as blithe could be.

Good Lord it was a pleasant sight,
　　To see them all on a row ;
With every man his good cigar,
　　And his little bag hanging low.

Bill Graham, of Skiers, he then stepped forth,
　　All buskined up to the knee ;
And he swore by all the fair maids there,
　　Their champion he would be.

When this the Captain he did hear,
    To Bill up stepped he ;
And thus he said before the face
    Of that goodly companie :—

"The devil a drop, thou proud fellow !
    Of my whiskey shalt thou see,
Until thy courage here be tried—
    Thou shalt not go scot-free."

"By my troth," cried Bill "thourt a gallant knight,
    And worthy of me for thy squire,
And I'll show thee how for a lady I'll fight,
    If thoul't meet me in good Yorkshire."

When sweet maid-Marian this did hear,
    With a hey down down and a derry ;
Her rosy cheek did bleach with fear,
    But sweet Meg it made merry.

"A boon, a boon," cried little John,
    "I'm sick, and fain would see,
What thou hast got in thy leather bottel,
    I pray thee show to me."

"Come hither, come hither, thou fine fellow,
    Hold up thy head again ;
I've that within my leather bottel,
    That shall not breed thee pain.

Then the Captain took little John by the hand,
    And they sat them under the tree ;
"If we drink water while this doth last,
    Then an ill death may we dee."

Then little John he rose up once more,
    Renewed with mirth and glee ;
And eke with a bound, he danced a round,
    In sight of that companie.

These fine fellows all, did then take hands,
    And danced about the green tree :
" For six merry men, for seven merry men,
    For nine merry men we be."

Then on they walked the rocks among,
    All on a midsummer day ;
Every youth with a maiden by his side,
    While the birds sang from each spray.

With kirtle tucked up to the knee,
    The maidens far did go ;
And Bob the tall to each and all,
    Great courtesie did show.

Some plucked the green leaf, some the rose,
    As to *Kinder-Scout* they sped ;
Or wiled away the sweet summer's day,
    At lovely *Derwent-Head*.

And some did shout, and some did sing,
    With the heart so blithe and merry ;
And some adown the hill did roll,
    With a hey derry down, down derry.

And ever and anon they'd sit,
    On a mossy bank to rest ;
While the bag and the whiskey glass went round,
    With the ringing glass and jest.

Then some among the heather strayed,
    Springing the bonny Moor-hen;
And some did climb the green hills' side,
    Or roam in the tangled glen.

The blackbird tried his golden bill,
    His sooty love to greet;
Upon the bough, the throstle cock,
    Did carol blithe and sweet.

And when the dews began to fall,
    And the glowworm's lamp to shine,
To *Ashupton* Inn they did repair,
    In order for to dine.

Then on the board did smoke roast beef,
    With pasties hot and cold;
And many a right good stomach showed,
    And many a tale was told.

And when the table it was cleared,
    And landlord brought them wine;
He swore, that never there before,
    Such a companie did dine!

So a health to the Queene, and long may she reign,
    And Albert long live he;
Push the glass about,—old *Kinder-Scout*,
    We'll drink long life to thee.

And here's a health to those fine fellows,
    And to all those maidens merry;
May each take a heart from the *Ashupton-hills*,
    Singing hey derry down, down derry!

And here's a health unto James Oakes!
　　And many a year may he
Rise up, and call his merry men all,
　　Unto the greenwood tree.

Derbyshire Hills.

JAMES BANNARD, "a Wandering Poet, in his 74th year," is the writer of the following lines, which he says at the heading of the broad-sheet from which I reprint it, are "Views and reflections taken from Solomon's Temple, near Buxton." Of Bannard I know nothing, farther than that he was a poor man, and eked out his living by selling these verses "at the 'Cottage of Content,' Buxton."

　　At length my wand'ring feet have brought
　　　　Me on this Derby Hill;
　　Where my sweet muse and fancy both
　　　　May sit and take their fill.

　　Although I've trod the stage of life
　　　　Past seventy years and three:
　　'Tis the first time that ever I
　　　　These Derby Hills did see.

　　Reader, before I now proceed,
　　　　I pray you will excuse;
　　Your pardon humbly I do beg,
　　　　Intruding with my muse.

Born in an humble state of life,
    Grammar I could not attain ;
But from the school of Nature I,
    Did all my learning gain.

As on this eminence I stand,
    And view the Landscape round,
Here hills and dales, rivers and rocks,
    Most sweetly do abound.

Mark how the glorious setting sun
    Fair Buxton Town displays ;
Buxton whose healing streams and air,
    Give hope for length of days.

The next that did attract the muse
    Was the fine noble Church,
Where sinners every Sabbath day
    Their wicked hearts should search.

What numbers there already lie,
    Now sleeping at its feet ;
Waiting the great and awful day,
    When they their Judge must meet.

Their dust then joins its better part,
    I hope in realms above ;
And all its dross be pressed away,
    By the Redeemer's love.

The fine Hotels I next remarked,
    The walks and lawns so gay,
Where gentry their amusements take,
    In this sweet month of May.

To Solomon's Temple I repaired,
    To take a wider view;
And as I was a stranger there,
    All things appeared new.

How dare the wicked infidel
    Say that there is no God!
These mountains high and these firm rocks
    May crumble at His nod.

In Him I live, in Him I move,
    In Him I have my being;
In Him I on this mount now stand
    And paint this beauteous scene.

Brierlow and Foxlow I remark'd,
    Haddon and Croome likewise;
But Axedge overcap'd them all,
    And struck me with surprise.

The Lover's Leap likewise I view'd,
    Shootingslow did appear;
The Cat-and-Fiddle I have seen
    But I was never there.

Chee Tor, Bakewell, and Matlock too,
    Likewise the Diamond Hill;
The Shivering Tor for to describe
    Is far beyond my skill.

Now from this mount I do descend
    Into the vale below,
From whence the River Wye doth spring,
    And sweetly on doth flow.

For to describe the beauties all,
    Display'd in Derbyshire ;
Instead of musing for one day,
    Methinks 'twould take a year.

Having seen seventy years and three,
    My days are not a few ;
I may expect in a short time,
    To bid this world adieu.

May blessings rest on all your heads,
    Ye rich, likewise ye poor ;
Something forebodes within my mind,
    I must see these Derby Hills no more.

Derbyshire Dales.

HAVING given some lines on "Derbyshire Hills," by a "Wandering poet" totally unknown to fame, it will be well to follow it by others on "Derbyshire Dales," by one whose name is known throughout the length and breadth of the land—Eliza Cooke.

I sigh for the land where the orange-tree flingeth
    Its prodigal bloom on the myrtle below ;
Where the moonlight is warm, and the gondolier singeth,
    And clear waters take up the strain as they go.

Oh ! fond is the longing, and rapt is the vision
    That stirs up my soul over Italy's tales ;
But the *present* was bright as the *far-off* Elysian,
    When I roved in the sun-flood through Derbyshire Dales.

There was joy for my eye, there was balm for my breathing;
    Green branches above me—blue streams at my side:
The hand of Creation seemed proudly bequeathing
    The beauty reserved for a festival tide.

I was bound, like a child, by some magical story,
    Forgetting the "South" and "Ionian Vales;"
And felt that dear England had temples of Glory,
    Where any might worship, in Derbyshire Dales.

Sweet pass of the "Dove!" 'mid rock, river, and dingle,
    How great is thy charm for the wanderer's breast!
With thy moss-girdled towers and foam-jewelled shingle,
    Thy mountains of might, and thy valleys of rest.

I gazed on thy wonders—lone, silent, adoring,
    I bent at the altar whose "fire never pales:"
The Great Father was with me—Devotion was pouring
    Its holiest praises in Derbyshire Dales.

Wild glen of dark "Taddington"—rich in thy robing
    Of forest-green cloak, with grey lacing bedight;
How I lingered to watch the red Western rays probing
    Thy leaf-mantled bosom with lances of light!

And "Monsal," thou mine of Arcadian treasure,
    Need we seek for "Greek Islands" and spice-laden gales,
While a Tempe like thee of enchantment and pleasure
    May be found in our own native Derbyshire Dales?

There is much in my Past bearing way-marks and flowers,
    The purest and rarest in odour and bloom;
There are beings and breathings, and places and hours,
    Still trailing in roses o'er Memory's tomb.

And when I shall count o'er the bliss that's departed,
  And Old Age be telling its garrulous tales,
Those days will be first when the kind and true-hearted
  Were nursing my spirit in Derbyshire Dales.

A RHAPSODY

On the Peak of Derbyshire.

THE following exquisite lines by my late highly-gifted father,[*] on the land he loved so well,—the glorious district of the Peak of Derbyshire,—may well claim a place in this part of my present volume. I give them, not as being the most favourable example I could choose of his style, but as being the most appropriate for my present purpose.

O, GIVE me the land where the wild thyme grows,
  The heathery dales among ;
Where Sol's own flow'er with crimson eye
  Creeps the sun-burnt banks along !
Where the beetling Tor hangs over the dell,
  While its pinnacles pierce the sky,
And its foot is laved by the waters pure,
  Of the lively murmuring Wye ;
Oh ! give me the land, where the crimson heather,
The thyme and the bilberry grow together.

O ! where upon earth is another land
  So green, so fine, so fair !

---

[*] Author of the " History of Buxton," " History of Lincoln," &c., &c.

Can any within Old England's bounds
    With this heathery land compare ?
The mountain air, the crystal springs,
    Where health has established her throne,
The flood-swollen torrent, the bright cascade,
    Belong to this land alone ;
O ! give me the land where grow together
The marj'ram, cistus, and purple heather.

Oxford may boast of its hundred spires,
    Its colleges, halls, and towers ;
Built in an ague-producing marsh,
    Are the Muses' and Learning's bowers ;
O ! tell me not of the sluggish stream,
    Too lazy to creep along ;
Too dull to inspire a poet's dream !
    This is not the land of song !
No ! give me the land where grow together
The cistus, the thyme, and the purple heather.

The Derby Hero.

THE two following productions of some local muse, written in the year 1822, are intended to do honour to a young pedestrian of Derby, who no doubt was thought famous in those days of foot-racing and pugilism.

    OF all your modern Heroes
        That rank so high in fame,
    There's one that takes the lead of all,
        Young Wantling is his name ;

For when he takes the field
   So nimbly he doth run,
His feet is at the destin'd mark
   Ere the race is well begun !
     Fol de rol, &c.

This youth's been lately tried
   Against a man of great renown,
And to run the Stafford hero
   He was back'd for fifty pounds ;
O he is the bravest lad
   That ever eyes did see,
For he won the race quite easy,
   When the bets were five to three !
     Fol de rol, &c.

Now ye men of sporting talent
   I would have you all to know,
On the eighteenth day of March
   You've a chance to see him go,
For this Hero he is match'd to run
   Three hundred yards we're told,
Against the Stafford Bragger
   For one hundred guineas in gold !
     Fol de rol, &c.

Then keep your spirits up, my lads,
   For he will show the way,
He is as swift as Mercury,
   And is sure to win the day ;

For Wantling's of such good mettle,
    And his honour is as good,
He is sure not to deceive you,
    As some other Runners would.
        Fol de rol, &c.

Of all the Runners now in vogue
    Young Wantling takes the lead;
You would think him jealous of the wind
    When you view him in his speed:
He will make that Braggadocia
    Afraid to show his face,
To be beat by an apprentice boy—
    It will be such disgrace.
        Fol de rol, &c.

We've another Hero on the list
    That runs but now and then,
But he's well known upon the turf
    By the name of Little Ben;
He's lately been to try his strength
    Some miles from Derby town,
And there he well confirmed his name
    As a youth of some renown.
        Fol de rol, &c.

Then drink success to Derby town,
    For it stands high in fame,
Its lads will yield to none,
    For they're Chickens of true Game;

Their strength has oft been tried
    By men both far and near,
But they never yet was beat,
    For their hearts are void of fear.
        Fol de rol, &c.

A New Song

On the great Foot Race that was contested on the London Road, near Derby, on the 18th day of March, 1822, betwixt Jas. Wantling, of Derby, and Shaw, the Staffordshire Hero, for 2 Hundred Guineas.

THE eighteenth day of March
    Will long be handed down,
When thousands came from far
    Into famed Derby town,
To see the great Foot Race
    For one hundred guineas aside,
Betwixt Shaw, the Stafford Hero,
    And Wantling, Derby's pride!
        Fol de rol, &c.

Now the time is come
    That these Heroes try their skill,
Whilst numbers flock together
    Offering to lay who will;

Large sums are laid around
  Ere they begin to run,
And mingled sounds you hear
  Crying I take your bet—done, done.
    Fol de rol, &c.

And now you see them striving
  Which shall get the first,
Straining each nerve and muscle
  Till their veins are almost burst;
But Wantling takes the lead,
  And labours hard to gain
The money for his friends,
  And establish his own fame.
    Fol de rol, &c.

The race it soon was over,
  Whilst women, men, and boys
Cried "Wantling still for ever!"
  In shouts that rend the skies.
His name this day is raised,
  As a Runner of great fame,
For Shaw, the Stafford Hero,
  Has been beat by him again!
    Fol de rol, &c.

All ye wise men of Staffordshire,
  Who back'd Shaw on that day,
Having ventured all your money,
  Leaving none your shots to pay,

Be wiser for the future,
    If again you chance to come,
And bring more money with you,
    Lest you go empty home.
        Fol de rol, &c.

Then let us drink the Hero's health,
    Whilst Fame proclaims his name,
May he never sell his honour
    For the sake of sordid gain :
All base attempts to bias him
    With scorn from him be hurl'd,
Then he will rise a wonder,
    And astonish all the world.
        Fol de rol, &c.

But let us act with honour,
    And not run the Hero down,
Although he lost the race,
    He's a claim to great renown ;
For Shaw and his supporters
    Have acted manly parts,
And any thing contrary
    Is quite foreign to their hearts.
        Fol de rol, &c.

ON THE DEATH OF THE LATE
Rev. Bache Thornhill, M.A.,
Perpetual Curate of Winster, Ashford, and Longstone.

MR. THORNHILL, on whose death through accident the following verses were written, was son of Bache Thornhill, Esq., of Stanton in the Peak. He was a man of refined tastes, fond of antiquarian pursuits, and was highly esteemed in the county of Derby. He was M.A. of St. John's College, Cambridge, where he was a fellow-student with Sir Robert Peel, with whom to the period of his untimely death he kept up an intimate friendship. On the 13th of December, 1827, Mr. Thornhill was accidentally shot by the discharge of the fowling-piece of a friend. He lingered until the 27th, when he died, at the age of forty-two. He was buried at Youlgreave, the coffin bearing the inscription—"Rev. Bache Thornhill, Vicar of Winster, and Vice-Vicar of Ashford and Longstone, died the 27th day of December, 1827; aged forty-two."

The writer of these verses was John Brimlow, of Winster. Brimlow had been a soldier in Colonel Thornhill's regiment, under which gallant officer he served in Egypt. He afterwards suffered from opthalmia, became blind, and got a precarious livelihood by rambling about the country with a basket, gathering "rags and bones." The verses are here reprinted from a broad-sheet.

> As I sat musing by the fire
>   I heard some people say
> A dreadful accident has befel
>   A worthy man this day.
>
> Then I got up, went out of door
>   For to see, and likewise hear,
> On every tongue enquiry sat,
>   And, in many an eye, a tear,

Saying our worthy Pastor he has fall'n,
    Oh! how hard has been his lot,
By accident a gun went off,
    And this good man was shot.

The rich, the poor, in groups they meet,
    Their sorrow for to express,
Saying if fifty come there will be none like Bache
    To those that are in distress.

For he was a friend to every one,
    To all alike was kind,
He was the same to rich and poor,
    Likewise sick, lame, or blind.

Oh! cruel Fate, what have we done,
    That this good man should fall,
But the die was cast, and the thing is past,
    And there must be an end to all.

But, hark! a messenger has just arrived,
    Glad tidings doth he bring,
This good man he is still alive,
    Oh! let us praise the King of kings.

Rejoice, my friends, he better gets,
    For the Lord has heard our prayer,
And He has promised when a few does meet
    That He always will be there.

But adieu, vain hope, thou art for ever fled,
    For this good man is no more,
For he is now numbered amongst the dead,
    So adieu, adieu, farewell for evermore.

                JOHN BRIMLOW, Winster.

A Journey into the Peak.

TO SIR ASTON COKAINE.

CHARLES COTTON, the "honoured friend" of good old Izaac Walton, and of most of the celebrated men of his day, was born at Beresford Hall, on the banks of his

"—— beloved Nymph! fair Dove,
Princess of Rivers,"

whose praises he has sung, and whose beauties he has rendered immortal by his pen, and by his fishing-house, dedicated to lovers of the angle. He was the only child of Charles Cotton, Esq., by Olive, daughter of Sir John Stanhope, of Elvaston Castle, near Derby (ancestor of the Earl of Harrington, and of the same family as the Earl of Chesterfield, Earl Stanhope, &c.) He married, first, Isabella, daughter of Sir Thomas Hutchinson, of Owthorpe; and, second, the widowed Countess of Ardglass (daughter of Sir William Russel, of Strensham). He died in 1687.

Charles Cotton was a profuse writer. Among his principal works are the second part of "The Complete Angler," "The Wonders of the Peak," "Virgil Travestie," "Moral Philosophy of the Stoics," "The Planter's Manual," "Life of the Duke of Espernon," "The Commentaries of De Montluc," "The Complete Gamester," "The Fair One of Tunis," "Burlesque upon Burlesque," "Montaigne's Essays," &c., &c. After his death, a collection of "Poems on several Occasions," by Charles Cotton, was published.

The following characteristic lines I here print from the original MS. copy, in my own possession. The volume of manuscript is of the highest interest, and is in the autograph writing of Charles Cotton himself. It is entitled, in his own writing, "Charles Cotton, His Verses," and is in folio, in the old binding with clasps. This volume is described in Sir Harris Nicholas' Life of Cotton, attached to his edition of the Complete Angler. It contains some pieces not printed, and others very different from those in his "Poems on Several Occasions," printed sur-

S

reptitiously after his death in 1689. The following varies in many parts from the copy printed in the volume alluded to.

S'R,

Coming home into this frozen Clime,
Grown cold, and almost senselesse, as my rythme,
I found, that Winter's bold impetuous rage
Prevented time and antidated age :
For, in my veins did nought but crystall dwell,
Each hair was frozen to an iccicle.
My flesh was marble, so that, as I went,
I did appear a walking monument.
'T might have been judged, rather than marble, flint,
Had there been any spark of fier in't.
  My mother looking back (to bid good night)
Was metamorphos'd, like the Sodomite.
Like Sinons horse, our horses were become,
And, since they could not go, they slided home.
The hills were hard to such a qualitie,
So beyond Reason in Philosophie ;
If Pegasus had kickt at one of those,
Homer's Odysses had been writ in prose.
  These are strange stories, S'r, to you, who sweat
Under the warm Sun's comfortable heat ;
Whose happy seat of Pooley farre outvies
The fabled pleasures of blest Paradise.
Whose Canaan fills your hous with wyne and oyl,[1]
Till't crack with burdens of a fruitful soil.
Which hous, if it were plac't above the sphear,
Would be a palace fit for Jupiter.
The humble chappell for religious Rites,
The inner rooms for honest, free delights,

And Providence, that these miscarrie, loth,
Has plac't the Tower a centinell to both :
So that there's nothing wanting to improve
Either your pietie, or peace, or love.
  Without, you have the pleasure of ye woods,
Fair plains, sweet meadows, and transparent flouds,
With all that's good, and excellent, beside
The tempting apples by Euphrates' side.
But, that, which does above all these aspire,
Is Delphos, brought from Greece to Warwick-shire.
  But Oh ! ungodly Hodge ! that valu'd not
The saving juice o'th' ænigmaticke pot.
Whose charming virtue made mee to forget
T'enquire of Fate, else I had stayed there yet.
Nor had I then once dar'd to venture on
The cutting ayr of this our Freezland zone.
  But once again, Dear Sir, I mean to come
  And learn to thank, as to be troublesome.

Another "Journey into the Peak" by Charles Cotton, which is but little known, is the following, which is an admirable specimen of his style. It is entitled an

Epistle to John Bradshaw, Esq.

FROM *Porto Nova* as pale wretches go,
To swing on fatal *Tripus*, even so
My dearest Friend, I went last day from thee,
Whilst for five Miles, the figure of that Tree
Was ever in my guilty Fancy's eye,
As if in earnest I'd been doom'd to die

For, what deserv'd it, so unworthily
Stealing so early, *Jack*, away from thee.
And that which (as't well might) encreas'd my fear,
Was the ill luck of my vile Chariotier,
Who drove so nicely too, t'increase my dread,
As if his Horses with my vital thread
Had Harness'd been, which being, alas ! so weak
He fear'd might snap, and would not it should break,
Till he himself the honour had to do't
With one thrice stronger, and my neck to boot.
Thus far in hanging posture then I went.
(And sting of Conscience is a punishment
On Earth they say the greatest, and some tell
It is moreo'er the onely one in Hell,
The Worm that never dies being alone
The thing they call endless Damnation :)
But leaving that unto the Wise that made it,
And knowing best the Gulf, can best evade it,
I'll tell you, that being pass'd through *Highgate*, there
I was saluted by the Countrey Air,
With such a pleasing Gale, as made me smell
The *Peak* it self; nor is't a Miracle,
For all that pass that *Portico* this way
Are *Transontani*, as the Courtiers say ;
Which suppos'd true, one then may boldly speak,
That all of th' North-side *High-gate* are i'th' *Peak ;*
And so to hanging when I thought to come,
Wak'd from the Dream, I found my self at home.

   Wonder not then if I, in such a case
So over-joy'd, forgot thee for a space ;

And but a little space, for, by this light,
I thought on thee again ten times e'er night;
Though when the night was come, I then indeed
Thought all on one of whom I'd greater need:
But being now cur'd of that Malady,
I'm at full leisure to remember thee,
And (which I'm sure you long to know) set forth
In Northern Song, my Journey to the North.

Know then with Horses twain, one sound, one lame,
On *Sunday*'s Eve I to St. *Alban's* came,
Where, finding by my Body's lusty state
I could not hold out home at that slow rate,
I found a Coach-man, who, my case bemoaning,
With three stout Geldings, and one able Stoning,
For eight good Pounds did bravely undertake,
Or for my own, or for my Money's sake,
Through thick and thin, fall out what could befall,
To bring me safe and sound to *Basford*-hall*.
Which having drank upon, he bid good-night,
And (Heaven forgive us) with the Morning's light,
Not fearing God, nor his Vice-gerent Constable,
We roundly rowling were the Road to *Dunstable*,
Which, as they chim'd to Prayers, we trotted through,
And 'fore elev'n ten minutes came unto
The Town that *Brickhill* height, where we did rest,
And din'd indifferent well both man and beast.
'Twixt two and four to *Stratford*, 'twas well driven,
And came to *Tocester* to lodge at Even

---

* Beresford Hall, Dove Dale, his residence.

Next day we din'd at *Dunchurch*, and did lie
That night four miles on our side *Coventry*.
Tuesday at Noon at *Lichfield* Town we baited,
But there some friends, who long that hour had waited,
So long detain'd me, that my Chariotier
Could drive that night but to *Uttoxiter*.
And there the *Wedn'sday*, being Market-day,
I was constrain'd with some kind Lads to stay
Tippling till afternoon, which made it night
When from my Hero's Tower I saw the light
Of her Flambeaux, and fanci'd as we drave
Each rising Hillock was a swelling wave,
And that I swimming was in *Neptune*' spight
To my long long'd-for Harbour of delight.

And now I'm here set down again in peace,
After my troubles, business, Voyages,
The same dull Northern clod I was before,
Gravely enquiring how Ewes are a Score,
How the Hay-Harvest, and the Corn was got,
And if or no there's like to be a Rot ;
Just the same Sot I was e'er I remov'd,
Nor by my travel, nor the Court improv'd ;
The same old fashion'd Squire, no whit refin'd,
And shall be wiser when the Devil's blind :
But find all here too in the self-same state,
And now begin to live at the old rate,
To bub old Ale, which nonsense does create,
Write leud Epistles, and sometimes translate
Old Tales of Tubs, of *Guyenne*, and *Provence*,
And keep a clutter with th'old Blades of *France*,

As *D'Avenant* did with those of *Lombardy*,
Which any will receive, but none will buy,
And that has set *H.B.** and me awry.
My River still through the same Chanel glides,
Clear from the Tumult, Salt, and dirt of Tides,
And my poor Fishing-house, my Seat's best grace,
Stands firm and faithfull in the self-same place
I left it four months since, and ten to one
I go a Fishing e'er two days are gone :
So that (my Friend) I nothing want but thee
To make me happy as I'd wish to be ;
And sure a day will come I shall be bless'd
In his enjoyment whom my heart loves best ;
Which when it comes will raise me above men
Greater than crowned Monarchs are, and then
I'll not exchange my Cottage for *White*-hall,
Windsor, the *Lauvre*, or th' *Escurial*.

Hugh Stenson and Molly Green.

THE following ballad has not, as far as I am aware, been "in print" before. I here give it from a MS. copy in my own possession. The Duke of Devonshire alluded to in the ballad as having acted so nobly in saving the life of "his countryman," Hugh Stenson, was, I presume, William, fourth Duke of Devonshire, who was Lord Lieutenant of Ireland in 1756.

THEN oh, Hugh Stenson is my name,
From Ashborne in the Peak I came,
And at the age of seventeen
I fell in love with Molly Green.

---

* "Henry Brome at the Gun in St. Paul's Churchyard," who published many of Cotton's works.

She is a beauty I do declare,
She came from Highchurch in Shropshire;
She was an angel in my eye,
Which caused me from my colours to fly.

Long time I courted her for her love,
But she would never constant prove;
A thought then I did entertain,
To cross the roaring ocean main.

But when I was upon the seas,
I could not have one moment's ease;
For she was daily in my sigh,
Which made me from my colours to fly.

But when I did return again,
I went unto this youthful dame,
Desiring she would not disdain
A bleeding heart and dying swain.

"Stenson," said she, "I pray forbear,
I know that you a deserter are,
And if my parents come to know,
They sure would prove your overthrow."

When I heard she made this reply,
I from her arms did swiftly fly,
And with a kiss I took my leave,
Although I'm bound a captive slave.

At Woolaton near Nottingham
I put my trust in a false man,
I took him for my friend to be,
But he, like Judas, betrayed me.

Derbyshire Ballads.

Then a court marshall there was call'd,
And I was brought amongst them all,
And for deserting they did me try,
And they condemned me for to die.

Oh Lord, oh Lord, it grieved me sore
To lay my bones on an Irish shore ;
One General Pearcey he did cry,
" It's by the Law that you must die."

From January to July
Upon the boards and stones I did lie,
Praying to Heavens both night and day
To take this thread of life away.

Oh then bespoke the President,
Hoping of me for to repent,
" I have done the best for you I can,
But O you are a dying man."

Twenty-five days I had to live,
And bread and water I did receive ;
The Clergyman came twice a day,
And for my soul did daily pray.

But at that time from England came
The Duke of Devonshire by name,
Our Lord Lieutenant for to be,
And he from death did set me free.

And when this Lord appeared in land,
I wrote to him with my own hand,
Desiring that his Grace would save
A dying mortal from the grave.

But when he looked these lines upon,
And saw I was his own countryman,
He said, " I'll ease him of his care,
And send him home into Derbyshire."

Oh then he gave a strict command
For to release me out of hand ;
A free discharge to me he gave,
And so his Grace my life did save.

So whilst I live I'm in duty bound
To kneel and pray upon the ground,
That when I die without control,
Sweet Jesus may receive my soul.

You soldiers all, where e'er you be,
And hear of this my misery,
I beg you'll warning take by me,
And so I end my tragedy.

FINIS.

The Beggar's Ramble.

THERE are at least three or four different versions of the "Ramble ;" or rather I should say there are at least three or four different metrical "Rambles" through Derbyshire, of this character. I give two. The first I reprint from a broad-sheet, and the second from an old MS. copy, both in my own collection. The allusions to places, persons, inns, &c., in the county, are curious and interesting.

HARK ye well, my neighbours all, and pray now can you tell
Which is the nearest way unto the Begger's Well ?

There is Eaton, and Toten, and Brancot on the hill,
There's Beggerly Beeston, and lousy Chilwell.

There's Trowel, and there's Cosel, from there to Cimberly
    Knowl,
I would have call'd at Watnall, but I thought it would
    not do,
There's Beaver, and there's Hansley, & so for Perkin Wood,
I meant to have call'd at Selson, but there ale is not good.

There's Snelson green, and Pinstone green, and Blackwell
    old hall,
An old place where I had lived I had a mind to call;
I got a good refreshment, and something else beside,
So turning up the closes, South Normanton I 'spied.

There's Blackwell, and there's Newton, from there to
    Marrot Moor,
There's Tipshall, and there's Hardstaff, where I had been
    before,
I cross o'er Hardstaff Common, from there to Pilsley lane
Where once a noted butcher lived, Geo. Holland was his
    name.

There's Wingfield, and Tupton, from there to the Claycross,
From there I went to Chesterfield,—was almost cut to loss,
There's Asher, and there's Firbeck, and Stretton on the hill,
There's Hickam, and Oakerthorpe, and so for Wiremill.

There's Brankenfield, & Wessenton, from there to Morat
    Moor,
There's Pentrich, and Alfreton, where I had been before,

There's Swanick, and Ripley, then to the hillocks I came,
From there to Denby Common, for to see old Dolly Green.

There's Denby and Bottlebrook, from there to the Lane ends,
From there I went to Horseley, in hopes to meet a friend,
So turning down Coxbench, I made a sudden stop,
Thinks I I'll up the closes go, for Potters of th' hill top.

In Woodhouse lane, as I've been told, they used to get good coal,
And Stansby is a pretty place, and so for the Dob hole,
There's the Justice room, and Smalley Bell, likewise the Rose and Crown,
And at Morley Smithey, I've been told there lives one Saml. Brown.

There's Morley, and Stansby, and so for Lockey Grange,
There's Spondon and Ockbrook, and so for Chaddeson came ;
There's Ferby, and Breadsall, and so for Alestree,
From there to Little Eaton went, George Milward for to see.

There's Duffield down by Derwent side, & Milford, in a line,
There's Belper, and there's Shottle, if I can get there in time ;
There's Turnditch, and Kirk Ireton, and so for Cross-in hand,
And when I got to Wardgate, I was almost at a stand.

There's Hollington and Middleton by Youlgrave I've heard tell,
There's Bonsal and there's Winster, from and to Bakewell,

There's Wardlemire & Uckler, from there to Hoyland came,
And when that I did thither get, I began to feel quite
  lame.

There's Calver, & there's Rowsley, that most delightful
  place,
From there went to Chatsworth, the mansion of his Grace;
There's Darley Dale, & Matlock, where I once stopt a week,
There's Cromford, & Wirksworth, & Ashbourn in the Peak.

There's Ashbourn Green, & Hognaston, and so for Atlow-win,
Then on by Shepherd Folly, and from there to Ginglers' Inn.
There's Yeldersly, and Alderwasley, and Langley, and
  Longford,
There's Brailford, and Mugington, and Weston Underwood.

There's Quarndon, and Markeaton, oft times I have heard
  tell,
From there I went to Kedleston, where there is a useful
  well;
And at Windy Mill, I do sure you very pleasant looks,
If you will only stop and drink with Honest Puss-in-Boots.

There's Darley by Derby, for that is a shady bower,
And Derby is a county town; there's handsome Micklover.
There's Litlover, and Mackworth, and so for Etwell I went,
Until at last I did arrive at Burton-upon-Trent.

There's Findon, and Repton, and Ashton also,
And there's another little place, I think they call Shardlow;
There's Elvaston, and Allvaston, I have travelled o'er
  and o'er,
There's wind mills and south mills, and Barrow-upon-Soar.

There's Swarston Bridge and Smalley Bridge, as plain it
 doth appear,
There's Keyworth, and Hathenturns, that lieth very near,
There's Sheepshead, and Thingstun, and Whitrick also
Across the Sherwood Forest, and from there to Lough-
 borough.

There's Gotham rare for wisdom, and Bunny's rare for game,
There's Clifton Grove and Rudington, Wilford down the
 lane ;
There's Cropwell, and there's Ratliffe, and Bridgeford on
 the hill,
There's Gunthorpe, and Calthorpe, and Overington Mill.

There's Southwell, and Westhorpe, and Eperston so green,
There's Lowtom and Burton Joice, and Bulcott lies between,
There's Lambley, and Woodborough, from there to Cal-
 verton,
And there's a place at Arnold, they call it Foxen Den.

There's Redhill and Maperly hills, from there to Thorny-
 wood,
Where once a noted robber lived, his name was Robin
 Hood ;
There's Gedling, and Carlton, as plainly it does appear,
There's Keyworth, and Hatherturns, that lieth very near.

There's Lenton, and Radford, and so for Bobber's Mill,
There's Hyson Green, and Basford, and so for Sinder hill ;
There's Broxter, and there's Nuttel, and Greasley lieth nigh,
There's Giltbrook, and Newthorpe, from there to Beggerley.

There's Moregreen and Nether Green, where lives a man
    of sport,
And Eastwood is a pretty place of trade and resort ;
And at Langley Mill I stopt a while, to see a noble fight,
And when I came to Brunsley Gin, thinks I I'll light
    my pipe.

There's Oldacre and Bentley, and so for the lime kilns,
There's Woodend, and Heaner, and famous Tag Hill,
There's Lee lane, and Marpole, where lives one Mr. Clay,
There's Shipley, and Shipley wood, and so for Cotnermay.

And there's another little place, if I am not mistaken,
I think some people call it Mapley by name,
There's Little Hallam, and Hilson, and so for Gallows Inn,
And when I came to Sandacre I was looken very thin.

There's Stapleford, and Risley, and Dracott also,
At last I came to Breaston, where I wish'd for long ago,
So I hope these lines which I have wrote no one they will
    offend,
For at every door there stands a whore, at Leak Town end.

The Beggar's Ramble.

COME hark you well, my masters, pray can you me tell
Which is the nearest road unto the beggar's wells?
There's Shoobottams of Womfords, and Bessicks in the
    Flash,
There's ropemakers of Mansfield, and Dales of bordbast.

There's Sigsmore and Staysmore, and Clackmore so rough,
There's Winster and Cotsworth, and merry Locksclough;
There's Longnor and Buxton, and outside the shade,
From thence you may go to Leechurch* and call at the west gaites.

There's Caldon and Caulton, there's the waterfall and grinn,
And these are four of the foulest places that ever man was in;
There's Haymore by Ashbourn, and then to the Peak Hills,
For Wool and Lead is the chiefest thing that the country yields.

There's Oaker† Hall and Blesford Hall,‡ and Mappleton in the sands,
There's Thorpe Cloud and Bentley, and at Tissington lies good land;
There's Parrich§ and Braston,‖ there's Bradburn and Wet Wilnn,¶
There's Hopton and Carsdale, Park Nook and Pusses Inn.**

There's Middleton and Cromford, and so to Gosley bank,
And if you taste of Wirksworth ale it's sure to make you drunk;
There's Hognaston and Atlow, and Atlor in the fall,
And from thence you may go to Bradley, and there's a pretty hall.

---

* Query Ludchurch.   † Okeover Hall.   ‡ Brailsford.
§ Parwich.   ‖ Brassington.   ¶ Wilne.
** "Puss-in-boots" at Windley.

There's Marston and Mugginton and Allestree and Quarn,
And in that pretty country there does grow good corn;
There's Donington and Diseworth, and Breedon-on-the Hill,
And from thence you go to Newton, and so to the King's
  Mills.

There's Mackworth and Marton,* and so to the Nun's
  Green,
There's Harehill and Hogdeston, a little way between;
There's Longford and Mammaton, and so to Harton forge,
And from thence you may go to Tidbury,† and in at the
  old George.

There's Foston and Roston, and so to Darley moor,
There's Yeavely and Radgley, and thence you may be sure
For why I did ramble to the far end of the town,
And there's a pretty landlady that keeps the Rose and Crown.

At Ellaston and Wooton, and at Stanton there's good ale,
And from thence you may go to Swinsor and Pantons in
  the Dale:
There's Crumpwood and Prestwood, and Rosemary hill,
There's Wotten Lodge and Alton Lodge, and so on to the
  Wire Mill.

There's Alton and Farley, and Rempstone so high,
There's Cheadle and Oakamoor is a little hard by;
There's Quicksall and Rosley‡ and Camebridge beyond,
And from thence you may go to Uteetter,§ and there lies
  good land.

* Markeaton. † Tutbury. ‡ Rodsley. § Uttoxeter.

There's Eaton and Crapnidge and Perwolt in the clay,
There's Stramshall and Bramshall and merry Loxley,
There's Overton and Netherton, and Bramest and Fole,
There's Leechurch and Park Hall, and Checkley-in-the-hole.

There's Dubberidge and Blyfield, and so to Coloten Green,
There's Boslem* and Handley† green a little way between,
For potmen and great carriers they bear the bell away,
But the old stock of Borleyash is quite gone to decay.

Henry and Clara.

A PEAK BALLAD.

IN the middle of last century as brutal and cold-blooded a murder as ever disgraced the annals of this kingdom was perpetrated in the Winnats (a corruption of "wind gates") at Castleton, the victims being a young gentleman and lady of "gentle," if not of "noble," blood, on their wedding-day, and the murderers being five miners of the place. The following ballad, the production, in his early days, of my late brother, the Rev. Arthur George Jewitt,‡ was printed by him in his "*Wanderings of Memory*," in 1815. The following explanatory note appears in "*Wanderings of Memory:*"—

"In the year 1768,§ a young gentleman and lady, each mounted on a fine horse, but unattended by any servants, had been up to the Chapel of Peak Forest to be married, (as being extra-parochial, the Vicar at that time exercised the same privilege as the parson of Gretna Green, and married any couple that came to him, without making any

---

* Burs'em. † Hanley.
‡ The Rev. A. G. Jewitt, who was the author of several well-known works, was born at Chesterfield in 1794, and died in 1828.
§ Another account says 1758.

impertinent enquiries concerning them,) and on their return, wishing to take Castleton in their way home, and being strangers in the country, found themselves benighted at the Winnats." "Here they were seized by five miners, dragged into a barn, robbed of a great sum of money, and then murdered. In vain the lady sought them to spare her husband; vainly he strove to defend his wife. While one part of them were employed in cutting the gentleman's throat, another of the villains, stepping behind the lady, struck a pick-axe into her head, which instantly killed her. Their horses were found, some days after, with their saddles and bridles still on them, in that great waste called Peak Forest; and Eldon Hole was examined for their riders, but without effect. They were then taken to Chatsworth, (the Duke of Devonshire being Lord of the Manor,) and ran there as '*waifs*,' but never were claimed, and it is said the saddles are yet preserved there. This murder, thus perpetrated in silence, though committed by so large a company, remained a secret till the death of the last of the murderers; but Heaven, ever watchful to punish such horrid wretches, rendered the fate of all the five singularly awful. One, named Nicholas Cock, fell down one of the Winnats, and was killed on the spot. John Bradshaw, another of the murderers, was crushed to death by a stone which fell upon him near the place where the poor victims were buried. A third, named Thomas Hall, became a suicide; a fourth, Francis Butler, after many attempts to destroy himself, died raging mad; and the fifth, after experiencing all the torments of remorse and despair which an ill-spent life can inflict on a sinner's death-bed, could not expire till he had disclosed the particulars of the horrid deed."

> CHRISTIANS, to my tragic ditty
> Deign to lend a patient ear,
> If your breasts e'er heav'd with pity,
> Now prepare to shed a tear.
>
> Once there lived a tender virgin,
> Virtuous, fair, and young was she,
> Daughter of a wealthy lordling,
> But a haughty man was he.

Many suitors, rich and mighty,
    For this beauteous damsel strove,
But she all their offers slighted,
    None could wake her soul to love.

One alone, of manners noble,
    Yet with slender fortune blessed,
Caus'd this lady's bosom trouble,
    Raised the flame within her breast.

Mutual was the blissful passion,
    Stronger and stronger still it grew;
Henry liv'd but for his Clara,
    Clara but her Henry knew.

But, alas! their bliss how transient,
    Earthly joy but leads to care:
Henry sought her haughty parent
    And implor'd his daughter fair—

Dar'd to ask the wealthy lordling,
    For the damsel's willing hand,—
Pleaded with respectful fervour,
    Who could his request withstand?

Clara's father,—he withstood it,
    He the ardent suit denied,—
To a house so poor, though noble,
    Never would he be allied.

Bade him seek a love more equal,
    Banish Clara from his mind,
For he should no more behold her,—
    She,—poor maid, he close confin'd.

Hapless Henry, thus rejected,
   Lost, unfriended, and forlorn,
Wretched, sad, by all neglected,
   His fond heart with anguish torn.

Then, to crown his bosom's sorrow,
   News was whisper'd in his ear,
Clara on the coming morrow,
   Would a lordling's bride appear.

Wild, distracted, mad with phrenzy,
   To the father's house he flew,
There determin'd to behold her,
   And to breathe his last adieu.

Joyous on the nuptial even,
   Round the sparkling festal board,
With a crowd of guests carousing,
   Sat this rich and haughty lord.

Left a moment unattended,
   Clara soon that moment seiz'd,
First to heav'n her sire commended,
   Then fled from home, tho' weeping, pleas'd.

Henry gain'd the castle portal,
   A footstep Clara's fears alarm'd;
She stops,—she lists,—they came,—fast panting,
   Henry caught her in his arms.

Now no time for fond endearments,
   Swift on wings of love they fled;
Till from father's house far distant,
   Father's frowns no more they dread.

Then before the sacred altar,
    They in wedlock join'd their hands :
Long their souls had been united
    In indissoluble bands.

Now with virtuous rapture burning,
    Whilst fond hope encreas'd the flame :
Tow'rds their home again returning,
    To this lonesome place they came.

Christian, shall I close my story ?
    Words can never tell the tale ;—
To relate a scene so bloody,
    All the pow'rs of language fail.

In that glen so dark and dismal,
    Five ruffians met this youthful pair :
Long the lover bravely struggled,
    Fought to save his bride so fair.

But at last, o'erpowr'd and breathless,
    Faint he sinks beneath their pow'r :
Joyful shouts the demon Murder,
    In this gloomy midnight hour.

Bids them not to rest with plunder,
    But their souls with rage inspires,
All their dark and flinty bosoms,
    With infernal malice fires.

High they lift the murd'rous weapon,
    Wretches, hear ye not her cries !
High they lift the murd'rous weapon !
    Lo ! her love, her husband dies !

Derbyshire Ballads.

Rocks, why stood ye so unmoved ?
   Earth, why op'dst thou not thy womb ?
Lightnings, tempests, did ye slumber ?
   Scap'd these hell-hounds instant doom !

High they lift the murd'rous weapon,
   Who can 'bide her piercing shriek ?
'Tis done——the dale is wrapt in silence,
   On their hands her life-blood reeks.

Dark and darker grows the welkin,
   Through the dale the whirlwind howls ;
On its head the black cloud low'ring,
   Threat'ning now, the grey rock scowls.

Conscience, where are now thine arrows ?
   Does the murd'rer feel the smart ?
Death and Grave, where are your terrors ?
   Written in the murd'rer's heart.

Yes, he sees their ghastly spectres
   Ever rising on his view ;
Eyes wide glaring,—face distorted,
   Quiv'ring lips of livid hue.

Ever sees the life-blood flowing,
   Ever feels the reeking stream,
Ever hears *his* last weak groaning,
   Mingled with *her* dying scream.

Christians, I have told my ditty,
   If you shudder not with fear,
If your breasts can glow with pity,
   Can you now withhold a tear ?

The Gipsies' Song.

FOR the following curious old Derbyshire song I am indebted to my good friend James Orchard Halliwell, F.S.A. It occurs in Playford's "Musical Companion," printed in 1673, and has not, so far as I am aware, been reprinted till now. "Honest John Playford," who was a printer as well as clerk of the Temple Church, London, published several of the most famous music-books of his day, and which at the present time are of the most service of any in determining the dates and names of tunes to which the old ballads, &c., were sung. In 1651 he published "A Musical Banquet, in three books, consisting of Lessons for the Lyra Viol, Allmains, and Sarabands, choice Catches and Rounds, &c.;" and again with the title, "A Banquet of Musick, set forth in three several varieties of Musick: first, Lessons for the Lyra Violl; the second, Ayres and Jiggs for the Violin; the third, Rounds and Catches: all which are fitted to the capacity of young practitioners in Music." Among his many other publications, his most famous was "The English Dancing Master, or Plaine and Easie Rules for the Dancing of Country Dances, with the Tune to each Dance," which passed through many editions, with additional tunes, &c. The "Musical Companion" was first published in 1673, and from this edition the following "Gipsies' Song" and music are taken. The work contained two hundred and eighteen compositions, of which one hundred and forty-three were catches and rounds, and the remainder glees, airs, part-songs, &c. This work was highly popular, and between the years 1673 and 1730 it passed through ten editions.

The "Gipsies' Song" here given was for two voices, and was composed by Robert Johnson.

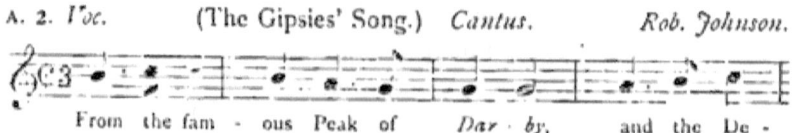

Derbyshire Ballads. 281

vil's A— that's hard by; where we year-ly make our mus-ters; There the *Gyp-sies* throng in clus-ters. Be not fright-ed with our fashion, though we seem a tatter'd Na-tion; We account our Raggs our Rich-es, so our tricks ex-ceed our stitches: Give us Ba-con, Rinds of Wal-nuts, Shells of Cockels and of Small Nuts: Ribonds, Bells, and Saffron Lin-nin; And all the World is ours to win in.

THE

Flax-Dresser's Wife of Spondon,

AND THE POUND OF TEA.

THE following ballad, recounting the droll mistake made by a woman at Spondon, near Derby, who thought *green* tea was to be boiled as *greens*, and eaten accordingly as "cabbage and bacon," was printed in the "spirit of English wit," in 1809. It tells its own tale. It may be well to remark that flax was, some years ago, much grown in this part of Derbyshire: some meadows at Duffield through which the turnpike road passes, are still known by the name of *Flax-holmes*.

'TWAS more than fifty years ago,
    In Spondon's simple village,
Spondon, in Derbyshire, I trow,
    Well known for useful tillage.

There dwelt a pair of simple souls—
    The husband a flax-dresser;
His wife dressed victuals for his jowls,
    And darn'd his hose—God bless her.

Now these poor folks had got a friend,
    Who dwelt in London city;
And oft some present he would send
    To John and dame, in pity.

Now, reader, if you'll backwards turn,
    And read this tale's beginning,
Full half-a-century you'll learn
    This story has been spinning.

Now near that time, you must be told,
    Tea first came into fashion;
Tea, which oft made a husband scold,
    And bounce about in passion.

At least, 'mongst those of middling life
    It made a hideous riot;
To have a gay tea-drinking wife,
    A man could ne'er be quiet.

'Twas thought as bad as now, I ween,—
  A sin since then grown bigger,—
Were a man's wife, by guzzling gin,
  To cut a reeling figure.

But London, who drank tea the first,
  Grew reconcil'd unto it;
And, though 'twas thought of crimes the worst,
  The ladies still would do it.

Now, reader, the flax-dresser's friend
  (The flax-dresser of Spondon)
Thought a good pound of tea he'd send
  To please them both from London.

But he forgot, good man, I trow,
  That in this favoured nation,
Good things, or bad, still travel slow,
  Like cow-inoculation.

Nor ever dreamt, you may believe,
  That they had no more notion
What was the gift they did receive,
  Than of the Western Ocean.

So when it came, long ponder'd they
  How 'twas to be devour'd;
They wish'd he'd sent some hint to say,
  For they were quite o'erpower'd.

At length, right well they both agreed
  'Twere best it should be taken,
By way of greens, when next they'd need,
  With some of their fat bacon.

Next day arrived, the flax-man's wife
    Set on her sauce-pan flattish,
Popp'd in the tea, then took a knife
    And cut some bacon fattish.

The bacon soon enough was done,
    But still the tea, so evil,
Kept very tough—the clock struck One;
    She wish'd it at the devil.

For at the hour of noon each day,
    These humble friends of labour
Took their plain meal—nor only they,
    For so did every neighbour.

Finding it hard, though tasted oft,
    She bawl'd out like a sinner,
"This cursed stuff will ne'er be soft,
    So, John! come down to dinner."

The Ashborne Foot-Ball Song.

ON page 118 I have spoken of the game of foot-ball as played at Derby. Ashborne was also one of the strongholds of this manly game, and in that pleasant little town it has been played from time immemorial, until "put down" by the strong arm of the law—not without much unpleasantness and strenuous opposition—a few years ago. The following song was sung (and I believe written) by Mr. Fawcett, the comedian, at the Ashborne theatre, on the 26th of February, 1821.

I'll sing you a song of a neat little place,
    Top full of good humour and beauty and grace;

Where coaches are rolling by day and by night,
And in playing at Foot-Ball the people delight.
Where health and good humour does always abound,
And hospitality's cup flows freely around,
Where friendship and harmony are to be found,
In the neat little town of Ashborne.

Shrove Tuesday, you know, is always the day,
When pancake's the prelude, and Foot-Ball's the play,
Where upwards and downwards men ready for fun,
Like the French at the Battle of Waterloo run.
And well may they run like the devil to pay,
'Tis always the case as I have heard say,
If a Derbyshire Foot-Ball man comes in the way,
In the neat little town of Ashborne.

There's Mappleton, Mayfield, Okeover and Thorpe,
Can furnish some men that nothing can whop,
And Bentley and Tissington always in tune,
And Clifton and Sturston are ready as soon.
Then there's Snelston and Wyaston, Shirley and all,
Who all are good men at brave Whittaker's call;
And who come to kick at Paul Gettliffe's Foot-Ball,
In the neat little town of Ashborne.

The Ball is turn'd up, and the Bull Ring's the place,
And as fierce as a bull-dog's is every man's face;
Whilst kicking and shouting and howling they run,
Until every stitch in the Ball comes undone.
There's Faulkner and Smith, Bodge Hand and some
    more,
Who hide it and hug it and kick it so sore,

And deserve a good whopping at every man's door
In the neat little town of Ashborne.

If they get to the Park the upwards men shout
And think all the downwards men put to the rout,
But a right about face they soon have to learn,
And the upwards men shout and huzza in their turn.
Then into Shaw Croft where the bold and the brave,
Get a ducking in trying the Foot-Ball to save;
For 'tis well known they fear not a watery grave,
In defence of the Foot-Ball at Ashborne.

If into Church Street should the Ball take its way,
The White Hart and Wheat Sheaf will cause some
  delay,
For from tasting their liquor no man can refrain,
Till he rolls like the Foot-Ball in Warin's tear-brain.
Then they run and they shout, they bawl and they
  laugh,
They kick and huzza, still the liquor they quaff
Till another Foot-Ball has been cut into half,
By the unfair players of Ashborne.

The Parson's Torr.

THE following admirable ballad, the production of the Rev. W. R. Bell, formerly curate of Bakewell, is founded partly on *facts*, and partly on *local traditions*. The unfortunate hero of the story was the Rev. Robert Lomas, Incumbent of Monyash, who was found dead, as described in the ballad, on the 12th of October, 1776. The scene of the ballad comprises the towns of Bakewell and

Monyash, and the mountainous country between them, the western part of which—that bordering on Lathkiln and Harlow Dales—being one of the most romantic districts of the Peak. The ballad first appeared in the "Reliquary," in 1864.

THE Parson of Monyash, late one eve,
    Sat in his old oak arm-chair:
And a playful flame in the low turf fire
    Oft-times shewed him sitting there.

What was it that made that kind-hearted man
    Sit pensively there alone?
Did other men's sorrows make sad his heart?
    Or, say—a glimpse of his own?

Black dark was that night and stormy withal,
    It rained as 'twould rain a sea;
And round and within the old Parsonage house
    The wind moaned piteously.

Still sat he deep musing till midnight hour,
    And then in a waking dream—
He quailed to hear mid the tempest a crash,
    And eke a wild piercing scream.

O mercy! cried he, with faltering breath,
    What sounds are these which I hear?
May evil be far from both me and mine!
    Good Lord, be thou to us near!

No longer sat he in that old arm-chair,
    But prayed and lay down in bed:
And strove hard to sleep, and not hear the storm
    That scowled and raged o'er his head.

But sleep seldom comes when 'tis most desired,
    And least to a troubled mind ;
And the Parson lay wake long time, I ween,
    Ere soft repose he could find.

As the dark hours of night passed slowly on,
    He slept as weary man will ;
But light was his sleep, and broken his rest,
    And sad his fore-dread of ill.

Thus restless he lay, and at early dawn
    He dream'd that he fell amain,
Down —down an abyss of fathomless depth,
    Loud shrieking for help in vain.

He woke up at once with a sudden shock,
    And threw out his arms wide-spread ;
"Good heavens!" he gasped, "what ill-omen is this?
    "Where am I—with quick or dead?"

Right well was he pleased to find 'twas a dream—
    That still he was safe and sound :
With the last shades of night, fear passed away,
    And joy once again came round.

The morning was calm, and the storm was hushed,
    Nor wind nor rain swept the sky ;
And betimes he arose, for bound was he
    To Bakewell that day to hie.

Old Hugh brought his horse to the garden gate,
    And saw him all safe astride ;
"Good-bye!" quoth the Parson : quoth Hugh, "good-bye !
    I wish you a pleasant ride !"

Forth rode he across the lone trackless moor,
    His thoughts on his errand bent
And hoped he right soon to come back again
    The very same way he went.

The journey to Bakewell he safely made
    A little before mid-day:
But Vicar and people were all at church,*
    Where they were oft wont to pray.

"I'll put up my beast," quoth the Parson, "here,
    At the White Horse hostelry; †
And go up to Church, that when prayers are done,
    The Vicar I there may see."

But ere he could reach the Old Newark door, ‡
    Both Priest and people were gone;
And the Vicar to soothe a dying man,
    To Over-Haddon sped on.

'Twas three past noon when the Vicar came back,
    The Parson he asked to dine,
And time stole a march on the heedless guest,
    Six struck as he sat at wine.

Up rose he from table and took his leave,
    Quite startled to find it late;
He called for his horse at the hostelry,
    And homeward was soon agate.

---

* At the *Friday* morning service.   † Now called the *Rutland Arms*.
‡ The door in the south transept, locally called the *Newark* door.

As he rode up the hill, past All Saints' Church,
    The moon just one glance bestowed,
And the wierd-like form of the old Stone Cross,
    In the Church-yard, dimly shewed.

Still higher and higher he climbed the hill,
    Yet more and more dark it grew;
The drizzling rain became sleet as he climbed,
    And the wind more keenly blew.

Ah! thick was the mist on the moor that night,
    Poor wight, he had lost his way!
The north-east wind blowing strong on his right,
    To the left had made him stray.

And now he was close to lone Haddon Grove,
    Bewildered upon the moor;
Slow leading his horse that followed behind,
    Himself groping on before.

Still onward and leeward, at last he came
    To the edge of Harlow Dale;
From his cave* the Lathkil a warning roared,
    But louder then howled the gale.

On the brink of Fox Torr the doomed man stood,
    And tugged the bridle in vain;
His horse would not move—then quick started back,
    And, snap, went each bridle-rein!

---

* The river Lathkil issues from a cavern in the limestone rock, directly opposite the Parson's Torr.

Then headlong fell he o'er the lofty cliff,
    He shrieked, and sank in the gloom;
Down—down to the bottom he swiftly sped,
    And death was his dreadful doom.

The dead man lay cold on the blood-stained rocks—
    The darkness did him enshroud;—
And the owls high up in the ivy-clad Torr,
    Bewailed him all night full loud.

O little thought they in the old thatched cot,
    Hard by the Parsonage gate;
Their master they never again should see,
    Nor ope to him soon nor late!

"This night is no better than last," quoth Hugh,
    "And master has not come back;
I hope he is hale and safe housed with friends,
    And has of good cheer no lack."

Quoth Betty, "I liked not his morning ride—
    I fear he's in evil plight—
A Friday's venture's, no luck! I've heard say,
    God help him if out this night."

At dawn of next day, old Betty went forth
    To milk the cow in the shed;—
And saw him sitting upon a large stone,
    All pale, and mute—with bare head.

But a moment she turned her eyes away,
    A fall she heard and a groan;

She looked again, but, no Parson was there,
    He'd vanished from off the stone!

Soon spread the dread tale through Monyash town—
    They made a great hue and cry;
And some off to this place—and some to that,
    To seek the lost man did hie.

Bad tidings from Bakewell—no Parson there—
    No parson could else be found;
'Twas noon, yet no tidings—they still searched on,
    And missed they no likely ground.

At last the searchers went into the Dale,
    And there at the foot of Fox Torr—
They found the Parson, all cold and dead,
    'Mong the rocks all stained with gore.

They took up his corse—and six stalwart men,
    Slowly bore it along the Dale;
And they laid the dead in his house that night,
    And many did him bewail.

When time had passed over—a day or twain,
    They buried him in the grave;
And his bones now rest in the lone Churchyard,
    Till doomsday them thence shall crave.

O dread was the death of that luckless man—
    Not soon will it be forgot;
The dismal story—for ages to come—
    Will often be told, I wot.

You may not now see in Monyash town
   The deadman's sear tuft of grass ;
But still it is there, in memory stored,
   And thence it never shall pass.

You may not now find Fox Torr by that name,
   The swain thus knows it no more ;
But pointing thereat from the Lathkil grot,
   He'll shew you the Parson's Torr.

And now, my dear friends, what more need I say?
   I've told you the story through :—
If you've in the least been pleased with my song,
   Then I am well-pleased with you.

INDEX.

∗ In the following Index the titles of the Ballads are given in SMALL CAPITALS, and the first lines in *italics*.

A BALLAD OF DERBYSHIRE, 7
A DAY IN THE WOODLANDS, 237
A JOURNEY INTO THE PEAK, 257, 259
A NEW SONG ON THE GREAT FOOT-RACE AT DERBY, 252
A PEAK BALLAD, 274
A POEM FOUND BY MR. * * * AND DEDICATED TO MAJOR TROWELL, 190
A RHAPSODY ON THE PEAK OF DERBYSHIRE, 248
A STRANGE BANQUET, OR THE DEVIL'S ENTERTAINMENT BY COOK LAUREL AT THE PEAK IN DERBYSHIRE, 125
Abington, 180
Adam Bell, 75
ADDRESS TO "DICKIE," 226
Agincourt, Battle of, et seq., 8
AGRICULTURAL MEETING, 160
Alderwasley, 269
Ale, Derby, 11, 129, 142
—— Cakes and, 60
Aldermary Church Yard, 1
"*All you that delight in merriment,*" 119
Allestree, 268, 273
ALL SAINTS' CHURCH, DERBY, 206
Alfreton, 267
Alvaston, 269
Allan-a-Dale, 100
Alroes, Lord, 52
Alton Towers, 134, 135, 273
Alton Lodge, 273
Amber, 151
AN ADDRESS TO "DICKIE," 226
"Angler, Complete," 257

AN ELEGY UPON THE DEATH OF THE GREATEST GENTRY IN DARLEY DALE, 146
Anne, St. Well, 10
ANTHONY BABINGTON'S COMPLAINTE, 164
Ap. Thomas, Sir Rees, 45, 49, 52
Arabella Stuart, 222
Archer's Wall, 102
Ardglass, Countess of, 257
Arnold, 270
"*As I sat musing by the fire,*" 255
"*As our king lay musing in his bed,*" 2, 3, 4
"*As I was going to Darby, Sir,*" 115
"*Arthur a Bradley,*" 83
"*As I on Oker Hill one day did stand,*" 147
"*As I to Ireland did pass,*" 223
Ashborne, 6, 83, 132, 133, 135, 263, et seq., 269, 272, 284—286
ASHBORNE FOOT-BALL SONG, 284
Ashborne Inns, 286
—————— bull-ring, 285
—————— "tear brain," 286
—————— theatre, 284
Ashop, river, 237
Ashopton, 237, 238, 242
Ashford-in-the-Water, 130, 255
Ashmole, Elias, 92
—————— autograph, 292
Ashover, 146, 152, 239 et seq., 267
Ashton, 269
ASHUPTON GARLAND, 237
Atlow, 269, 272
"*Attend, ye jolly gardeners,*" 184
"*At length my wandering feet have brought,*" 243

INDEX.

Audley End, 11
Autograph, Anthony Babington, 165
────── ────── Arabella Stuart, 222
────── ────── Elias Ashmole, 92
Aurora Borealis, ballad on, 64
Axe Edge, 143, 245
Ayscough, William, 65
Babington family, 151, 164—181
Babington, Antony, Complainte, 164
Bakewell, 66, 130, 131, 245, 268, 280, et seq
BALLAD OF DERBYSHIRE, 7
────── ────── Hero Robin Hood, 73
Bage, 148
Baske, 148
Ballard, 175
Bank Hall, 142, 143
Banks, Sir Joseph, 152
Bannard, James, 243, 246
Barking Barbers, 199
Barnwell, 175
Barrow-upon-Soar, 269
BACHELORS OF DARBY, THE UNCONSCIONABLE, 58
Basford, 270
Bath, 157
Ballad, a Peak, HENRY AND CLARA 274
Bateman, Thomas, 12, 129
Bath, 8
Beggars' Well, 266
Beeston, 267
Beaumaris, 25
BEGGAR'S RAMBLE, 266
BEGGAR'S WELLS, 176
Beggarley, 270
Bellamy, 176
Bell, Adam, 75
Belper, 268
Bellman of London, 126
Belvoir, 267
Bennett, William, 67, 96, 230
Beresford Hall, 257, 261
Bessy, Song of the Lady, 12
Begrammes Abbey, 39, 43
Bessel, J., Printer,) 61
Bentley, 271
Bell, Rev. W. R., 286
Bessick, 271
BEGGAR'S RAMBLE, THE, 271

Birchover, 147
Blackwell, 267
Blakely Oldhurst, 134
BLINK-EYED COBBLER, 119
BLUE'S VALOUR DISPLAYED, 129
Blesford Hall, 272
Blyfield, 274
Bonner, Sir William, 46
Boothby, ────── 7, 135
Boyce, Dr., 209
Bottle Brook, 268
Bolt Edge Moor, 232
Bosworth Field, 47, 48
Bolesworth field, 47, 48
Bonsall, 268
Boar, Blue, 49, 75
Bow Lane, 1
Bow, wow, wow, 199
Bowden, 231, 233
Bood, 142
Borleyash, 274
Broxter, 270
Brailsford, 261
Brown, Samuel, 268
Bridgeford, 270
Breadsall, 268
Bramcote, 267
Bradford, 135
Brickhill, 261
Brackenbury, 14, et seq.
Browne, 134
Brierlow, 245
Brereton, Humphry, 12, et seq.
BRADSHAW, EPISTLE TO JOHN, 258
Brimlow, John, 255, 256
Brome, Henry, 263
Bromefield, 13
Brightside, 153
Bradley, 272
Bradley, Arthur A', 83
Brunsley Gin, 271
Breaston, 271
Brailsford Hall, 272
Braston, 272
Brassington, 272
Bradburn, 272
Breedon on the Hill, 273
Branshall, 274
Bramest, 274
Butler, 275
Bradshaw, 275

INDEX.

Bull, 74, 75, 79—81
Bullets, 10
Buxton, 8, 66, 68, 96—103, 227, 228, 243, 244, 272
—— Advertiser, 228
BUCKSTONE, LAY OF THE, 96
Buckingham, 30
Bulcote, 270
"Burlesque upon Burlesque," 257
Burning in a Tun, 17
Burton-on-Trent, 269
Burton Joyce, 270
Bull-running, 73, 74, 79, 80, 81
BUTCHER, DRUNKEN, OF TIDES-
    WELL, 66
Burslem, 274
Calverton, 270
Calton family, 148
Carlton, 276
Calton, 148
Calthorpe, 270
Castle Naze works, 142
Cakes and ale, 60
Calver, 269
Callcott, 115, 269
CAT, WHITTINGTON AND HIS, 103
Cat and Fiddle, 245
Cambridge, Duke of, 2, 273
—— 7, 255, 273
Castleton, 68, 92, 125—129, 274, 275, 280
—— a strange banquet at, 125, 230, 331
Cards, game at, for a kingdom, 64
Candles, 23
Cap of maintenance, 128
Carnarvon, 25
"Cavalier," 67
Cavendish, Sir William, 222
—— Elizabeth, Countess of, 222
Caldon, 272
Caulton, 272
Carsdale, 272
Cecil, 222
Celestial bard, 193
Chappell, W., 3, 62, 110
Chapel-en-le-Frith, 62, 68, 69, 97, 102, 142, 143, 204, 226, 231
Chamber Knoll, 71
Charcoal, 23

Chatsworth, 11, 222, 269, 275
Chaddesden, 268
Cheadle, 273
Checkley in the Hole, 274
Cheetham, Library, 1
Chester, Ranulph, Earl of, 236
Cheshire, 5, 13 et seq., 39, 40, 56, 58, 230
Chesterfield, 104, 267
—— Earl of, 257
Chee Tor, 245
Cheetham Hill, 230
Chester,
—— West, 26
Chevy Chace, 196
Chilwell, 267
Chirk Land, 13
Choir of All Saints' Church, 206
"*Christians, to my tragic ditty,*" 274
—— thunder at, 274, 275
Cider, 60
Cinder Hills, 270
CLARA, HENRY AND, 274
Claret, 11
Clay Cross, 267
Clarence, Duke of, 14, et seq.
Clifton, 285
Clifton Grove, 270
Clim of the Clough, 75, 100
Clorinda (Maid Marian), 74 et seq.
Clough, Clim of the, 75, 100
Clowdeslee, William of, 75, 100
COBLER, THE BLINK-EYED, 119
COCK TAIL REEL, 153
Cock Lorel, or Cook Laurel, 125
Comical Scotch dialogue, 64
Coke family, 135, 137, et seq., 187 to 203
Cokain, Sir Aston, notice of, 6, 7
—— Ballad of Derbyshire, 6
—— Poems, 7
—— portrait of, 7
—— Journey into the Peak, 257
Cokain, Thomas, 6, **7**
Coke, Daniel Parker, 187—
COOK LAUREL'S ENTERTAINMENT
    TO THE DEVIL, 125
—— note, 126
Cook, Eliza, 246

Cook, 275
"Cook Laurel would have the Devil his guest," 126
Colepepper Col., 55
Coloton Green, 274
Collyer, J. Payne, 179
Colvile, C. R., 161
Collumbell, 149
"Complete Gamester," 257
"Commentaries of De Montlac," 257
COMPLAINTE OF ANTHONIE BABINGTON, 164
Combs Moss, 97, 102
"Come lasses and lads," 61
"Come all you gallant lasses of courage stout and bold," 129
"Come gather round and form a throng," 160
"Complete Angler," 257, et seq.
"Come hark you well, my masters, pray can you me tell," 271
"Coming home into this frozen clime," 258
Congleton, 143
Cooper, W. Durant, 164
Coopland, 24
Cosel, 267
Cottage of Content, 243
Cotherm: y. 271
Cotton, Charles, 7, 257--263
——————— Journey into the Peak, 257
——————— Epistle to John Bradshaw, 259
——————— list of his works, 257
——————— MS. poems, 257
——————— Poems on Several Occasions, 257
——————— life of, 257
——————— Complete Angler, 257
Coventry, 262
Coventry, 75
Cowley, 169
Coxbench, 268
Crapnidge, 274
Crich, 152, 162
Cromford, 269, 272
Crompton, John Bell, 162

Croome, 245
Cropwell, 270
Cross-o'th-hands, 268
Crumpswood, 273
Cubley, 207
Dakin, 152
Dale, 271
DANBY, LORD, DEVONSHIRE'S NOBLE DUEL WITH, 55
Darnall Park, 25
Darley, 273
Darley Abbey, 269
DARLEY DALE, ELEGY UPON THE DEATH OF THE GREATEST GENTRY, 146
——————— 269
Date Obelum Belisario, 199
DEATH OF REV. BACHE THORNHILL, 255
Deaf Stone, 11
"Dear Polyhymnie be," 7
"Declare, O Muse, what demon 'twas," 111
Deincourt, 210
Delamere forest, 13, et seq.
——————— Lord, 55, et seq.
Delaware, Lord, 58
Deloney, Thomas, 179
Denby, 268
Derby, Earl of, 8, 12, et seq.
Derby, 6, 7, 115, et seq., 269
DERBY RAM, 115
Derby, 182, 183, 280, 281
Derby, Agricultural Meeting, 160
——————— Nun's Green, Songs on, 187—
DERBY BLUES, 129, 184
DERBY HERO, 249
Derby hills, 1, 243
——————— ale, 11, 129
——————— UNCONSCIONABLE BACHELORS OF, 58
——————— lasses of, 58
——————— races, 118
——————— FLORIST'S SONG, 206
Derbyshire Volunteers, 2, 131
——————— Militia, 115, 182, 192
DERBYSHIRE, A BALLAD OF, 6
DERBYSHIRE, NEW BALLAD OF ROBIN HOOD, 73
DERBYSHIRE MILLER, 110

DERBYSHIRE MEN, 145
DERBYSHIRE MILITIA, SONG IN PRAISE OF, 182
DERBYSHIRE HILLS, 243
DERBYSHIRE DALES, 246
DERBYSHIRE, A RHAPSODY ON, 248
Derrick, Samuel, 157
Derwent, river, 8, 237, 241, 268
——— village, 237
Derwentwater, Lord, 55
Dethick, 151, 164—181
DEVONSHIRE'S NOBLE DUEL, 55
——— ——— Duke of, 55, et seq., 157, 183, 263, 265, 275
——— ——— Long-Arm'd Duke, 55
——— ——— Duchess of, 57
——— ——— Yorkshire Pie, 157
Diamond Hill, 245
Dibden, 198
Dicey, W., 74
Dick Whittington, 103
Dickie of Tunstead, 226
"DICKIE," AN ADDRESS TO, 226
Diseworth, 273
Dixon, H., 1
Donnington, 273
Dob Holes, 268
Doctor Double Ale, 126
Dove, river, 247
Doveridge, 83, 274
Dove Dale, 247, 257, et seq.
——— river, 257 et seq.
Doune, 7
Draycott, 271
Drawn with wild horses, 17
Drayton, 7
Draycott, Philip, 170
DRIVING OF THE DEER, 230
Dronfield, 153
DRUNKEN BUTCHER OF TIDESWELL, 66
Duckinfield, 230
Dudley, W., 207
——— S., 207
Duel, Devonshire's noble, 55
Duffield, 268, 281
Dunstable, 261
Dunchurch, 262
Durham, Bishop of, 46

Durintwood, 134
Eagles Foot, 35
Eastwood, 271
Eaton, 267, 274
Ebbing and flowing well, 10
Edale, 230
Edward IV., 12
Edwards, 149
Eldon Hole, 10, 275
——— Hill, 232
Ellaston, 273
ELEGY UPON THE DEATH OF THE GREATEST GENTRY OF DARLEY DALE, 146
Elizabeth of York, 12
Elvaston, 6, 257, 269
Entcliffe Hill, 130, 131
Eperstone, 270
EPISTLE TO JOHN BRADSHAW, ESQ., 258
Epsom, 10
Espernon, Duke of, 257
Etwall 269
Eyre, family, 129, 147
"Fair one of Tunis," 257
Fairfield, 78
Fair, Humours of Hayfield, 61
——— Nottingham Goose, 58, et seq.
"*Farewell our daddies and our mammies*," 182
Farley, 273
Farnfield, 24
Faulkner, 285
Fawcett's Ashborne Foot-ball Song, 284
Ferrars, Lord, 41, 132
Findern, 269
Firby, 268
Firbeck, 267
Fitzwarine, Sir Hugh, 104
——— ——— Alice, 104
——— ——— Maud, 104
Flash, 271
FLAX-DRESSER'S WIFE OF STONDON AND THE POUND OF TEA, 281
Flax-holmes, 281
FLORISTS' SONG, 206
FLORIST'S SONG, 184
Florist's society, 184
Fludyer, 157

INDEX.

Fole. 274
Foljamb, 67
Forest, Delamere, 13, et seq.
"*For Jesus' sake be merry and glad*," 12
Foston, 273
Foot-ball, game of, 118
────── Derby, 118, 284
FOOT-BALL SONG, ASHBORNE, 284
Foot-ball at Ashborne, 284, et seq.
FOX CHASE, SQUIRE VERNON'S, 131
Fox, family, 118, 227
Fox Low, 245
Fox Torr, 290, 292, 293
France, conquest of, 1
French King, 1, 4
FRITH, SQUIRE, HUNTING SONG, 142
Frith, Samuel, 142
Fools, strips of, 16
"*From the famous Peak of Darby*," 281
Gage, 180
Gallow's Inn, 271
Game at cards for a kingdom, 64
────── cakes and ale, 60
"Gamester, Complete," 257
Gamwell of Gamwell Hall, 75, 76
GARLAND OF MERRIMENT, 64
GARLAND, ASHUPTON, 237
Gaunt, John of, 79, 188—203
Gautriss Dale, 232
Gawn, 118
Gawsworth, 143
Gedling, 270
Gell, Colonel Thomas, 210
────── Sir John, 210
George Inn, 273
George III., 2
Gerrard, Sir Gilbert, 177
Getliffe, 285
Ghent, John of, 79, 188—203
Ghost, 71, 72
Giltbrook, 270
Gingler's Inn, 269
Gipsies metamorphosed, 126
GIPSIES' SONG, THE, 280
"*God that is moste of myghte*," 54
"*God prosper long fair Derby town*," 196

"*Good people give attention to a story you shall hear*," 55
Gosley Bank, 272
Goose Fair, 58, et seq.
Gotham, 210, 270
Gray, 210
Graceley, 143
Greaves, 147
Greensmith, 149
Greene, 209
GREEN, HUGH STENSON AND MOLLY, 263
Gresley, 270
Greswark, 144
Gretna Green, 274
Grindleford Bridge, 92
Guards, brigade of, 2
Gunthorpe, 270
Gutch, John Mathew, 73
Guy, Earl of Warwick, 75
Habbington, 7
Haddon Hall, 131, 148, 245
────── Over, 289
────── Grove, 290
Haines, William, 92
Hall, 275
Halliwell, J. O., 280
Hand, 285
Halliwell Collection, 1, 12
Handford, Tom, 136—142
Hansley, 267
Handel, 209
Harpham, 157
Harden, 13
Harestan, 210
Harrington, Earl of, 6, 257
"*Hark, hark, brother sportsmen, what a melodious sound*," 143
Harehill, 273
Harton, 273
Harlow Dale, 280, 290
Harleian MSS., 54
Hardstaff, 267
"*Hark you well, you neighbours all, and pray now can you tell*," 266
Harrington, Sir William, 46, 51
Hardwick, Earl of, 160, 161
────── Bess of, 222
Hartington, "strange and wonderful sight" there, 64
Hartington, 64, 66

Hathersage, 85, 91, 92
Hassop, 147
———— and Little John, 85, et seq., 91, et seq.
———— Little John's grave, &c., 91, 92
Hathenturns, 270
HAYFIELD FAIR, HUMOURS OF, 61
Hayfield, 61, 62
Haymore, 272
Heanor, 271
Helldon Hill, 232
HENRY AND CLARA, a Peak Ballad, 274
"Here must I tell the praise," 105
HERO, DERBY, 249
———— Stafford, 250—254
Hertford, Earl of, 222, 225
Hickham, 267
High Peak, 61, 64, 67, 248, 274, 280
High Church in Shropshire, 264
Highlander, 64
Highgate, 260
Hilson (Ilkeston), 271
Hills, Derby, 1, 5
Hillary, 210
Hood, Robin, 73—103
Hodgkinson, 152
Hogdeston, 273
Hognaston, 269, 272
Holland, George, 267
Hollington, 268
Holt Castle, 12, 19, 24, 45
Holy poker, 199
Horsley, 268
Howitt, Richard, 210
Howsley, 143
Hoyland, 269
HUGH STENSON AND MOLLY GREEN, 263
HUMOURS OF HAYFIELD FAIR, 61
Hunter, Rev. Joseph, 73
Hunting songs, Squire Vernon's Fox Chace, 131
———————— Trusley, 137
———————— Squire Frith's, 142
Hurdle, 17
Hutchinson, Tour through the Peak, 61, 227
———— of Owthorpe, 257
Hyde Park, 2

Hyson Green, 270
"I'll sing you a song of a neat little place," 284
"I sigh for the land where the orange tree flingeth," 246
"I' Darbyshire who're born an' bred," 145
Ilam Hall, 134
Ilkeston, 271
"In summer time when leaves are green," 237
Isle of Man, 13, 18
"Jack Asses' trot," 193
James, King, 56
———— taxes, 55, et seq.
———— treachery of, 57
Jenkinson, 149
Jewitt, Arthur, 248
———— Rev. Arthur George,, 274
————'s "Wanderings of Memory," 274
———————— HENRY AND CLARA, a Peak Ballad, 274
Johnson, 280
Jonson, Ben, 7
Jones, 179, 180
JOURNEY INTO THE PEAK, 257, 259
Kedleston, 269
Kendall, 24
Kent, 26, 73
—— Earl of, 46
Keyworth, 270
"Kind gentlemen will you be patient awhile," 74
King's Mills, 273
KING HENRY V., HIS CONQUEST OF FRANCE, 1
—— Edward IV., 12
—— George III., 2
—— Henry VII., 12
—— Charles II., 12
—— Richard, 50, et seq.
—— James, 56
"—— of the Peak," 67, 133
—— Henry VIII., 67
—— Richard II., 79
—— Castile and Leon, 79
—— George IV., 111
—— George I., 146
—— James I., 164, 222
—— Charles I., 211

INDEX. 301

King William I., 230
Kimberworth, 153
Kimberley, 267
Kinder Scout, 67, 241, 242
Kirk Ireton, 268
Kirke, H., 204
Kirkland, Walter, 145
Kirklees Priory, 91, 93
Kniveton, Sir Gilbert, 7
——————— Mary, 7
Knolls, Sir Frederick, 179
Konynges Dale, 232
Langley Mill, 271
LADY BESSY, Song of the, 12
Lady Low, 97
Lady Arabella Stuart, 222—
Lambley, 270
Lancashire, 5, 49, 105
Lancaster, Duke of, 79, 187—
Langley, 143, 144, 269
Lasses of Darby pawned by their sweethearts, 58
"*Last night as slumbering on my bed I lay,*" 188
Latham House, 24, et seq.
Lathkiln Dale, 287, 290
——————— River, 290
Latimer, Lord, 46
LAY OF THE BUCKSTONE, 96
Laycock, Samuel, 229
Layksley (see Loxley)
Lead, 272
Lead, 10, 11
Leak, 210
Leake, or Leke, family, 210 et seq.
Lee Lane, 271
Lee, Lord, 41
Leech, Mrs., of Tideswell, 114
Leech Arch, 272, 274
Leicestershire, 117
Leigh, Lord, 41
Leicester, 44, 53
LEKE, SIR FRANCIS, 210
Lennox, Earl of, 222
Lenton, 270
Lichfield, 48, 262
"Life of the Duke of Espernon," 257
Lincoln, 76, 98
Lincolnshire, 58
LINES OCCASIONED BY A YORKSHIRE PIE, 157

Lislay, Lord, 38
Little Hallam, 271
Little Britain, 39, 47
——— Stoone, 47
——— Eaton, 268
Little John, 73—103, 238, et seq.
LITTLE JOHN AND ROBIN HOOD, 85
LITTLE JOHN'S END, 91
Littleover, 269
Liverpool, 39
Locko Grange, 268
Lomas, 286
Longnor, 272
London, 16, et seq., 55, 104, 105, 121, 157, 280, 282, 283
——— great fire of, 104
——— Tower of, 225
Long-Armed Duke, 55
Longstone, 255
Longford, 135, 137, 269, 273
Lordis Seat, 230, 231
"*Lord Pevered stood on the Lordis Seat*" 231
LOST AND DEAD, 204
Loughborough, 270
Lovell, Lord, 46
Lovers' Leap, 244
Lowton, 270
Loxley, 73—103, 274
Ludlow, 14
Lysons, 210
Mackworth, 269, 273
Macclesfield Forest, 143, 144
Maid Marian, 73—103, 238, et seq.
Malpas, 40
Mam Tor, 245
Mammaton, 273
Manners, 148
Manchester, 1, 24, et seq.
Mansfield, 271
Mapperley, 270, 271
Mappleton, 272
Markeaton, 269, 273
Marrot Moor, 267
Mar routed, 64
Martin Markall, 126
Marston, 273
Marpole, 271
Marton, 273
Mary Queen of Scots, 222

Masbro', 153
Massinger, 7
Matlock, 150, 245, 269
May, 7
May pole, 61
Mayfield, 285
Mead, 60
Mercaston, 7
Mercer's Company, 104
Merriment, garland of, 64
Meverell, 67
Mickleover, 269
Middleton, 272
Middleton by Youlgrave, 268
Milford Haven, 43
Militia, Derbyshire, 115, 182
——————— Song in praise of, 182
Milnes, 239, et seq.
Milward, 150, 268
MILLER, THE DERBYSHIRE, 110
Minstrels, 79, 80
Minstrels' Court, 79, 80
——— King of the, 79, 80
Monsal Dale, 247
"Montaigne's Essays," 257
Montlac De, 257
Monyash, 286, et seq.
Moregreen, 271
Morley, 149, 268
Morgan, 173
"Moral Philosophy of the Stoics," 257
Moules dale, 13
Music of "As our King lay musing in his bed," 2
Music of "The Derbyshire Miller," 110
Music of "The Gipsies' Song,"
Mugginton, 269, 273
Mullins, Tom, 132—134
Mundy family, 198, 203
Nares, 209
"Neaw, Dickie, be quiet wi' thee, lad," 228
Nether Green, 271
Netherton, 274
NEW BALLAD OF ROBIN HOOD, shewing his Birth, Breeding, Valour, and Marriage, at Tutbury Bull Running, 73

NEW SONG IN PRAISE OF THE DERBYSHIRE MILITIA, 182
Newton, 267, 273
Newthorpe, 270
Norfolk, Duke of, 46, 52
Northampton, 74
Northern Lights, ballad on, 64
Nottingham, 58, 65, 73, 98, 264
——————— Goose Fair, 58, et seq.
Nottinghamshire, 73—103
NUN'S GREEN RANGERS, 199
Nun's Green, ballads on, 187—203
Nuttall, 270
Oaker Hall, 272
Oakes, James, 237, et seq.
Oakamoor, 273
Obstinate lady, 7
Ockbrook, 268
"Of all your modern heroes," 249
"O give me the land where the wild thyme grows," 248
Ogston, 151
Oker Hill, 147, 153
Okerthorpe, 267
Okeover Hall, 272, 285
Oldacre, 271
OLD NUN'S GREEN, 187
"One Valentine's day in the morning," 137
ON THE STRANGE AND WONDERFUL SIGHT THAT WAS SEEN IN THE AIR ON THE 6TH OF MARCH, 1716..64
ON THE DEATH OF THE LATE REV. BACHE THORNHILL, M.A., 255
"O say not so, Sir Francis," 210
Osgathorpe, 230, et seq.
Osmaston by Ashborne, 133
Over Haddon, 289
Overton, 152
Overton, 274
Overington, 270
Owen, Jack, 143
Owthorpe, 257
Oxford, Earl of, 41
Oxford, 249
Paget, 173
Paislow Moss, 68, 71
Pain, 149
Pantons in the Dale, 273

Paris, 6, 42
Park Nook, 272
Park Hall, 274
PARSON'S TORR, 286
Parwich, 272
PAVING AND LIGHTING. A NEW SONG, 196
Paynslee, 170
Pearcey, General, 265
Peel, Sir Robert, 255
Peak Hills, 272
— — Ballad, HENRY AND CLARA, 274
" Peak, Wonders of the," 257
— — — Tradition of, 2
— — — High, 61, 64, 67, 248, 274, 280
— — — A RHAPSODY ON, 248
— — — JOURNEY INTO THE, 257, 259
— — — Forest, 67, 103, 204, 230, 275
Pedlar and Robin Hood, 3
Percy Society, 1, 12
— — Lord, 46, 52
Pentrich, 267
Perkin Wood, 267
Perwolt, 274
Perry Dale, 232
PEVEREL AND THE DRIVING OF THE DEER, 230
Peverel family, 230, 231, et seq.
PIE, YORKSHIRE, 157
Pills to purge melancholy, 61, 126
Pilsley, 267
Pinder of Wakefield, 74
Pinxstone, 267
Playford, 280
Poems on Nun's Green, 187—203
— — — dedicated to Major Trowel, 192
" — — — upon Several Occasions," 257
Polesworth, 7
Pooley, 6, 7
Poole's Hole, 10
Potter of Hill Top, 268
Pott, 149
POWER OF LOVE, 210
PRESSED MAN'S LAMENTATION, 182
Prestwood, 273

PRINCELY DIVERSION, or the Jovial Hunting Match, 137
PRINCE IN THE TOWN, AND DEVIL IN THE CHURCH, 111
Prince of Wales, George, 111
Printers, J. Bessel, 61
— — — William Ayscough, 65
— — — Wynkende Worde, 73, 126
— — — W. Dicey, 74
— — — R. Raikes, 74
— — — W. O., 126, 137
— — — A. M., 126
— — — J. Deacon, 126
" Planter's Manual," 257
" Puss in Boots," 269, 272
Pursglove, Bishop, 67
QUADRUPEDS, THE, 193
Quarndon, 269, 273
Queen Elizabeth, 164, 165, 225
— — of Scots, Mary, 166—181
Quicksall, 273
Quin, 157
Quintin, St., family, 157, 158
— — — Sir William, 157, 158
Radborne, 137
Radford, 270
Radgley, 273
Raikes, R., 74
Raleigh, Sir Walter, 222
RAM, THE DERBY, 115
RAMBLE, BEGGAR'S, 266
RAMBLE, THE BEGGAR'S, 271
Randolph, 7
Ratcliffe, 270
Rees Ap Thomas, Sir, 45, 49, 52
Red Hill, 270
REEL, COCKTAIL, 157
Recruiting Derby hills, 1, 5
Red Rose, 49—53
Rempstone, 273
Repton, 269
" Reliquary," 65, 73, 92, 97, 145, 164, 287
RHAPSODY ON THE PEAK OF DERBYSHIRE, 248
Riber Hall, 150
Richmond, Duke of, 161
Richard, King, 50, et seq.
Richmond, Margaret, 12, et seq.
— — — Earl of, 12, et seq.
Riddings, 238, et seq.

Ripley, 268
Risley, 271
Robin Hood and the Pedlar, 32
——— A NEW BALLAD OF, 73
——— Lytell geste of, 73
——— AND LITTLE JOHN, 85
——— 73—103, 238, et seq., 270
Robin Hood's marks, 102
Rodsley, 273
Rosemary Hill,
Rosley, 273
Roston, 273
Ross, Lord, 46
Rose of England, 6
Rose, red, 49, 53
Rose, Union of, 53
Rose of Lancaster, 69
Rose and Crown, 268
Rowlands, 126
Row (or Roo) Tor, 147
Rowsley, 269
Rowland of Warburton, 45
Roxburghe Collection, 1, 58, 74, 126
Ruddington, 270
Runcorn, 144
Rural dance about the May-pole, 61
Rushop Edge, 230
Russell, Sir William, 257
Sack, 11
Salisbury, 30, 54
Salford, 24
——— Bridge, 24
Sandall Castle, 19
Sandiacre, 271
Sandys, 7
Sandy Way Head, 68
Savage, 175
Savage, Sir John, 19, 49
Scarsdale, 210
——— Lord, 210
Scarlet, Will, 100
Scotch dialogue, 64
Scrope, Lord, 46
Selston, 267
Seymour, Lord, 222
Shallcross, 144
Shardlow, 269
Shaw, the Staffordshire hero, 252
Shaws Croft, 286
Sheepshead, 270

Sheffield, 31, 74, 239, et seq.
——— Castle, 31
Sheppards Folly, 269
Sherwood Forest, 73—103, 270
Sherry, Cary, 7
——— Mary, 7
Ship of fools, 126
Shipley Wood, 271
Shipley, 271
Shirley Park, 132, 285
——— family, 132
Shoolbottam, 271
Shottle, 268
Shootingslow, 245
"*Should the French but presume on our coast to appear*," 182
Shrewsbury, Earl of, 12, et seq., 222
——— 43, 45
Shrove Tuesday, 285
Sign of the Eagle's foot, 35
——— Bull, 75
——— George, 112
——— Angel, 126, 184
——— White Horse, 131
——— Rutland Arms, 289
——— White Hart, 286, 289
——— Wheat Sheaf, 286
——— Sun, 263
——— Rose and Crown, 268
——— Puss in Boots, 269
Sigsmore, 272
Sinfin Moor, 118
SIR RICHARD WHITTINGTON'S ADVANCEMENT, 104
SIR FRANCIS LEKE; or the Power of Love, 210
Skiers, 238, et seq.
Skull at Tunstead, 226
Slack, 71
Sloman, Charles, 110
Smalley, 268
Smith, 197, 285
Smock frock, 64
Snelston, 267, 285
Snitterton, 150
Solomon's Temple, 243, 245
SONG, 206
SONG OF THE LADY BESSY, 12
SONG, ASHBORNE FOOT-BALL, 284
SONG, THE GIPSIES', 280
"*Soon as old Ball was got better*," 153

SONG (a satirical attack on the Choir of All Saints' Church, Derby) 206
South Normanton, 267
Southwell, 270
Sparrowpit, 68
Spencer, Earl 161
SPONDON, THE FLAX-DRESSER'S WIFE OF, AND THE POUND OF TEA, 281
Spondon, 268, 281–284
SQUIRE VERNON'S FOX CHACE, 131
St. Albans, 261
St. Ann's Well, 10
St. Michael's ground, 93
St. Quintin Sir William, 157
Stafford, 45, 47, 250, et seq.
——— Hero, 250, et seq.
Staffordshire, 73, 230
Stainsby, 268
Stancliffe Hall, 148
Stanhope, Sir John, 6, 257
——— Earl, 257
Stanley, Earls of Derby, 12, et seq.
——— family, 12, et seq.
Stapleford, 271
Stanton 255, 273
Staysmore 272
STENSON, HUGH, AND MOLLY GREEN, 263
Steare, 148
Stoics, Moral Philosophy of, 257
Stone, Staffordshire, 47, 48
Stone, Little, 47
Stoone, Little, 47
Stramshall, 274
STRANGE AND WONDERFUL SIGHT AT HARTINGTON, 64
Strange, Lord George, 12, et seq.
Stratford, 261
Strensham, 257
Stretton on the Hill, 267
Strutt, 197
Stuart, Arabella, 222—
——— Charles, 222
Sturston, 285
Stutely, Will, 89, 90
Suckling, 7
Sudbury Hall, 131, 136
Surrey, Earl of, 46

Sutton-on-the-Hill, 140
Sutton-in-Scarsdale, 210, 211
Swarkstone, 270
Swanwick, 268
Swinsor, 273
Swinscoe Moor, 118
Swift, 210
Swithamly, 143, 144
Taddington, 247
Tag Hill, 271
Talbot, 19
Tamworth, Lord, 132
TAYLOR'S RAMBLE, 129
Tea pound of 281
Team's balls, 1, 5
Teneriffe, 10
Terrill, James, 14
Tewkesbury, 26
THE AGRICULTURAL MEETING,
THE ASHBORNE FOOT-BALL SONG, 284
THE ASHPTON GARLAND, OR A DAY IN THE WOODLANDS, 237
THE BEGGAR'S RAMBLE, 271
THE DERBY HERO 249
THE DRIVING OF THE DEER, 230
"The eighteenth day of March," 252
"The fire burns brightly on the hearth," 204
THE FLAX-DRESSER'S WIFE OF SPONDON, 281
THE FLORISTS' SONG, 184
THE GIPSIES' SONG, 280
THE HUMOURS OF HAYFIELD FAIR 61
"The Miller he caught the maid by the toe," 110
THE MOST PLEASANT SONG OF THE LADY BESSY, 12
THE NUN'S GREEN RANGERS, or the Triple Alliance, consisting of a Sergeant, a Tinker, and a Bear, 199
THE POWER OF LOVE; SIR FRANCIS LEKE, OR, 210
THE QUADRUPEDS, or Four-Footed Petitioners against the Sale of Nun's Green 193
THE SORROWFUL LAMENTATION, LAST DYING SPEECH AND CONFESSION OF OLD NUN'S GREEN, 187

"*The sixth of March, kind neighbours this is true,*" 65
THE TAILOR'S RAMBLE, or the Blues' Valour Displayed, 129
THE TRUE LOVER'S KNOT UNTIED (Arabella Stuart) 222
THE UNCONSCIONABLE BATCHELORS OF DARBY, 58
"*Then, oh Hugh Stenson is my name,* 263
Thirsk, 157
Thomas Rees, Ap, 45, 49, 52
Thompson, 157
Thorpe, 285
Thorpe Cloud, 272
Thornywood, 270
Thornhill family, 148, 255
—— —— Thomas Bache, Elegy on, 252
Thringstone, 270
Tibshelf, 267
TIDESWELL IN AN UPROAR, or the Prince in the Town, and the Devil in the Church, 111
TIDESWELL, DRUNKEN BUTCHER OF, 66
Tideswell, 66, et seq., 111, 112, 113, 114, 155
Tinker's Inn, 133
Tipling school, 59
"'*Tis merry in the High Peak Forest,*" 97
Tissington, 272
Titbury (see Tutbury)
Tixhall Poetry, 62
Ton of tennis balls, 1
Toton, 267
Tower Hill, 17, 31, 47
Towcester, 261
Tragedy of Ovid, 7
Tragnel, 144
Trapalin supposed a Prince, 7
Trent, river, 8
Tribute, 1, 4
TRIPLE ALLIANCE, consisting of an old Sergeant, a Tinker, and a Bear, 199
Trowel, 267
Trowell, Major, 190
TRUE LOVERS' KNOT UNTIED, 222
Trusley, 137—142

TRUSLEY HUNTING SONG, 137
Tudor, Henry, 45
Tune, "To thee, to thee," 58
—— "As our King lay musing on his bed," 2, 3
—— Derbyshire Miller,
—— Cook Laurel, 125
—— King of the Cannibal Islands, 160
—— Chevy Chace, 196
—— Bow, wow, wow, 199
—— Barking Barber, 199
—— Date Obolum Beliario, 199
—— Vicar and Moses, 206
—— Gipsies' Song,
Tun, burning in a, 17
Tunbridge, 10
"Tunis, Fair one of," 257
Tunstead, Dickie of, 226
Tunstead, 226, 227
Tupton, 267
Turbutt, Gladwin, 151
Turnditch, 268
Tutbury, 13 et seq., 273
Tutbury bull-running, 73, 74, 79
"'*Twas more than fifty years ago,*" 282
"*Two jackasses, the father and the son,*" 193
Tydder, Henry, 45
Ucklow, 269
UNCONSCIONABLE BATCHELORS OF DERBY, 58
Union of the Roses, 53
Utceter, 273
Uttoxeter, 262, 273
VERNON, SQUIRE, FOX CHACE, 131
—— —— family, 131, et seq.
—— —— Lord, 131, 135
—— —— George, 132—136
—— —— Dorothy, 132
Victoria, Queen, 2
"Virgil Travestie," 257
Volunteers, Derbyshire, 2, 131
Wakefield, Pinder of, 74
Walker, 133, 134
Walton, Isaac, 257
"Wanderings of Memory," 274
Wantling, 249—252
Warburton, 45

INDEX.

"*The Parson of Monyash late one eve*," 286
Wardgate. 268
Wardlowmier, 269
Warin. 286
Warwick, Guy, Earl of, 75
Warwickshire, 75, 259
Waterloo, 285
Wathall, 267
Wells, Lady, 22
"*Were but my muse inspired by Fludyer's taste*," 157
West Chester, 26
—— Smithfield, 61
Westminster, 15, et seq.
Weston-under-wood, 269
Westhorpe, 270
Wessington, 267
Wet Willm. 272
Weever Hills, 154
Whaley Bridge, 69, 227
"*What will it availe on fortune to exclayme*," 167
Wheatcroft, Leonard, 146, 152
"*When Apollo thinks fit to handle his lyre*," 206
"*When Heaven from Earth had shut out day*," 190
"*When Robin Hood was about twenty years old*," 58
Whittaker, 285
WHITTINGTON, SIR RICHARD'S, ADVANCEMENT, 104
Whittington and his Cat, 104
———— De, 104
———— in Derbyshire, 104, 231, 233
———— Sir William, 104
Whitrick, 270
Whitehall, 263
Whitworth guns, 148

Whitworth, Joseph, 148
Wilford, 270
Williams, Richard, 164—166
Willoughby, Lord, 57
Will Stutely, 89, 90
Willett, 142
Winnats, 274, 275
Winnats, murder at, 274, 275
Windsor, 11, 263
Winster, 255—257, 268, 272
Wilson, Jack, 139
Wire Mill 273
Windley, 272
Wirksworth, 269, 272
Wood end 271
Woodlands, 237, et seq.
WOODLANDS, A DAY IN THE, 237
Woodborough, 270
Wool, 272
Woolaton, 264
Wooley, 133—136, 150, 151
Womfords, 271
"Wonders of the Peak," 257
Worde, Wynken de, 73, 126
Worcestershire, 26
Wootton, 135, 273
Wotton Lodge, 273
Wyaston, 133, 285
Wye river, 245, 248
Wynken de Worde, 73, 126
Yeaveley, 273
"*Ye Tideswellites can this be true*," 114
Yeldersley, 269
York, 157
York, Duke of, 14, et seq.
YORKSHIRE PIE, 157
"*You lovers of mirth attend awhile*," 59
Young lasses pawned by their sweethearts, 58

www.ingramcontent.com/pod-product-compliance
Lightning Source LLC
Chambersburg PA
CBHW022023240426
43667CB00042B/1069